FTCE
GENERAL KNOWLEDGE

By: Sharon Wynne, M.S.

XAMonline, INC.
Boston

To obtain permission(s) to use the material from this work for any purpose including workshops or seminars, please submit a written request to:

XAMonline, Inc.
25 First Street, Suite 106
Cambridge, MA 02141
Toll Free 1-800-509-4128
Email: info@xamonline.com
Web: www.xamonline.com
Fax: 1-617-583-5552

Library of Congress Cataloging-in-Publication Data

Wynne, Sharon A.
    FTCE General Knowledge / Sharon A. Wynne. 3rd ed
    ISBN 978-1-60787-016-6
    1. FTCE General Knowledge
    2. Study Guides
    3. FTCE
    4. Teachers' Certification & Licensure
    5. Careers

Disclaimer:

The opinions expressed in this publication are the sole works of XAMonline and were created independently from the National Education Association, Educational Testing Service, or any State Department of Education, National Evaluation Systems or other testing affiliates.

Between the time of publication and printing, state specific standards as well as testing formats and Web site information may change and therefore would not be included in part or in whole within this product. Sample test questions are developed by XAMonline and reflect content similar to that on real tests; however, they are not former test questions. XAMonline assembles content that aligns with state standards but makes no claims nor guarantees teacher candidates a passing score. Numerical scores are determined by testing companies such as NES or ETS and then are compared with individual state standards. A passing score varies from state to state.

Printed in the United States of America   œ-1

FTCE General Knowledge
ISBN: 978-1-60787-016-6

Table of Contents

COMPETENCY 4
KNOWLEDGE OF ALGEBRAIC THINKING..54

COMPETENCY 5
KNOWLEDGE OF DATA ANALYSIS AND PROBABILITY 70

DOMAIN II
ENGLISH...85

COMPETENCY 6
CONCEPTUAL AND ORGANIZATIONAL SKILLS 87

COMPETENCY 7
WORD CHOICE SKILLS 91

DOMAIN IV
ESSAY 167

SAMPLE TEST

FTCE
GENERAL KNOWLEDGE

SECTION 1
ABOUT XAMONLINE

XAMonline—A Specialty Teacher Certification Company

Created in 1996, XAMonline was the first company to publish study guides for state-specific teacher certification examinations. Founder Sharon Wynne found it frustrating that materials were not available for teacher certification preparation and decided to create the first single, state-specific guide. XAMonline has grown into a company of over 1,800 contributors and writers and offers over 300 titles for the entire PRAXIS series and every state examination. No matter what state you plan on teaching in, XAMonline has a unique teacher certification study guide just for you.

XAMonline—Value and Innovation

We are committed to providing value and innovation. Our print-on-demand technology allows us to be the first in the market to reflect changes in test standards and user feedback as they occur. Our guides are written by experienced teachers who are experts in their fields. And our content reflects the highest standards of quality. Comprehensive practice tests with varied levels of rigor means that your study experience will closely match the actual in-test experience.

To date, XAMonline has helped nearly 600,000 teachers pass their certification or licensing exams. Our commitment to preparation exceeds simply providing the proper material for study—it extends to helping teachers **gain mastery** of the subject matter, giving them the **tools** to become the most effective classroom leaders possible, and ushering today's students toward a **successful future**.

SECTION 2
ABOUT THIS STUDY GUIDE

Purpose of This Guide

Is there a little voice inside of you saying, "Am I ready?" Our goal is to replace that little voice and remove all doubt with a new voice that says, "I AM READY. **Bring it on!**" by offering the highest quality of teacher certification study guides.

Organization of Content

You will see that while every test may start with overlapping general topics, each is very unique in the skills they wish to test. Only XAMonline presents custom content that analyzes deeper than a title, a subarea, or an objective. Only XAMonline presents content and sample test assessments along with **focus statements**, the deepest-level rationale and interpretation of the skills that are unique to the exam.

Title and field number of test

→Each exam has its own name and number. XAMonline's guides are written to give you the content you need to know for the specific exam you are taking. You can be confident when you buy our guide that it contains the information you need to study for the specific test you are taking.

Subareas

→These are the major content categories found on the exam. XAMonline's guides are written to cover all of the subareas found in the test frameworks developed for the exam.

Objectives

→These are standards that are unique to the exam and represent the main subcategories of the subareas/content categories. XAMonline's guides are written to address every specific objective required to pass the exam.

Focus statements

→These are examples and interpretations of the objectives. You find them in parenthesis directly following the objective. They provide detailed examples of the range, type, and level of content that appear on the test questions. **Only XAMonline's guides drill down to this level.**

How Do We Compare with Our Competitors?

XAMonline—drills down to the focus statement level.
CliffsNotes and REA—organized at the objective level
Kaplan—provides only links to content
MoMedia—content not specific to the state test

Each subarea is divided into manageable sections that cover the specific skill areas. Explanations are easy to understand and thorough. You'll find that every test answer contains a rejoinder so if you need a refresher or further review after taking the test, you'll know exactly to which section you must return.

How to Use This Book

Our informal polls show that most people begin studying up to eight weeks prior to the test date, so start early. Then ask yourself some questions: How much do you really know? Are you coming to the test straight from your teacher-education program or are you having to review subjects you haven't considered in ten years? Either way, take a **diagnostic or assessment test** first. Also, spend time on sample tests so that you become accustomed to the way the actual test will appear.

This guide comes with an online diagnostic test of 30 questions found online at *www.XAMonline.com*. It is a little boot camp to get you up for the task and reveal things about your compendium of knowledge in general. Although this guide is structured to follow the order of the test, you are not required to study in that order. By finding a time-management and study plan that fits your life you will be more effective. The results of your diagnostic or self-assessment test can be a guide for how to manage your time and point you toward an area that needs more attention.

After taking the diagnostic exam, fill out the **Personalized Study Plan** page at the beginning of each chapter. Review the competencies and skills covered in that chapter and check the boxes that apply to your study needs. If there are sections you already know you can skip, check the "skip it" box. Taking this step will give you a study plan for each chapter.

Week	Activity
8 weeks prior to test	Take a diagnostic test found at www.XAMonline.com
7 weeks prior to test	Build your Personalized Study Plan for each chapter. Check the "skip it" box for sections you feel you are already strong in. ✗ SKIP IT ☐
6-3 weeks prior to test	For each of these four weeks, choose a content area to study. You don't have to go in the order of the book. It may be that you start with the content that needs the most review. Alternately, you may want to ease yourself into plan by starting with the most familiar material.
2 weeks prior to test	Take the sample test, score it, and create a review plan for the final week before the test.
1 week prior to test	Following your plan (which will likely be aligned with the areas that need the most review) go back and study the sections that align with the questions you may have gotten wrong. Then go back and study the sections related to the questions you answered correctly. If need be, create flashcards and drill yourself on any area that you makes you anxious.

SECTION 3
ABOUT THE FTCE GENERAL KNOWLEDGE EXAM

What Is the FTCE General Knowledge Exam?

The FTCE General Knowledge exam is meant to assess mastery of the basic skills required to teach in Florida public schools. It covers the general areas of reading, writing, and mathematics and is administered by Pearson Education on behalf of the Florida Department of Education.

Often **your own state's requirements** determine whether or not you should take any particular test. The most reliable source of information regarding this is your state's Department of Education. This resource should have a complete list of testing centers and dates. Test dates vary by subject area and not all test dates necessarily include your particular test, so be sure to check carefully.

If you are in a teacher-education program, check with the Education Department or the Certification Officer for specific information for testing and testing timelines. The Certification Office should have most of the information you need.

If you choose an alternative route to certification you can either rely on our website at *www.XAMonline.com* or on the resources provided by an alternative certification program. Many states now have specific agencies devoted to alternative certification and there are some national organizations as well, for example:

National Association for Alternative Certification
http://www.alt-teachercert.org/index.asp

Interpreting Test Results

Contrary to what you may have heard, the results of the FTCE General Knowledge test are not based on time. More accurately, you will be scored on the raw number of points you earn in relation to the raw number of points available. Each question is worth one raw point. It is likely to your benefit to complete as many questions in the time allotted, but it will not necessarily work to your advantage if you hurry through the test.

Follow the guidelines provided by Pearson for interpreting your score. The website offers a sample test score sheet and clearly explains how/whether the scores are scaled and what to expect if you have an essay portion on your test.

Scores are available approximately 6 weeks after the test date and scores will be sent to you and your chosen institution(s).

What's on the Test?

The FTCE General Knowledge exam consists of four subtests, each of which can be taken as separate exams or all at once. Each subtest consists of multiple-choice questions and there is also 1 essay. The breakdown of the questions is as follows:

Category	Approximate Number of Questions	Approximate Percentage of the test	Testing Time
I: Essay	1 essay	–	50 minutes
II: English Language Skills	40 multiple choice	32%	40 minutes
III: Reading	40 multiple choice	32%	40 minutes
IV: Mathematics	45 multiple choice	36%	1 hr, 40 minutes

Question Types

You're probably thinking, enough already, I want to study! Indulge us a little longer while we explain that there is actually more than one type of multiple-choice question. You can thank us later after you realize how well prepared you are for your exam.

1. Complete the Statement. The name says it all. In this question type you'll be asked to choose the correct completion of a given statement. For example:

> **The Dolch Basic Sight Words consist of a relatively short list of words that children should be able to:**
>
> A. Sound out
>
> B. Know the meaning of
>
> C. Recognize on sight
>
> D. Use in a sentence

The correct answer is A. In order to check your answer, test out the statement by adding the choices to the end of it.

2. **Which of the Following.** One way to test your answer choice for this type of question is to replace the phrase "which of the following" with your selection. Use this example:

> **Which of the following words is one of the twelve most frequently used in children's reading texts:**
>
> A. There
>
> B. This
>
> C. The
>
> D. An

Don't look! Test your answer. _____ is one of the twelve most frequently used in children's reading texts. Did you guess C? Then you guessed correctly.

3. **Roman Numeral Choices.** This question type is used when there is more than one possible correct answer. For example:

> **Which of the following two arguments accurately supports the use of cooperative learning as an effective method of instruction?**
>
> I. Cooperative learning groups facilitate healthy competition between individuals in the group.
>
> II. Cooperative learning groups allow academic achievers to carry or cover for academic underachievers.
>
> III. Cooperative learning groups make each student in the group accountable for the success of the group.
>
> IV. Cooperative learning groups make it possible for students to reward other group members for achieving.
>
> A. I and II
>
> B. II and III
>
> C. I and III
>
> D. III and IV

Notice that the question states there are **two** possible answers. It's best to read all the possibilities first before looking at the answer choices. In this case, the correct answer is D.

4. **Negative Questions.** This type of question contains words such as "not," "least," and "except." Each correct answer will be the statement that does **not** fit the situation described in the question. Such as:

> **Multicultural education is not**
>
> A. An idea or concept
>
> B. A "tack-on" to the school curriculum
>
> C. An educational reform movement
>
> D. A process

Think to yourself that the statement could be anything but the correct answer. This question form is more open to interpretation than other types, so read carefully and don't forget that you're answering a negative statement.

5. **Questions that Include Graphs, Tables, or Reading Passages.** As always, read the question carefully. It likely asks for a very specific answer and not a broad interpretation of the visual. Here is a simple (though not statistically accurate) example of a graph question:

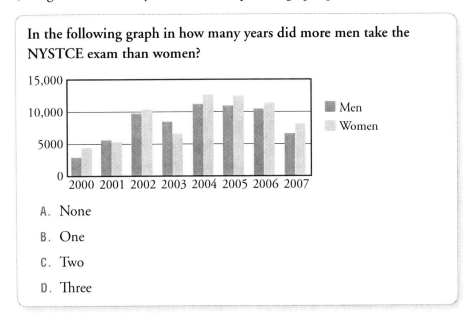

> **In the following graph in how many years did more men take the NYSTCE exam than women?**
>
> A. None
>
> B. One
>
> C. Two
>
> D. Three

It may help you to simply circle the two years that answer the question. Make sure you've read the question thoroughly and once you've made your determination, double check your work. The correct answer is C.

SECTION 4
HELPFUL HINTS

Study Tips

1. **You are what you eat.** Certain foods aid the learning process by releasing natural memory enhancers called CCKs (cholecystokinin) composed of tryptophan, choline, and phenylalanine. All of these chemicals enhance the neurotransmitters associated with memory and certain foods release memory enhancing chemicals. A light meal or snacks of one of the following foods fall into this category:

   - Milk
   - Rice
   - Eggs
   - Fish
   - Nuts and seeds
   - Oats
   - Turkey

   The better the connections, the more you comprehend!

2. **See the forest for the trees.** In other words, get the concept before you look at the details. One way to do this is to take notes as you read, paraphrasing or summarizing in your own words. Putting the concept in terms that are comfortable and familiar may increase retention.

3. **Question authority.** Ask why, why, why? Pull apart written material paragraph by paragraph and don't forget the captions under the illustrations. For example, if a heading reads *Stream Erosion* put it in the form of a question (Why do streams erode? What is stream erosion?) then find the answer within the material. If you train your mind to think in this manner you will learn more and prepare yourself for answering test questions.

4. **Play mind games.** Using your brain for reading or puzzles keeps it flexible. Even with a limited amount of time your brain can take in data (much like a computer) and store it for later use. In ten minutes you can: read two paragraphs (at least), quiz yourself with flash cards, or review notes. Even if you don't fully understand something on the first pass, your mind stores it for recall, which is why frequent reading or review increases chances of retention and comprehension.

5. **Get pointed in the right direction.** Use arrows to point to important passages or pieces of information. It's easier to read than a page full of yellow highlights. Highlighting can be used sparingly, but add an arrow to the margin to call attention to it.

6. **The pen is mightier than the sword.** Learn to take great notes. A by-product of our modern culture is that we have grown accustomed to getting our information in short doses. We've subconsciously trained ourselves to assimilate information into neat little packages. Messy notes fragment the flow of information. Your notes can be much clearer with proper formatting. *The Cornell Method* is one such format. This method was popularized in *How to Study in College*, Ninth Edition, by Walter Pauk. You can benefit from the method without purchasing an additional book by simply looking up the method online. Below is a sample of how *The Cornell Method* can be adapted for use with this guide.

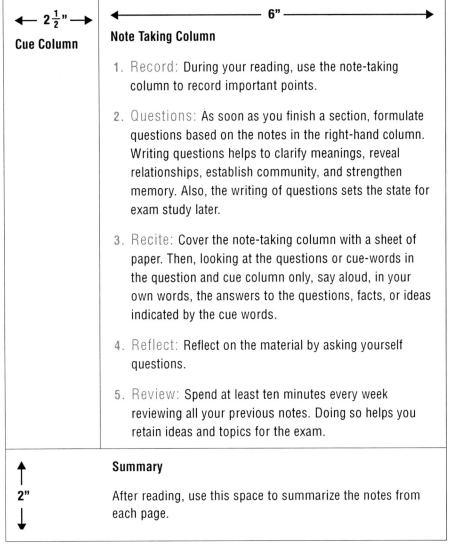

← 2½" → **Cue Column**	←——————— 6" ———————→ **Note Taking Column** 1. Record: During your reading, use the note-taking column to record important points. 2. Questions: As soon as you finish a section, formulate questions based on the notes in the right-hand column. Writing questions helps to clarify meanings, reveal relationships, establish community, and strengthen memory. Also, the writing of questions sets the state for exam study later. 3. Recite: Cover the note-taking column with a sheet of paper. Then, looking at the questions or cue-words in the question and cue column only, say aloud, in your own words, the answers to the questions, facts, or ideas indicated by the cue words. 4. Reflect: Reflect on the material by asking yourself questions. 5. Review: Spend at least ten minutes every week reviewing all your previous notes. Doing so helps you retain ideas and topics for the exam.
↑ 2" ↓	**Summary** After reading, use this space to summarize the notes from each page.

Adapted from How to Study in College, Ninth Edition, by Walter Pauk, ©2008 Wadsworth

The proctor will write the start time where it can be seen and then, later, provide the time remaining, typically fifteen minutes before the end of the test.

7. Place yourself in exile and set the mood. Set aside a particular place and time to study that best suits your personal needs and biorhythms. If you're a night person, burn the midnight oil. If you're a morning person set yourself up with some coffee and get to it. Make your study time and place as free from distraction as possible and surround yourself with what you need, be it silence or music. Studies have shown that music can aid in concentration, absorption, and retrieval of information. Not all music, though. Classical music is said to work best

8. Check your budget. You should at least review all the content material before your test, but allocate the most amount of time to the areas that need the most refreshing. It sounds obvious, but it's easy to forget. You can use the study rubric above to balance your study budget.

Testing Tips

1. Get smart, play dumb. Sometimes a question is just a question. No one is out to trick you, so don't assume that the test writer is looking for something other than what was asked. Stick to the question as written and don't overanalyze.

2. Do a double take. Read test questions and answer choices at least twice because it's easy to miss something, to transpose a word or some letters. If you have no idea what the correct answer is, skip it and come back later if there's time. If you're still clueless, it's okay to guess. Remember, you're scored on the number of questions you answer correctly and you're not penalized for wrong answers. The worst case scenario is that you miss a point from a good guess.

3. Turn it on its ear. The syntax of a question can often provide a clue, so make things interesting and turn the question into a statement to see if it changes the meaning or relates better (or worse) to the answer choices.

4. Get out your magnifying glass. Look for hidden clues in the questions because it's difficult to write a multiple-choice question without giving away part of the answer in the options presented. In most questions you can readily eliminate one or two potential answers, increasing your chances of answering correctly to 50/50, which will help out if you've skipped a question and gone back to it (see tip #2).

5. Call it intuition. Often your first instinct is correct. If you've been studying the content you've likely absorbed something and have subconsciously retained the knowledge. On questions you're not sure about trust your instincts because a first impression is usually correct.

6. Graffiti. Sometimes it's a good idea to mark your answers directly on the test booklet and go back to fill in the optical scan sheet later. You don't get extra points for perfectly blackened ovals. If you choose to manage your test this way, be sure not to mismark your answers when you transcribe to the scan sheet.

7. Become a clock-watcher. You have a set amount of time to answer the questions. Don't get bogged down laboring over a question you're not sure about when there are ten others you could answer more readily. If you choose to follow the advice of tip #6, be sure you leave time near the end to go back and fill in the scan sheet.

Do the Drill

No matter how prepared you feel it's sometimes a good idea to apply Murphy's Law. So the following tips might seem silly, mundane, or obvious, but we're including them anyway.

1. Remember, you are what you eat, so bring a snack. Choose from the list of energizing foods that appear earlier in the introduction.

2. You're not too sexy for your test. Wear comfortable clothes. You'll be distracted if your belt is too tight or if you're too cold or too hot.

3. Lie to yourself. Even if you think you're a prompt person, pretend you're not and leave plenty of time to get to the testing center. Map it out ahead of time and do a dry run if you have to. There's no need to add road rage to your list of anxieties.

4. Bring sharp number 2 pencils. It may seem impossible to forget this need from your school days, but you might. And make sure the erasers are intact, too.

5. No ticket, no test. Bring your admission ticket as well as **two** forms of identification, including one with a picture and signature. You will not be admitted to the test without these things.

6. You can't take it with you. Leave any study aids, dictionaries, notebooks, computers, and the like at home. Certain tests **do** allow a scientific or four-function calculator, so check ahead of time to see if your test does.

7. Prepare for the desert. Any time spent on a bathroom break **cannot** be made up later, so use your judgment on the amount you eat or drink.

8. Quiet, Please! Keeping your own time is a good idea, but not with a timepiece that has a loud ticker. If you use a watch, take it off and place it nearby but not so that it distracts you. And **silence your cell phone**.

To the best of our ability, we have compiled the content you need to know in this book and in the accompanying online resources. The rest is up to you. You can use the study and testing tips or you can follow your own methods. Either way, you can be confident that there aren't any missing pieces of information and there shouldn't be any surprises in the content on the test.

If you have questions about test fees, registration, electronic testing, or other content verification issues please visit *www.fl.nesinc.org.*

Good luck!

Sharon Wynne
Founder, XAMonline

DOMAIN I
MATHEMATICS

PERSONALIZED STUDY PLAN

KNOWN MATERIAL/ SKIP IT

PAGE	COMPETENCY AND SKILL	
5	**1: Knowledge of number sense, concepts, and operations**	☐
	1.1: Compare the relative value of real numbers	☐
	1.2: Solve addition, subtraction, multiplication, and division of rational numbers problems	☐
	1.3: Apply basic number theory concepts	☐
	1.4: Apply the Order of Operations with or without grouping symbols	☐
22	**2: Knowledge of measurement (using customary or metric units)**	☐
	2.1: Solve length, weight, mass, perimeter, area, capacity, and volume problems	☐
	2.2: Solve real-world problems involving rated measures	☐
	2.3: Solve real-world problems involving scaled drawings	☐
	2.4: Solve problems involving units of measures	☐
	2.5: Solve problems involving estimates of measures	☐
	2.6: Choose the correct reading, using instruments	☐
39	**3: Knowledge of geometry and spatial sense**	☐
	3.1: Identify simple two- and three-dimensional figures	☐
	3.2: Solve ratio, proportion, similarity, congruence, and the Pythagorean relationship problems	☐
	3.3: Identify integers in a coordinate system (graph) and apply the concepts of slope and distance to solve problems	☐
	3.4: Identify geometric concepts including perpendicularity, parallelism, tangency, symmetry, and transformations	☐
54	**4: Knowledge of algebraic thinking**	☐
	4.1: Analyze and generalize patterns	☐
	4.2: Interpret algebraic expressions using words, symbols, variables, tables, and graphs	☐
	4.3: Solve equations and inequalities graphically or algebraically	☐
	4.4: Determine whether a number or ordered pair is among the solutions of given equations or inequalities	☐

PERSONALIZED STUDY PLAN

KNOWN MATERIAL/ SKIP IT

PAGE	COMPETENCY AND SKILL	
70	**5:** **Knowledge of data analysis and probability**	☐
	5.1: Analyze data presented in histograms, bar graphs, circle graphs, pictographs, tables, and charts	☐
	5.2: Identify how data can lead to different or inappropriate interpretations	☐
	5.3: Calculate range, mean, median, and mode(s) and interpret the meaning of the measures of central tendency and dispersion	☐
	5.4: Identify how the measures of central tendency can lead to different interpretations	☐
	5.5: Calculate the probability of a specified outcome	☐
	5.6: Solve problems involving probability using counting procedures, tables, tree diagrams, and the concepts of permutations and combination	☐

COMPETENCY 1
KNOWLEDGE OF NUMBER SENSE, CONCEPTS, AND OPERATIONS

SKILL 1.1 **Compare the relative value of real numbers** *(e.g., integers, fractions, decimals, percents, irrational numbers, and numbers expressed in exponential or scientific notation)*

Rational numbers can be expressed as the ratio of two integers, $\frac{a}{b}$, where $b \neq 0$, for example, $\frac{2}{3}$, $-\frac{4}{5}$, $5 = \frac{5}{1}$ are all rational numbers.

Rational numbers include integers, fractions, mixed numbers, and terminating and repeating decimals. Every rational number can be expressed as a repeating or terminating decimal and can be shown on a number line.

INTEGERS are the positive and negative whole numbers and zero.

...-6, –5, –4, –3, –2, –1, 0, 1, 2, 3, 4, 5, 6,...

WHOLE NUMBERS are the natural numbers and zero.

0, 1, 2, 3, 4, 5, 6...

NATURAL NUMBERS are the counting numbers.

1, 2, 3, 4, 5, 6...

IRRATIONAL NUMBERS are real numbers that cannot be written as the ratio of two integers. They are infinite, nonrepeating decimals.

$\sqrt{5} = 2.2360$, pi $= \pi = 3.1415927...$

A FRACTION is an expression of numbers in the form of $\frac{x}{y}$, where x is the numerator and y is the denominator, which cannot be zero.

$\frac{3}{7}$ 3 is the numerator; 7 is the denominator

If the fraction has common factors for the numerator and denominator, divide both by the common factor to reduce the fraction to its lowest form.

$\frac{13}{39} = \frac{1 \times 13}{3 \times 13} = \frac{1}{3}$ Divide by the common factor 13.

A MIXED NUMBER has an integer part and a fractional part.

$2\frac{1}{4}, -5\frac{1}{6}, 7\frac{1}{3}$

PERCENT means per 100 (written with the symbol %).

$10\% = \frac{10}{100} = \frac{1}{10}$

> **INTEGERS:** the positive and negative whole numbers and zero

> **WHOLE NUMBERS:** the natural numbers and zero

> **NATURAL NUMBERS:** the counting numbers

> **IRRATIONAL NUMBERS:** real numbers that cannot be written as the ratio of two integers

> **FRACTION:** an expression of numbers in the form of $\frac{x}{y}$, where x is the numerator and y is the denominator

> **MIXED NUMBER:** a number that has an integer part and a fractional part

> **PERCENT:** means "per 100;" ten percent is 10 parts out of 100

DECIMAL: a number written with a whole-number part, a decimal point, and a decimal part

EXPONENT FORM: a shorthand way of writing repeated multiplication

BASE: the number to be multiplied as many times as indicated by the exponent

EXPONET: tells how many times the base is multiplied by itself

DECIMALS means deci or part of ten. To find the decimal equivalent of a fraction, use the denominator to divide the numerator, as shown in the following example.

Find the decimal equivalent of $\frac{7}{10}$.

Because 10 cannot divide into 7 evenly, $\frac{7}{10} = 0.7$

The EXPONENT FORM is a shortcut method to write repeated multiplication. The basic form is b^n, where b is called the BASE and n is the EXPONENT. Both b and n are real numbers. The b^n implies that the base b is multiplied by itself n times.

Examples:

$3^4 = 3 \times 3 \times 3 \times 3 = 81$
$2^3 = 2 \times 2 \times 2 = 8$
$(-2)^4 = (-2) \times (-2) \times (-2) \times (-2) = 16$
$-2^4 = -(2 \times 2 \times 2 \times 2) = 16$

Caution: The exponent does not affect the sign unless the negative sign is inside the parentheses and the exponent is outside the parentheses.

$(-2)^4$ implies that -2 is multiplied by itself 4 times.

-2^4 implies that 2 is multiplied by itself 4 times, and then the answer becomes. negative.

KEY EXPONENT RULES: FOR 'a' NONZERO AND 'm' AND 'n' REAL NUMBERS	
Product Rule	$a^m \times a^n = a^{(m+n)}$
Quotient Rule	$\frac{a^m}{a^n} = a^{(m-n)}$
Rule of Negative Exponents	$\frac{a^{-m}}{a^{-n}} = \frac{a^n}{a^m}$

When 10 is raised to any power, the exponent tells the numbers of zeros in the product.

Example:

$10^7 = 10,000,000$

SCIENTIFIC NOTATION: a convenient method for writing very large and very small numbers

SCIENTIFIC NOTATION is a convenient method for writing very large and very small numbers. It employs two factors. The first factor is a number between 1 and 10. The second factor is a power of 10. This notation is considered "shorthand" for expressing very large numbers (such as the weight of 100 elephants) or very small numbers (such as the weight of an atom in pounds).

Recall that:

10^n	=	Ten multiplied by itself n times
10^n	=	Any nonzero number raised to the zero power is 1
10^1	=	10
10^2	=	$10 \times 10 = 100$
10^3	=	$10 \times 10 \times 10 = 1000$
10^{-1}	=	$\frac{1}{10}$ (deci)
10^{-2}	=	$\frac{1}{100}$ (centi)
10^{-3}	=	$\frac{1}{1000}$ (milli)
10^{-6}	=	$\frac{1}{1,000,000}$ (micro)

Example: Write 46,368,000 in scientific notation.

1. Introduce a decimal point and decimal places.
   $46{,}368{,}000 = 46{,}368{,}000.0000$

2. Make a mark between the two digits that give a number between
   -9.9 and 9.9.
   $4 \wedge 6{,}368{,}000.0000$

3. Count the number of digit places between the decimal point and the $\wedge$
   mark. This number is the *nth* power of ten.
   So, $46{,}368{,}000 = 4.6368 \times 10^7$.

Example: Write 0.00397 in scientific notation.

1. Decimal place is already in place.

2. Make a mark between 3 and 9 to obtain a number between -9.9 and. 9.9.

3. Move decimal place to the mark (three hops).
   $0.003 \wedge 97$
   Motion is to the right, so n on 10^n is negative.
   Therefore, $0.00397 = 3.97 \times 10^{-3}$.

Solve real-world problems involving addition, subtraction, multiplication, and division of rational numbers *(e.g., whole numbers, integers, decimals, percents, and fractions including mixed numbers)*

PROPERTIES: rules that apply for addition, subtraction, multiplication, or division of real numbers

PROPERTIES are rules that apply for addition, subtraction, multiplication, or division of real numbers. These properties are:

Commutative	You can change the order of the terms or factors as follows.
	For addition: $\qquad a + b = b + a$
	For multiplication: $\qquad ab = ba$
	Since addition is the inverse operation of subtraction and multiplication is the inverse operation of division, no separate laws are needed for subtraction and division.
	Example: 5 + 8 = 8 + 5 = 13
	Example: 2 × 6 = 6 × 2 = 12
Associative	You can regroup the terms as you like.
	For addition: $\qquad a + (b + c) = (a + b) + c$
	For multiplication: $\qquad a(bc) = (ab)c$
	This rule does not apply for division and subtraction.
	Example: (2 + 7) + 5 = 2 + (7 + 5) *9 + 5 = 2 + 12 = 14*
	Example: (3 × 7) × 5 = 3 × (7 × 5) *21 × 5 = 3 × 35 = 105*
Identity	Finding a number so that when added to a term results in that number (additive identity); finding a number such that when multiplied by a term results in that number (multiplicative identity).
	For addition: $\qquad a + 0 = a$ (zero is additive identity)
	For multiplication: $\qquad a \times 1 = a$ (one is multiplicative)
	Example: 17 + 0 = 17
	Example: 34 × 1 = 34
	The product of any number and one is that number.

Continued on next page

Inverse	Finding a number such that when added to the number, it results in zero; or when multiplied by the number, it results in 1.
	For addition: $\quad\quad a - a = 0$
	For multiplication: $\quad a \times (\frac{1}{a}) = 1$
	$(-a)$ is the additive inverse of a; $(\frac{1}{a})$, also called the reciprocal, is the multiplicative inverse of a.
	Example: 25 − 25 = 0
	Example: $5 \times \frac{1}{5} = 1$
	The product of any number and its reciprocal is one.
Distributive	This technique allows us to operate on terms within parentheses without first performing operations within the parentheses. This is especially helpful when terms within the parentheses cannot be combined.
	$a(b + c) = ab + ac$
	Example: $6 \times (4 + 9) = (6 \times 4) + (6 \times 9)$
	$\quad\quad\quad\quad 6 \times 13 = 24 + 54 = 78$
	To multiply a sum by a number, multiply each addend by the number, then add the products.

Addition of Whole Numbers

Example: At the end of a day of shopping, a shopper had $24 remaining in his wallet. He spent $45 on various goods. How much money did the shopper have at the beginning of the day?

The total amount of money the shopper started with is the sum of the amount spent and the amount remaining at the end of the day.

$$\begin{array}{r} \$\ 24 \\ +\ 45 \\ \hline \$\ 69 \end{array}$$ The original total was $69.

Example: A race took the winner 1 hr. 58 min. 12 sec. on the first half of the race and 2 hr. 9 min. 57 sec. on the second. How much time did the entire race take?

$$1 \text{ hr } 58 \text{ min } 12 \text{ sec}$$
$$\underline{+ \ 2 \text{ hr } \ \ 9 \text{ min } 57 \text{ sec}}$$

Add these numbers.

$$3 \text{ hr } 67 \text{ min } 69 \text{ sec}$$
$$\underline{+ \ 1 \text{ min } - 60 \text{ sec}}$$

Change 60 sec to 1 min.

$$3 \text{ hr } 68 \text{ min } \ \ 9 \text{ sec}$$
$$\underline{+ \ 1 \text{ hr } - 60 \text{ min}}$$

Change 60 min to 1 hr.

$$4 \text{ hr } 8 \text{ min } 9 \text{ sec}$$

Final answer.

Subtraction of Whole Numbers

Example: At the end of his shift, a cashier has $96 in the cash register. At the beginning of his shift, he had $15. How much money did the cashier collect during his shift?

The total collected is the difference between the ending amount and the starting amount.

$$\$ \ 96$$
$$\underline{-15}$$
$$\$ \ 81$$ The total collected was $81.

Multiplication of Whole Numbers

> *Another way of conceptualizing multiplication is to think in terms of groups.*

Multiplication is one of the four basic number operations. In simple terms, multiplication is the addition of a number to itself a certain number of times. For example, 4 multiplied by 3 is equal to $4 + 4 + 4$ or $3 + 3 + 3 + 3$. Another way of conceptualizing multiplication is to think in terms of groups. For example, if we have 4 groups of 3 students, the total number of students is 4 multiplied by 3. We call the solution to a multiplication problem the PRODUCT.

> **PRODUCT:** the answer to a multiplication problem

The basic algorithm for whole number multiplication begins with aligning the numbers by place value, with the number containing more places on top.

$$172$$
$$\underline{\times \ 43}$$

Note that we placed 172 on top because it has more places than 43 does.

Next, we multiply the ones place of the bottom number by each place value of the top number sequentially.

$$(2)$$
$$172$$
$$\underline{\times \ 43}$$
$$516$$

$\{3 \times 2 = 6, \ 3 \times 7 = 21, \ 3 \times 1 = 3\}$ Note that we had to carry a 2 to the hundreds column because $3 \times 7 = 21$. Note also that we add carried numbers to the product.

Next, we multiply the number in the tens place of the bottom number by each place value of the top number sequentially. Because we are multiplying by a number in the tens place, we place a zero at the end of this product.

```
   (2)
   172
 × 43        {4 × 2 = 8, 4 × 7 = 28, 4 = 1 = 4}
   516
  6880
```

Finally, to determine the final product, we add the two partial products.

```
     172
   × 43
     516
  + 6880
    7396      The product of 172 and 43 is 7,396.
```

Example: A student buys 4 boxes of crayons. Each box contains 16 crayons. How many total crayons does the student have?

The total number of crayons is 16 × 4.

```
    16
  × 4
    64      The total number of crayons equals 64.
```

Division of Whole Numbers

Division, the inverse of multiplication, is another of the four basic number operations. When we divide one number by another, we determine how many times we can multiply the divisor (number divided by) before we exceed the number we are dividing (dividend). For example, 8 divided by 2 equals 4 because we can multiply 2 four times to reach 8 (2 × 4 = 8 or 2 + 2 + 2 + 2 = 8). Using the grouping conceptualization we used with multiplication, we can divide 8 into 4 groups of 2 or 2 groups of 4. We call the answer to a division problem the QUOTIENT.

QUOTIENT: the answer to a division problem

If the divisor does not divide evenly into the dividend, we express the leftover amount either as a remainder or as a fraction with the divisor as the denominator. For example, 9 divided by 2 equals 4 with a remainder of 1, or $4 \frac{1}{2}$.

The basic algorithm for division is long division. We start by representing the quotient as follows.

$14\overline{)293}$ → 14 is the divisor and 293 is the dividend.
This represents 293 ÷ 14.

Next, we divide the divisor into the dividend, starting from the left.

$$\begin{array}{r} 2 \\ 14\overline{)293} \end{array} \rightarrow \quad \text{14 divides into 29 two times with a remainder.}$$

Next, we multiply the partial quotient by the divisor, subtract this value from the first digits of the dividend, and bring down the remaining dividend digits to complete the number.

$$\begin{array}{r} 2 \\ 14\overline{)293} \\ -\ 28 \downarrow \\ \hline 13 \end{array} \rightarrow \quad 2 \times 14 = 28,\ 29 - 28 = 1,\ \text{and bringing down the 3 yields 13.}$$

Finally, we divide again (the divisor into the remaining value) and repeat the preceding process. The number left after the subtraction represents the remainder.

$$\begin{array}{r} 20 \\ 14\overline{)293} \\ -\ 28 \\ \hline 13 \\ -\ 0 \\ \hline 13 \end{array} \rightarrow$$

The final quotient is 20 with a remainder of 13. We can also represent this quotient as $20\frac{13}{14}$.

Example: Each box of apples contains 24 apples. How many boxes must a grocer purchase to supply a group of 252 people with one apple each?

The grocer needs 252 apples. Because he must buy apples in groups of 24, we divide 252 by 24 to determine how many boxes he needs to buy.

$$\begin{array}{r} 10 \\ 24\overline{)252} \\ -\ 24 \\ \hline 12 \\ -\ 0 \\ \hline 12 \end{array} \rightarrow \quad \text{The quotient is 10 with a remainder of 12.}$$

Thus, the grocer needs 10 boxes plus 12 more apples. Therefore, the minimum number of boxes the grocer can purchase is 11.

Example: At his job, John gets paid $20 for every hour he works. If John made $940 in a week, how many hours did he work?

This is a division problem. To determine the number of hours John worked, we divide the total amount made ($940) by the hourly rate of pay ($20). Thus, the number of hours worked equals 940 divided by 20.

$$\begin{array}{r} 47 \\ 20\overline{)940} \\ -\,80 \\ \hline 140 \\ -140 \\ \hline 0 \end{array}$$

$0 \rightarrow 20$ Divides into 940 a total of 47 times with no remainder.

John worked 47 hours.

Addition and Subtraction of Decimals

When adding and subtracting decimals, we align the numbers by place value as we do with whole numbers. After adding or subtracting each column, we bring the decimal down, placing it in the same location as in the numbers added or subtracted.

Example: Find the sum of 152.3 and 36.342.

$$\begin{array}{r} 152.300 \\ +\ 36.342 \\ \hline 188.642 \end{array}$$

Note that we placed two zeros after the final place value in 152.3 to clarify the column addition.

Example: Find the difference of 152.3 and 36.342.

$$\begin{array}{r} 2\ 9\ 10 \\ 152.\cancel{300} \\ -\ 36.342 \\ \hline 58 \end{array} \qquad \begin{array}{r} (4)11(12) \\ 1\cancel{52.300} \\ -\ 36.342 \\ \hline 115.958 \end{array}$$

Note how we borrowed to subtract from the zeros in the hundredths and thousandths places of 152.300.

Multiplication of Decimals

When multiplying decimal numbers, we multiply exactly as with whole numbers and place the decimal in from the right the total number of decimal places contained in the two numbers multiplied. For example, when multiplying 1.5 and 2.35, we place the decimal in the product 3 places in from the right (3.525).

> When adding and subtracting decimals, we align the numbers by place value as we do with whole numbers.

Example: Find the product of 3.52 and 4.1.

$$3.52$$
$$\underline{\times\ 4.1}$$
$$352$$
$$\underline{+\ 14080}$$
$$14.432$$

Note that there are three decimal places in total in the two numbers.

We place the decimal three places in from the right.

Thus, the final product is 14.432.

Example: A shopper has 5 one-dollar bills, 6 quarters, 3 nickels, and 4 pennies in his pocket. How much money does he have?

$$5 \times \$1.00 = \$5.00$$

$$
\begin{array}{ccc}
1\ 3 & 1 & \\
\$0.25 & \$0.05 & \$0.01 \\
\underline{\times\ 6} & \underline{\times\ 3} & \underline{\times\ 4} \\
\$1.50 & \$0.15 & \$0.04
\end{array}
$$

Note the placement of the decimals in the multiplication products. Thus, the total amount of money in the shopper's pocket is:

$$\$5.00$$
$$1.50$$
$$0.15$$
$$\underline{+\ 0.04}$$
$$\$6.69$$

Division of Decimals

When dividing decimal numbers, we first remove the decimal in the divisor by moving the decimal in the dividend the same number of spaces to the right. For example, when dividing 1.45 into 5.3, we convert the numbers to 145 and 530 and perform normal whole-number division.

Example: Find the quotient of 5.3 divided by 1.45.

Convert to 145 and 530.

Divide.

$$
\begin{array}{r}
3 \\
145\overline{)530} \\
\underline{-435} \\
95
\end{array}
$$

$$
\begin{array}{r}
3.65 \\
145\overline{)530.00} \\
\underline{-435} \\
950 \\
\underline{-870} \\
800
\end{array}
$$

Note that we insert the decimal to continue division.

Because one of the numbers divided contained one decimal place, we round the quotient to one decimal place. Thus, the final quotient is 3.7.

Operating with Percents

Example: 5 is what percent of 20?

This is the same as converting $\frac{5}{20}$ to % form.

$$\frac{5}{20} \times \frac{100}{1} = \frac{5}{1} \times \frac{5}{1} = 25\%$$

Example: There are 64 dogs in the kennel. 48 are collies. What percent are collies?

Restate the problem.	48 is what percent of 64?
Write an equation.	$48 = n \times 64$
Solve.	$\frac{48}{64} = n$

$n = \frac{3}{4} = 75\%$

75% of the dogs are collies.

Example: The auditorium was filled to 90% capacity. There were 558 seats occupied. What is the capacity of the auditorium?

Restate the problem.	90% of what number is 558?
Write an equation.	$0.9n = 558$
Solve.	$n = \frac{558}{.9}$

$n = 620$

The capacity of the auditorium is 620 people.

Example: A pair of shoes costs $42.00. The sales tax is 6%. What is the total cost of the shoes?

Restate the problem.	What is 6% of 42?
Write an equation.	$n = 0.06 \times 42$
Solve.	$n = 2.52$
Add the sales tax to the cost.	$42.00 + $2.52 = $44.52

The total cost of the shoes, including sales tax, is $44.52.

Addition and Subtraction of Fractions

Key points

1. You need a common denominator in order to add and subtract reduced and improper fractions.

   Example:

   $$\frac{1}{3} + \frac{7}{3} = \frac{1+7}{3} = \frac{8}{3} = 2\frac{2}{3}$$

   Example:

   $$\frac{4}{12} + \frac{6}{12} - \frac{3}{12} = \frac{4+6-3}{12} = \frac{7}{12}$$

2. Adding an integer and a fraction of the same sign results directly in a mixed fraction.

   Example:

   $$2 + \frac{2}{3} = 2\frac{2}{3}$$

   Example:

   $$\text{-}2 - \frac{2}{3} = \text{-}2\frac{2}{3}$$

3. Adding an integer and a fraction with different signs involves the following steps.

   - Get a common denominator

   - Add or subtract as needed

   - Change to a mixed fraction if possible

   Example:

   $$2 - \frac{1}{3} = \frac{2 \times 3 - 1}{3} = \frac{6 - 1}{3} = \frac{5}{3} = 1\frac{2}{3}$$

   Example:

   Add $7\frac{3}{8} + 5\frac{2}{7}$

   Add the whole numbers, add the fractions, and combine the two results:

   $$7\frac{3}{8} + 5\frac{2}{7} = (7 + 5) + \left(\frac{3}{8} + \frac{2}{7}\right)$$

   $$= 12 + \frac{(7 \times 3) + (8 \times 2)}{56} \qquad \text{(LCM of 8 and 7)}$$

   $$= 12 + \frac{21 + 16}{56} = 12 + \frac{37}{56} = 12\frac{37}{56}$$

   Example: Perform the operation.

   $$\frac{2}{3} - \frac{5}{6}$$

   We first find the LCM of 3 and 6, which is 6.

   $$\frac{2 \times 2}{3 \times 2} - \frac{5}{6} \rightarrow \frac{4 - 5}{6} = \frac{\text{-}1}{6} \qquad \text{(Using method A)}$$

   Example:

   $$\text{-}7\frac{1}{4} + 2\frac{7}{8}$$

   $$\text{-}7\frac{1}{4} + 2\frac{7}{8} = (\text{-}7 + 2) + \left(\frac{\text{-}1}{4} + \frac{7}{8}\right)$$

   $$= (\text{-}5) + \frac{\text{-}2 + 7}{8} = (\text{-}5) + \left(\frac{5}{8}\right)$$

   $$= (\text{-}5) + \frac{5}{8} = \frac{\text{-}5 \times 8}{1 \times 8} + \frac{5}{8} = \frac{\text{-}40 + 5}{8}$$

   $$= \frac{\text{-}35}{8} = \text{-}4\frac{3}{8}$$

   Divide 35 by 8 to get 4, remainder 3.

Example:

Caution: A common error would be:

$-7\frac{1}{4} + 2\frac{7}{8} = -7\frac{2}{8} + 2\frac{7}{8} = -5\frac{9}{8}$ Wrong.

It is correct to add -7 and 2 to get -5, but adding $\frac{2}{8} + \frac{7}{8} = \frac{9}{8}$ is wrong. It should have been $\frac{-2}{8} + \frac{7}{8} = \frac{5}{8}$. Then, $-5 + \frac{5}{8} = -4\frac{3}{8}$ as before.

Multiplication of Fractions

Using the following example: $3\frac{1}{4} \times \frac{5}{6}$

1. Convert each number to an improper fraction

   $3\frac{1}{4} = \frac{(12 + 1)}{4} = \frac{13}{4}$ $\qquad$ $\frac{5}{6}$ is already in reduced form.

2. Reduce (cancel) common factors of the numerator and denominator if they exist

   $\frac{13}{4} \times \frac{5}{6}$ $\qquad$ No common factors exist.

3. Multiply the numerators by each other and the denominators by each other

   $\frac{13}{4} \times \frac{5}{6} = \frac{65}{24}$

4. If possible, reduce the fraction to its lowest term

   $\frac{65}{24}$ $\qquad$ Cannot be reduced further.

5. Convert the improper fraction back to a mixed fraction by using long division

   $\frac{65}{24} = 24\overline{)65} = 2\frac{17}{24}$
   $\phantom{\frac{65}{24} = 24\overline{)}}\underline{48}$
   $\phantom{\frac{65}{24} = 24\overline{)6}}17$

Summary of Sign Changes for Multiplication

1. $(+) \times (+) = (+)$

2. $(-) \times (+) = (-)$

3. $(+) \times (-) = (-)$

4. $(-) \times (-) = (+)$

Example: $7\frac{1}{3} \times \frac{5}{11} = \frac{22}{3} \times \frac{5}{11}$

Reduce like terms (22 and 11).

$= \frac{2}{3} \times \frac{5}{1} = \frac{10}{3} = 3\frac{1}{3}$

Example: $-6\frac{1}{4} \times \frac{5}{9} = \frac{-25}{4} \times \frac{5}{9}$

$= \frac{-125}{36} = -3\frac{17}{36}$

Example: $\frac{-1}{4} \times \frac{-3}{7}$

A negative times a negative equals a positive.

$= \frac{1}{4} \times \frac{3}{7} = \frac{3}{28}$

Division of Fractions

1. Change mixed fractions to improper fractions

2. Change the division problem to a multiplication problem by using the reciprocal of the number after the division sign

3. Find the sign of the final product

4. Cancel if common factors exist between the numerator and the denominator

5. Multiply the numerators together and the denominators together

6. Change the improper fraction to a mixed number

Example: $3\frac{1}{5} + 2\frac{1}{4} = \frac{16}{5} + \frac{9}{4}$

$= \frac{16}{5} \times \frac{4}{9}$ The reciprocal of $\frac{9}{4}$ is $\frac{4}{9}$.

$= \frac{64}{65} = 1\frac{19}{45}$

Example: $7\frac{3}{4} + 11\frac{5}{8} = \frac{31}{4} + \frac{93}{8}$

$= \frac{31}{4} \times \frac{8}{93}$ Reduce like terms.

$= \frac{1}{1} \times \frac{2}{3} = \frac{2}{3}$

Example: $(-2\frac{1}{2}) + 4\frac{1}{6} = \frac{-5}{2} + \frac{25}{6}$

$= \frac{-5}{2} \times \frac{6}{25}$ Reduce like terms.

$= \frac{-1}{1} \times \frac{3}{5} = \frac{-3}{5}$

Example: $(-5\frac{3}{8}) + (\frac{7}{16}) = \frac{-43}{8} + \frac{27}{16}$

$= \frac{-43}{8} \times \frac{-16}{7}$ Reduce like terms.

$= \frac{43}{1} \times \frac{2}{7}$ A negative times a negative equals a positive.

$= \frac{86}{7} = 12\frac{2}{7}$

SKILL 1.3 Apply basic number theory concepts including the use of primes, composites, factors, and multiples in solving problems

The Greatest Common Factor (GCF)

GCF is the abbreviation for the greatest common factor. The GREATEST COMMON FACTOR is the largest number that is a factor of all the numbers in a given problem. The GCF can be no larger than the smallest number in the problem.

To find the GCF, list all possible factors of the smallest number given (including the number itself). Starting with the largest factor (which is the smallest number itself), determine if this number is also a factor of all the other numbers in the problem. If it is, that number is the GCF.

If the smallest number in the problem is not a factor of the other numbers, continue to test increasingly smaller possible factors until you find a common factor. That is the GCF. The GCF is not necessarily the only common factor.

Example: Find the GCF of 12, 20, and 36.
The smallest number in the problem is 12. The factors of 12 are 1, 2, 3, 4, 6, and 12. 12 is the largest of these factors, but it does not divide evenly into 20. Neither does 6. However, 4 will divide into both 20 and 36 evenly. Therefore, 4 is the GCF.

Example: Find the GCF of 14 and 15.
The factors of 14 are 1, 2, 7 and 14. 14 is the largest factor, but it does not divide evenly into 15. Neither does 7 or 2. Therefore, the only factor common to both 14 and 15 is the number 1, the GCF.

> **GREATEST COMMON FACTOR:** the largest number that is a factor of all the numbers in a problem

> *If no other number is a common factor, then the GCF of a group of numbers will be the number 1.*

The Least Common Multiple (LCM)

LCM is the abbreviation for LEAST COMMON MULTIPLE. The least common multiple of a group of numbers is the smallest number that all of the given numbers will divide into. The LCM will always be the largest of the given numbers or a multiple of the largest number.

Example: Find the LCM of 20, 30, and 40.
The largest number given is 40, but 30 will not divide evenly into 40. The next multiple of 40 is 80 (2×40), but 30 will not divide evenly into 80 either. The next multiple of 40 is 120 (3×40). 120 is divisible by both 20 and 30, so 120 is the LCM.

> **LEAST COMMON MULTIPLE:** the smallest number of a group of numbers that all the given numbers will divide into evenly

Example: Find the LCM of 96, 16, and 24.
The largest number is 96. 96 is divisible by both 16 and 24, so 96 is the LCM.

Example: Elly Mae can feed the animals in 15 minutes. Jethro can feed them in 10 minutes. How long will it take them to feed the animals if they work together?
If Elly Mae can feed the animals in 15 minutes, then she could feed $\frac{1}{15}$ of them in 1 minute, $\frac{2}{15}$ of them in 2 minutes, and $\frac{x}{15}$ of them in x minutes. In the same fashion, Jethro could feed $\frac{x}{10}$ of them in x minutes. Together they complete one job. The equation is:

$$\frac{x}{15} + \frac{x}{10} = 1$$

Multiply each term by the LCD (least common denominator) of 30:

$2x \times 3x = 30$

$x = 6$ minutes

Prime and Composite Numbers

COMPOSITE NUMBERS are whole numbers that have more than two different factors. For example, 9 is composite because, besides the factors of 1 and 9, 3 is also a factor. 70 is composite because, besides the factors of 1 and 70, the numbers 2, 5, 7, 10, 14, and 35 are also all factors.

PRIME NUMBERS are whole numbers greater than 1 that have only two factors: 1 and the number itself. Examples of prime numbers are 2, 3, 5, 7, 11, 13, 17, and 19. Note that 2 is the only even prime number.

When factoring into prime factors, all the factors must be numbers that cannot be factored again (without using 1). Initially, numbers can be factored into any two factors. Check each resulting factor to see whether it can be factored again. Continue factoring until all remaining factors are prime. This is the list of prime factors. Regardless of what way the original number was factored, the final list of prime factors will always be the same.

Remember that the number 1 is neither prime nor composite.

Example:
Factor 30 into prime factors.
Factor 30 into any two factors.

5×6	Now factor the 6.
$5 \times 2 \times 3$	These are all prime factors.

or

Factor 30 into any two factors.

COMPOSITE NUMBERS: whole numbers that have more than two different factors

PRIME NUMBERS: whole numbers greater than 1 that have only two factors: 1 and the number itself

| 3×10 | Now factor the 10. |
| $3 \times 2 \times 5$ | These are the same prime factors, even though the original factors were different. |

Example:

Factor 240 into prime factors.

Factor 240 into any two factors.

24×10	Now factor both 24 and 10.
$4 \times 6 \times 2 \times 5$	Now factor both 4 and 6.
$2 \times 2 \times 2 \times 3 \times 2 \times 5$	These are the prime factors.

This can also be written as $2^4 \times 3 \times 5$.

SKILL 1.4 Apply the Order of Operations with or without grouping symbols

Always follow the ORDER OF OPERATIONS when evaluating algebraic expressions. Follow these steps in order:

1. Simplify inside grouping characters such as parentheses, brackets, square root, and fraction bars

2. Multiply out expressions with exponents

3. Do multiplication and/or division, from left to right

4. Do addition and/or subtraction, from left to right

ORDER OF OPERATIONS: the order in which mathematical operations should be performed

Example: $3^3 - 5(b + 2)$

$= 3^3 - 5b - 10$

$= 27 - 5b - 10 = 17 - 5b$

Example: $2 - 4 \times 2^3 - 2(4 - 2 \times 3)$

$= 2 - 4 \times 2^3 - 2(4 - 6) = 2 - 4 \times 2^3 - 2\,(-2)$

$= 2 - 4 \times 2^3 + 4 = 2 - 4 \times 8 + 4$

$= 2 - 32 + 4 = 6 - 32 = -26$

COMPETENCY 2
KNOWLEDGE OF MEASUREMENT (USING CUSTOMARY OR METRIC UNITS)

> **SKILL 2.1** Solve real-world problems involving length, weight, mass, perimeter, area, capacity, and volume

MEASUREMENTS OF LENGTH (ENGLISH SYSTEM)		
12 inches (in)	=	1 foot (ft)
3 ft	=	1 yard (yd)
1760 yd	=	1 mile (mi)

MEASUREMENTS OF LENGTH (METRIC SYSTEM)		
kilometer (km)	=	1000 meters (m)
hectometer (hm)	=	100 meters (m)
decameter (dam)	=	1 mile (mi)
meter (m)	=	10 meters (m)
decimeter (dm)	=	1 meter (m)
centimeter (cm)	=	1/10 meter (m)
millimeter (mm)	=	1/100 meter (m)

CONVERSION OF LENGTH FROM ENGLISH TO METRIC		
1 inch	=	2.54 centimeters
1 foot	≈	30 centimeters
1 yard	≈	0.9 meters
1 mile	≈	1.6 kilometers

MEASUREMENTS OF WEIGHT (ENGLISH SYSTEM)		
28 grams (g)	=	1 ounce (oz)
16 ounces (oz)	=	1 pound (lb)
2000 pounds (lb)	=	1 ton (t) (short ton)
1.1 ton (t)	=	1 ton (t)

MEASUREMENTS OF WEIGHT (METRIC SYSTEM)		
kilogram (kg)	=	1000 grams (g)
gram (g)	=	1 gram (g)
milligram (mg)	=	1/1000 gram (g)

CONVERSION OF WEIGHT FROM ENGLISH TO METRIC		
1 ounce	≈	28 grams
1 pound	≈ ≈	0.45 kilogram 454 grams

MEASUREMENT OF VOLUME (ENGLISH SYSTEM)		
8 fluid ounces (oz)	=	1 cup (c)
2 cups (c)	=	1 pint (pt)
2 pints (pt)	=	1 quart (qt)
4 quarts (qt)	=	1 gallon (gal)

MEASUREMENT OF VOLUME (METRIC SYSTEM)		
kiloliter (kl)	=	1000 liters (l)
liter (l)	=	1 liter (l)
milliliter (ml)	=	1/1000 liters (ml)

CONVERSION OF VOLUME FROM ENGLISH TO METRIC		
1 teaspoon (tsp	≈	5 milliliters
1 fluid ounce	≈	15 milliliters
1 cup	≈	0.24 liters
1 pint	≈	0.47 liters
1 quart	≈	0.95 liters
1 gallon	≈	3.8 liters

MEASUREMENT OF TIME		
1 minute	=	60 seconds
1 hour	=	60 minutes
1 day	=	24 hours
1 week	=	7 days
1 year	=	365 days
1 century	=	100 years

Square Units

Square units can be derived with knowledge of basic units of length by squaring the equivalent measurements.

1 square foot (sq. ft.) = 144 sq. in.

1 sq. yd. = 9 sq. ft.

1 sq. yd. = 1296 sq. in.

Example:
14 sq. yd. = _____ sq. ft.
$14 \times 9 = 126$ sq. ft.

Weight

Example: Kathy has a bag of potatoes that weighs 5 lbs., 10 oz. She uses one third of the bag to make mashed potatoes. How much does the bag weigh now?

1 lb. = 16 oz.

5(16 oz.) + 10 oz.

= 80 oz + 10 oz = 90 oz.

$90 - (\frac{1}{3})90$ oz

= 90 oz − 30 oz

= 60 oz

60 ÷ 16 = 3.75 lb

.75 = 75%

$75\% = \frac{75}{100} = \frac{3}{4}$

$\frac{3}{4} \times 16$ oz = 12 oz

The bag now weighs 3 lb, 12 oz.

Example: The weight limit of a playground merry-go-round is 1000 pounds. There are 11 children on the merry-go-round. 3 children weigh 100 pounds. 6 children weigh 75 pounds. 2 children weigh 60 pounds. George weighs 80 pounds. Can he get on the merry-go-round?

3(100) + 6(75) + 2(60)

= 300 + 450 + 120

= 870

1000 − 870

= 130

George weighs less than 130, so he can get on the merry-go-round.

Perimeter and Area

The PERIMETER of any polygon is the sum of the lengths of the sides.

The AREA of a polygon is the number of square units covered by the figure.

FIGURE	AREA FORMULA	PERIMETER FORMULA
Rectangle	LW	$2(L + W)$
Triangle	$\frac{1}{2} bh$	$a + b + c$
Parallelogram	bh	sum of lengths of sides
Trapezoid	$\frac{1}{2} h(a + b)$	sum of lengths of sides

PERIMETER: the sum of the lengths of the sides of any polygon

AREA: the number of square units covered by a polygon

Example: A farmer has a piece of land shaped as shown below. He wishes to fence this land at an estimated cost of $25 per linear foot. What is the total cost of fencing this property to the nearest foot?

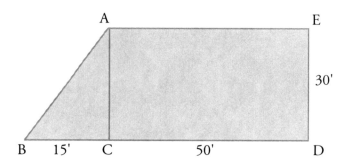

From the right triangle *ABC*, *AC* = 30 and *BC* = 15.

Since $(AB) = (AC)^2 + (BC)^2$

$(AB) = (30)^2 + (15)^2$

So feet $\sqrt{(AB)^2} = AB = \sqrt{1125} = 33.5410$ feet

To the nearest foot, *AB* = 34 feet.

Perimeter of the piece of land is = *AB* + *BC* + *CD* + *DE* + *EA*

= 34 + 15 + 50 + 30 + 50 = 179 feet

Cost of fencing = $25 × 179 = $4,475.00

Area of a Polygon

Example: What will be the cost of carpeting a rectangular office that measures 12 feet by 15 feet if the carpet costs $12.50 per square yard?

The problem is asking you to determine the area of the office. The area of a rectangle is *length × width = A.*

Substitute the given values in the equation $A = lw.$

$A = (12 \text{ ft.})(15 \text{ ft.})$

$A = 180 \text{ ft.}^2$

The problem asked you to determine the cost of carpet at $12.50 per square yard.

First, you need to convert 180 ft.^{2} into yards^2.

$\quad$ 1 yd =3 ft.

$\quad$ (1 yd)(1 yd.) = (3 ft.) (3 ft.)

$\quad$ 1 yd^2 = 9 ft^2

$\quad$ $\frac{180 \text{ ft}^2}{9 \text{ ft}^2} = 20$

The carpet costs \$12.50 per square yard; thus the cost of carpeting the office described is \$12.50 × 20 = \$250.00.

Example: Find the area of a parallelogram if its base is 6.5 cm long and the height of the altitude to that base is 3.7 cm.

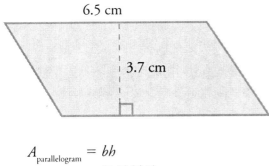

6.5 cm

3.7 cm

$A_{\text{parallelogram}} = bh$
$\quad\quad = (3.7)(6.5)$
$\quad\quad = 24.05 \text{ cm}^2$

Example: Find the area of this triangle.

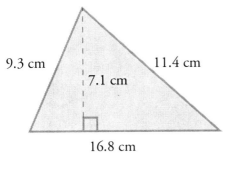

9.3 cm $\quad\quad$ 11.4 cm

7.1 cm

16.8 cm

$A_{\text{triangle}} = \frac{1}{2} bh$
$\quad\quad = 0.5(16.8)(7.1)$
$\quad\quad = 59.64 \text{ cm}^2$

Example: Find the area of this trapezoid.

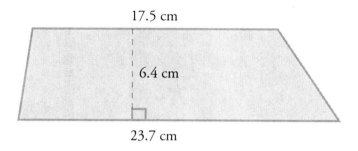

17.5 cm

6.4 cm

23.7 cm

The area of a trapezoid equals one-half the sum of the bases times the altitude.

$A_{trapezoid} = \frac{1}{2} h(b_1 + b_2)$
$A_{trapezoid} = 0.5(6.4)(17.5 + 23.7)$
$A_{trapezoid} = 131.84 \text{ cm}^2$

Circles

The distance around a circle is the CIRCUMFERENCE. The ratio of the circumference to the diameter is represented by the Greek letter pi, $\pi \sim 3.14 \sim \frac{22}{7}$.

The circumference of a circle is found by the formula $C = 2\pi r$ or $C = \pi d$, where r is the radius of the circle and d is the diameter.

The area of a circle is found by the formula $A = \pi r^2$.

Example: Find the circumference and area of a circle whose radius is 7 meters.

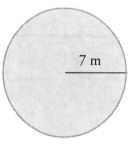

7 m

$C = \pi r$ $A = \pi r^2$
$= 2(3.14)(7)$ $= 3.14(7)(7)$
$= 43.96 \text{ m}$ $= 153.86 \text{ m}^2$

Volume and surface area are computed using the following formulas:

FIGURE	LATERAL AREA	TOTAL AREA	VOLUME
Regular Pyramid	$\frac{1}{2} Pl$	$\frac{1}{2} Pl + B$	$\frac{1}{3} Bh$

P = Perimeter, h = height, B = Area of Base, l = slant height

FIGURE	VOLUME	TOTAL SURFACE AREA
Right Cylinder	$\pi r^2 h$	$2\pi rh + 2\pi r^2$
Right Cone	$\dfrac{\pi r^2 h}{3}$	$\pi r \sqrt{r^2 + h^2} + \pi r^2$
Sphere	$\dfrac{4}{3} \pi r^3$	$4\pi r2$
Rectangular Solid	LWH	$2LW + 2WH + 2LH$

P = Perimeter, h = height, B = Area of Base, l = slant height

Example: What is the volume of a shoe box with a length of 35 cm, a width of 20 cm, and a height of 15 cm?

Volume of a rectangular solid

= Length × Width × Height

= 35 × 20 × 15

= 10500 cm^3

Example: A water company is trying to decide whether to use traditional cylindrical paper cups or to offer conical paper cups, since both cost the same. The traditional cups are 8 cm wide and 14 cm high. The conical cups are 12 cm wide and 19 cm high. The company will use the cup that holds the most water.

Draw and label a sketch of each.

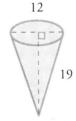

$V = \pi r^2 h$ $V = \dfrac{\pi r^2 h}{3}$ 1. Write a formula.

$V = \pi(4)^2(14)$ $V = \dfrac{1}{3}\pi(6)^2(19)$ 2. Substitute.

$V = 703.717$ cm^3 $V = 716.283$ cm^3 3. Solve.

The choice should be the conical cup since its volume is more.

Example: How much material is needed to make a basketball that has a diameter of 15 inches? How much air is needed to fill the basketball?

Draw and label a sketch:

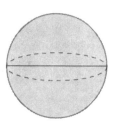

$D = 15$ inches

Total surface area	Volume	
$\text{TSA} = 4\pi r^2$	$V = \frac{4}{3}\pi r^3$	1. Write a formula.
$= 4\pi(7.5)^2$	$= \frac{4}{3}\pi(7.5)^3$	2. Substitute.
$= 706.858 \text{ in}^2$	$= 1767.1459 \text{ in}^3$	3. Solve.

SKILL 2.2 Solve real-world problems involving rated measures *(e.g., miles per hour, meters per second, cost per item, and cost per unit)*

Example: A class wants to take a field trip from New York City to Albany. The trip is approximately 160 miles. If they travel at 50 miles per hour, how long will it take for them to get to Albany (assuming that they are traveling at a steady rate)?

Set up the equation as a proportion and solve:

$$\frac{160 \text{ miles}}{x \text{ hours}} = \frac{50 \text{ miles}}{1 \text{ hour}}$$

$(160 \text{ miles})(1 \text{ hour}) = (50 \text{ miles})(x \text{ hours})$

$160 = 50x$

$x = 3.2 \text{ hours}$

Example: A salesman drove 480 miles from Pittsburgh to Hartford. The next day he returned the same distance to Pittsburgh in half an hour less time than his original trip took, because he increased his average speed by 4 mph. Find his original speed.

Since distance $=$ rate $\times$ time, then time $= \frac{\text{distance}}{\text{rate}}$

original time $- 1/2$ hour $=$ shorter return time

$$\frac{480}{x} - \frac{1}{2} = \frac{480}{x + 4}$$

Multiplying by the LCD of $2x(x + 4)$, the equation becomes:

$480[2(x + 4)] - 1[x(x + 4)] = 480(2x)$

$960x + 3840 - x^2 - 4x = 960x$

$x^2 + 4x - 3840 = 0$

$(x + 64)(x - 60) = 0$

$x = 60$

60 mph is the original speed, 64 mph is the faster return speed.

Cost per Unit

The unit rate for purchasing an item is its price divided by the number of units in the item. The item with the lower unit rate is the lower price.

Example: Find the item with the best unit cost.

$1.79 for 10 ounces

$1.89 for 12 ounces

$5.49 for 32 ounces

$\frac{1.79}{10} = 0.179$ per ounce $\frac{1.89}{12} = 0.1575$ per ounce $\frac{5.49}{32} = 0.172$ per ounce

$1.89 for 12 ounces is the best price.

SKILL Solve real-world problems involving scaled drawings *(e.g., maps,*
2.3 *blueprints, and models)*

Students need to understand that ratios and proportions are used to create scale models of real-life objects. They should understand the principles of ratio and proportion and how to calculate scale using ratio and proportion.

Scaled drawings (maps, blueprints, and models) are used in many real-world situations. Architects make blueprints and models of buildings. The contractors then use these drawings and models to build the buildings. Engineers make scaled drawings of bridges, machine parts, roads, airplanes, and many other things. Maps of the world, countries, states, roads, etc., are scaled drawings. Landscape designers use scaled drawings and models of plants, decks, and other structures to show how they should be placed around a house or other building. Models of cars, boats, and planes made from kits are scaled. Automobile engineers construct models of cars before the actual assembly is done. Many museum exhibits are actually scaled models because the real size of the items displayed would be too large.

Examples of real-world problems that students might solve using scaled drawings include:

- Reading road maps and determining the distance between locations by using the map scale

- Creating a scaled drawing (floor plan) of their classroom to determine the best use of space

- Creating an 8 ½" × 11" representation of a quilt to be pieced together

- Drawing a blueprint of their rooms and creating a model from it

---

SKILL 2.4 Solve real-world problems involving the change of units of measures of length, weight, capacity, and time

Length

Example: A car skidded 170 yards on an icy road before coming to a stop. How long is the skid distance in kilometers?

Since 1 yard 0.9 meter, multiply 170 yards by 0.9.

$$170 \times 0.9 = 153 \text{ meters}$$

Since 1000 meters = 1 kilometer, divide 153 by 1000.

$$\frac{153}{1000} = 0.153 \text{ kilometer}$$

Example: The distance around a race course is exactly 1 mile, 17 feet, and $9\frac{1}{4}$ inches. Approximate this distance to the nearest tenth of a foot.

Convert the distance to feet.

$$1 \text{ mile} = 1760 \text{ yards} = 1760 \times 3 \text{ feet} = 5280 \text{ feet}$$

$$9\frac{1}{4} \text{ inches} = \frac{37}{4} \times \frac{1}{12} = \frac{37}{48} \approx 0.77083 \text{ foot}$$

So 1 mile, 17 feet, and $9\frac{1}{4}$ inches = $5280 + 17 + 0.77083$ feet

$$= 5297.\underline{7}7083 \text{ feet.}$$

Now, we need to round to the nearest tenths digit. The underlined 7 is in the tenths place. The digit in the hundredths place, also a 7, is greater than 5, so the 7 in the tenths place must be rounded up to 8 to get a final answer of 5297.8 feet.

Weight

Example: Zachary weighs 150 pounds. Tom weighs 153 pounds. What is the difference in their weights in grams?

153 pounds − 150 pounds = 3 pounds

1 pound = 454 grams

3(454 grams) = 1362 grams

Capacity

Example: Students in a fourth grade class want to fill a 3-gallon jug using cups of water. How many cups of water are needed?

1 gallon = 16 cups of water

3 gallons × 16 cups = 48 cups of water are needed.

Time

Example: It takes Cynthia 45 minutes to get ready each morning. How many hours does she spend getting ready each week?

45 minutes × 7 days = 315 minutes

$$\frac{315 \text{ minutes}}{60 \text{ minutes in an hour}} = 5.25 \text{ hours}$$

SKILL 2.5 **Solve real-world problems involving estimates of measures including length, weight, mass, temperature, time, money, perimeter, area, and volume**

To estimate the measurements of familiar objects, it is first necessary to determine which units to use.

Examples:

LENGTH	
The coastline of Florida	miles or kilometers
The width of a ribbon	inches or millimeters
The thickness of a book	inches or centimeters
The length of a football field	yards or meters
The depth of water in a pool	feet or meters

WEIGHT OR MASS	
A bag of sugar	pounds or grams
A school bus	tons or kilograms
A dime	ounces or grams

CAPACITY OR VOLUME	
Paint to paint a bedroom	gallons or liters
Glass of milk	cups or liters
Bottle of soda	quarts or liters
Medicine for child	ounces or milliliters

It is necessary to be familiar with the metric and customary system in order to estimate measurements.

Some common equivalents include:

ITEM	APPROXIMATELY EQUAL TO	
	METRIC	CUSTOMARY
Large paper clip	1 gram	0.1 ounce
Average sized adult	75 kilograms	170 pounds
Length of an office desk	1 meter	1 yard
Length of dollar bill	15 centimeters	6 inches
Area of football field		6,400 sq. yd
Temperature of boiling water	100°C	212°F
Temperature of ice	0°C	32°F
1 cup of liquid	240 mL	8 fl oz
1 teaspoon	5 ml	

Example: Estimate the measurement of the following items:

The length of dollar bill = ____6____ inches

Weight of a baseball = ____1____ pound

Distance from New York to Florida = ____1100____ km

Volume of water to fill a medicine dropper = ____1____ milliliter

Length of a desk = ____2____ meters

Temperature of water in a swimming pool = ____80°____ F

Depending on the degree of accuracy needed, we can measure an object with different units. For example, a pencil may be 6 inches when measured to the nearest inch or $6\frac{3}{8}$ inches when measured to the nearest eighth of an inch.

Using the metric system, the pencil might be 15 cm when measured to the nearest cm or 154 mm when measured to the nearest mm.

Rounding Measurements

When rounding to a given place value, it is necessary to look at the number in the place smaller that than the place to which the number will be rounded, that is, the number to its right. If this number is 5 or more, increase the number in the place above and change all numbers to its right to zero. If the number is less than 5, leave the number in the place above as it is and change all numbers to its right to zero.

Given a set of objects and their measurements, rounding procedures are helpful when attempting to round to the nearest given unit.

Rounding measurements can require an additional step. When the measurement to be rounded is not in decimal form, convert the measurement to a decimal number before applying the rules of rounding.

Example: Round the measurements to the given units.

MEASUREMENT	ROUND TO NEAREST	ANSWER
1 foot 7 inches	foot	2 ft
5 pound 6 ounces	pound	5 pounds
$5\frac{9}{16}$ inches	inch	6 inches

Convert each measurement to a decimal number. Then apply the rules for rounding.

1 foot 7 inches = $1\frac{7}{12}$ ft = 1.58333 ft, round up to 2 ft.

5 pounds 6 ounces = $5\frac{6}{16}$ pounds = 5.375 pound, round to 5 pounds.

$5\frac{9}{16}$ inches = 5.5625 inches, round up to 6 inches.

Rounding numbers is a form of estimation that is useful in many mathematical operations. For example, when estimating the sum of two three-digit numbers it is helpful to round the two numbers to the nearest hundred prior to addition.

Rounding Whole Numbers

To round whole numbers, first find the place value you want to round to (the rounding digit). Look at the digit directly to the right. If the digit is less than 5, do not change the rounding digit and replace all numbers after the rounding digit with zeros. If the digit is greater than or equal to 5, increase the rounding digit by 1, and replace all numbers after the rounding digit with zeros.

Example: Round 517 to the nearest ten.
1 is the rounding digit because it occupies the tens place. 517 rounded to the nearest ten = 520; because $7 > 5$, we add 1 to the rounding digit.

Example: Round 15,449 to the nearest hundred.
The first 4 is the rounding digit because it occupies the hundreds place. 15,449 rounded to the nearest hundred = 15,400; because $4 < 5$, we do not add to the rounding digit.

Rounding Decimals

Rounding decimals is identical to rounding whole numbers except that you simply drop all the digits to the right of the rounding digit.

Example: Round 417.3621 to the nearest tenth.
3 is the rounding digit because it occupies the tenths place. 417.3621 rounded to the nearest tenth = 417.4; because $6 > 5$, we add 1 to the rounding digit.

Regrouping to Estimate Differences

Estimate the difference between two numbers by first rounding the numbers and then subtracting one of the rounded numbers from the other. When subtracting two rounded numbers, one rounded up and the other rounded down, regrouping improves the estimate.

The regrouping method of estimation only works when we round the two numbers in opposite directions.

For example, when estimating the difference of 540 and 355, round 540 down to 500 and 355 up to 400. Thus, the estimated difference is 500 minus 400, or 100. Note that 540 is rounded *down* by 40 and 355 is rounded *up* by 45.

Front-End Estimation

FRONT-END ESTIMATION is an elementary form of estimation of sums and differences. To estimate a sum or difference by front-end estimation, add or subtract only the two highest place values and fill the remaining place values with zeroes.

> **FRONT-END ESTIMATION:** an elementary form of estimation of sums and differences

Example: Estimate 4987 + 3512 by front-end estimation.
The estimated sum is 8400 (4900 + 3500).

Note that we do not round the numbers, but merely drop the digits after the two highest place values. In other words, we convert 4987 to 4900, not 5000.

Example: Estimate 3894 − 617 by front-end estimation.
The estimated difference is 3200 (3800 − 600).

Note that because 617 does not have a digit in the thousands place and 3894 does, we convert 617 to 600, not 610.

> *While we can add or subtract rounded numbers to estimate sums and differences, front-end estimation is simpler and usually delivers results that are just as accurate.*

Applied estimation example

Example: Janet goes into a store to purchase a CD that is on sale for $13.95. While shopping, she sees two pairs of shoes priced at $19.95 and $14.50. She only has $50. Can she purchase everything?

Solve by rounding:

$19.95 → $20.00
$14.50 → $15.00
$13.95 → $14.00
$49.00   Yes, she can purchase the CD and the shoes.

> **SKILL 2.6** **Choose the correct reading, to a specified degree of accuracy, using instruments** *(e.g., scales, rulers, thermometers, measuring cups, protractors, and gauges)*

When using a scale with a needle that has a mirrored plate behind it, view the scale so that the needle's reflection is hidden behind the needle itself. Do not look at the mirrored plate from an angle.

In order to read a balance scale accurately, place the scale on a level surface and make sure that the hand points precisely at 0. Place objects on the plate gently and take them away gently. Face the dial straight on to read the graduation accurately.

> *When reading an instrument of measurement, first determine the interval of scale on the instrument. To achieve the greatest accuracy, read the scale to the nearest measurement mark.*

If the dial hand points between two graduations, choose the number that is closest to the hand.

When reading inches on a ruler, remember that each inch is divided into halves by the longest mark in the middle of two inch marks, into fourths by the next longest marks, into eighths by the next, and into sixteenths by the shortest. When a measurement falls between two inch marks, add the fractional marks to the whole number of inches and give the measurement as the number and fraction of inches. A fraction should always be expressed in lowest terms.

> *Measurements using the metric system should always be written using the decimal system, for example, 3.756 centimeters.*

When using a metric system ruler, note that each centimeter is broken into tenths, with the longer mark in the middle indicating five tenths, or half a centimeter. Measure as accurately as possible to the nearest tenth of a centimeter, then the nearest hundredth, and finally the nearest thousandth.

When reading a thermometer, hold it vertically at eye level. Check the scale of the thermometer to read as many significant digits as possible. Thermometers with heavy or extended lines that are marked 10, 20, 30, and so on should be read to the nearest 0.1 degree. Thermometers with fine lines every two degrees should be read to the nearest 0.5 degree.

> **MENISCUS LINE:** the bottom of the concave arc of a liquid's surface

In order to get an accurate reading in a liquid measuring cup, set the cup on a level surface and read it at eye level. Read the measurement at the MENISCUS LINE, which is the bottom of the concave arc of a liquid's surface. When measuring dry ingredients, dip the appropriately sized measuring cup into the ingredient and sweep away the excess across the top with a straight-edged object.

Protractors measure angles in degrees. To measure accurately, find the center hole on the straight edge of the protractor and place it over the vertex of the angle to measure. Line up the zero on the straight edge with one of the sides of the angle. Find the point where the second side of the angle intersects the curved edge of the protractor and read the number that is written at the point of intersection.

When reading an instrument such as a rain gauge, read at eye level and at the meniscus line. The measuring tube is divided, marked, and labeled in tenths and hundredths. Measure to the nearest hundredth.

COMPETENCY 3
KNOWLEDGE OF GEOMETRY AND SPATIAL SENSE

SKILL 3.1 Identify and/or classify simple two- and three-dimensional figures according to their properties

Two-Dimensional Figures

We name **POLYGONS**—simple, closed, two-dimensional figures composed of line segments—according to the number of sides they have.

A **QUADRILATERAL** is a polygon with four sides.

The sum of the measures of the angles of a quadrilateral is 360°.

A **TRAPEZOID** is a quadrilateral with exactly one pair of parallel sides.

In an **ISOSCELES TRAPEZOID**, the nonparallel sides are congruent.

A **PARALLELOGRAM** is a quadrilateral with two pairs of parallel sides.

In a parallelogram:

- The diagonals bisect each other
- Each diagonal divides the parallelogram into two congruent triangles

> **POLYGON:** a simple, closed, two-dimensional figure composed of line segments

> **QUADRILATERAL:** a polygon with four sides

> **TRAPEZOID:** a quadrilateral with exactly *one* pair of parallel sides

> **ISOSCELES TRAPEZOID:** a quadrilateral in which the nonparallel sides are congruent

> **PARALLELOGRAM:** a quadrilateral with two pairs of parallel sides

- Both pairs of opposite sides are congruent
- Both pairs of opposite angles are congruent
- Two adjacent angles are supplementary

RECTANGLE: a parallelogram with a right angle

A RECTANGLE is a parallelogram with a right angle.

RHOMBUS: a parallelogram with all sides equal in length

A RHOMBUS is a parallelogram with all sides equal in length.

SQUARE: a rectangle with all sides equal in length

A SQUARE is a rectangle with all sides equal in length.

Example: True or false?

All squares are rhombuses	True
All parallelograms are rectangles	False—*some* parallelograms are rectangles
All rectangles are parallelograms	True
Some rhombuses are squares	True
Some rectangles are trapezoids	False—trapezoids have only *one* pair of parallel sides
All quadrilaterals are parallelograms	False—some quadrilaterals are parallelograms
Some squares are rectangles	False—all squares are rectangles
Some parallelograms are rhombuses	True

Triangles

A TRIANGLE is a polygon with three sides. We can classify triangles by the types of angles or the lengths of their sides.

An ACUTE TRIANGLE has exactly three *acute* angles. An ACUTE ANGLE is an angle that measures less than 90°.

A RIGHT TRIANGLE has one *right* angle. A RIGHT ANGLE is an angle that measures 90°.

An OBTUSE TRIANGLE has one *obtuse* angle. An OBTUSE ANGLE measures between 90° and 180°.

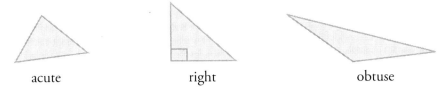

acute   right   obtuse

All three sides of an EQUILATERAL TRIANGLE are the same length.

Two sides of an ISOSCELES TRIANGLE are the same length.

None of the sides of a SCALENE TRIANGLE is the same length.

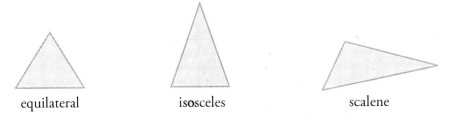

equilateral   isosceles   scalene

Example: Can a triangle have two right angles?
No. A right angle measures 90°; therefore, the sum of two right angles would be 180°, and there could not be a third angle.

Example: Can a triangle have two obtuse angles?
No. Since an obtuse angle measures more than 90°, the sum of two obtuse angles would be greater than 180°.

Three-dimensional figures

A CYLINDER is a space figure that has two parallel, congruent circular bases.

TRIANGLE: a polygon with three sides
ACUTE TRIANGLE: a triangle with exactly three *acute* angles
ACUTE ANGLE: an angle that measures less than 90°
RIGHT TRIANGLE: a triangle with one *right* angle
RIGHT ANGLE: an angle that measures 90°
OBTUSE TRIANGLE: a triangle with one *obtuse* angle
OBTUSE ANGLE: an angle that measures between 90° and 180°
EQUILATERAL TRIANGLE: a triangle in which all sides are the same length
ISOSCELES TRIANGLE: a triangle in which two sides are the same length
SCALENE TRIANGLE: a triangle in which no sides are the same length
CYLINDER: a space figure that has two parallel, congruent circular bases

SPHERE: a space figure having all its points the same distance from the center	A SPHERE is a space figure having all its points the same distance from the center.
CONE: a space figure having a circular base and a single vertex	A CONE is a space figure having a circular base and a single vertex.
PYRAMID: a space figure with a square base and four triangle-shaped sides	A PYRAMID is a space figure with a square base and four triangle-shaped sides.
TETRAHEDRON: a four-sided space triangle; each face is a triangle	A TETRAHEDRON is a four-sided space triangle. Each face is a triangle.
PRISM: a space figure with two congruent, parallel bases that are polygons	A PRISM is a space figure with two congruent, parallel bases that are polygons.

SKILL 3.2 Solve real-world and mathematical problems involving ratio, proportion, similarity, congruence, and the Pythagorean relationship

Ratios

RATIO: a comparison of two numbers

A RATIO is a comparison of two numbers. If a class had 11 boys and 14 girls, we can write the ratio of boys to girls in 3 ways:

- 11:14

- 11 to 14

- $\frac{11}{14}$

The ratio of girls to boys is:

- 14:11

- 14 to 11

- $\frac{14}{11}$

We should reduce ratios when possible. A ratio of 12 cats to 18 dogs reduces to 2:3, 2 to 3, or $\frac{2}{3}$.

Proportions

A PROPORTION is an equation in which one fraction is set equal to another. To solve the proportion, multiply each numerator by the other fraction's denominator. Set these two products equal to each other and solve the resulting equation. This is called cross-multiplying the proportion.

PROPORTION: an equation in which one fraction is set equal to another

Example: $\frac{4}{15} = \frac{x}{60}$ *is a proportion.*
  To solve, cross multiply.
  $(4)(60) = (15)(x)$
  $240 = 15x$
  $16 = x$

Example: $\frac{x+3}{3x+4} = \frac{2}{5}$ *is a proportion.*
  To solve, cross multiply.
  $5(x + 3) = 2(3x + 4)$
  $5x + 15 = 6x + 8$
  $7 = x$

Example: $\frac{x+2}{8} = \frac{2}{x-4}$ *is another proportion.*
  To solve, cross multiply.
  $(x + 2)(x - 4) = 8(2)$
  $x^2 - 2x - 8 = 16$
  $x^2 - 2x - 24 = 0$
  $(x - 6)(x + 4) = 0$
  $x = 6$ or $x = -4$

Proportions can be used to solve word problems whenever relationships are compared. Some situations include scale drawings and maps, similar polygons, speed, time and distance, cost, and comparison shopping.

Example: Which is the better buy, 6 items for $1.29 or 8 items for $1.69?

Find the unit price.

$$\frac{6}{1.29} = \frac{1}{x}$$
$$6x = 1.29$$
$$x = 0.215$$

$$\frac{8}{1.69} = \frac{1}{x}$$
$$8x = 1.69$$
$$x = 0.21125$$

Thus, 8 items for $1.69 is the better buy.

Example: A car travels 125 miles in 2.5 hours. How far will it go in 6 hours?

Write a proportion comparing the distances and times.

Let x represent distance in miles. Then,

$$\frac{miles}{hours} \qquad \frac{125}{2.5} = \frac{x}{6}$$
$$2.5x = 750$$
$$x = 300$$

Thus, the car can travel 300 miles in 6 hours.

Example: The scale on a map is $\frac{3}{4}$ inch = 6 miles. What is the actual distance between two cities if they are $1\frac{1}{2}$ inches apart on the map?

Write a proportion comparing the scale to the actual distance.

	Scale		Actual
	$\dfrac{\frac{3}{4}}{1\frac{1}{2}}$	=	$\dfrac{6}{x}$
	$\frac{3}{4}x$	=	$1\frac{1}{2} \times 6$
	$\frac{3}{4}x$	=	9
	x	=	12

Thus, the actual distance between the cities is 12 miles.

Congruence

CONGRUENT FIGURES have the same size and shape. If one is placed atop the other, it will fit exactly. Congruent lines have the same length. Congruent angles have equal measures.

The symbol for congruence is ≅.

Polygons (pentagons) *ABCDE* and *VWXYZ* are congruent. They are exactly the same size and shape.

CONGRUENT FIGURES: figures that have the same size and shape

The symbol for congruence is ≅.

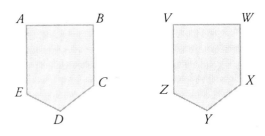

$$ABCDE \cong VWXYZ$$

The corresponding parts are these congruent angles and congruent sides:

Corresponding angles	Corresponding sides
$\angle A \leftrightarrow \angle V$	$AB \leftrightarrow VW$
$\angle B \leftrightarrow \angle W$	$BC \leftrightarrow WX$
$\angle C \leftrightarrow \angle X$	$CD \leftrightarrow XY$
$\angle D \leftrightarrow \angle Y$	$DE \leftrightarrow YZ$
$\angle E \leftrightarrow \angle Z$	$AE \leftrightarrow VZ$

Similarity

Two figures that have the same shape are SIMILAR. Polygons are similar if and only if corresponding angles are congruent and corresponding sides are in proportion. Corresponding parts of similar polygons are proportional.

SIMILAR: two figures that have the same shape

Example: Given the rectangles below, compare the area and perimeter.

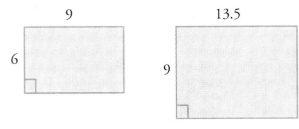

$A = LW$	$A = LW$	1. Write formula.
$A = (6)(9)$	$A = (9)(13.5)$	2. Substitute known values.
$A = 54$ sq. units	$A = 121.5$ sq. units	3. Compute.

$$P = 2(L + W) \qquad P = 2(L + W) \qquad \text{1. Write formula.}$$

$$P = 2(6 + 9) \qquad P = 2(9 + 13.5) \qquad \text{2. Substitute known values.}$$

$$P = 30 \text{ units} \qquad P = 45 \text{ units} \qquad \text{3. Compute.}$$

Notice that the areas are related to each other in the following manner:
Ratio of sides $\frac{9}{13.5} = \frac{2}{3}$

Multiply the first area by the square of the reciprocal $\left(\frac{3}{2}\right)^2$ to get the second area.
$$54 \times \left(\frac{3}{2}\right)^2 = 121.5$$

The perimeters are related to each other in the following manner:
Ratio of sides $\frac{9}{13.5} = \frac{2}{3}$

Multiply the perimeter of the first by the reciprocal of the ratio $\left(\frac{3}{2}\right)$ to get the perimeter of the second.
$$30 \times \frac{3}{2} = 45$$

Example: Given two similar quadrilaterals, find the lengths of sides x, y, and z.

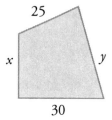
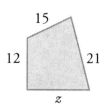

Since corresponding sides are proportional, the scale is:

$$\frac{12}{x} = \frac{3}{5} \qquad\qquad \frac{21}{y} = \frac{3}{5} \qquad\qquad \frac{z}{30} = \frac{3}{5}$$
$$3x = 60 \qquad\qquad 3y = 105 \qquad\qquad 5z = 90$$
$$x = 20 \qquad\qquad y = 35 \qquad\qquad z = 18$$

Example: Tommy draws and cuts out two triangles for a school project. One of them has sides of 3, 6, and 9 inches. The other triangle has sides of 2, 4, and 6 inches. Is there a relationship between the two triangles?

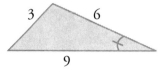
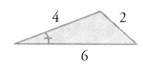

Take the proportion of the corresponding sides.
$$\frac{2}{3} \qquad\qquad \frac{4}{6} = \frac{2}{3} \qquad\qquad \frac{6}{9} = \frac{2}{3}$$
The smaller triangle is $\frac{2}{3}$ the size of the large triangle.

The Pythagorean Theorem

Given any right triangle $\triangle ABC$ the square of the hypotenuse is equal to the sum of the squares of the other two sides.

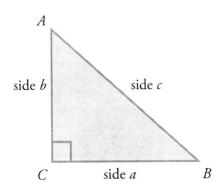

side b

side c

Hypotenuse (side opposite the 90° angle)

C side a B

This theorem says that $(AB)^2 = (BC)^2 + (AC)^2$ or $c^2 = a^2 + b^2$.

Example: Find the area and perimeter of a rectangle if its length is 12 inches and its diagonal is 15 inches.

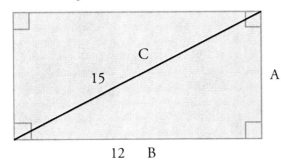

15

C

A

12   B

1. Draw and label sketch.
2. Since the height is still needed, use Pythagorean formula to find missing leg of the triangle.

$A^2 + B^2 = C^2$

$A^2 + 12^2 = 15^2$

$A^2 = 15^2 - 12^2$

$A^2 = 81$

$A = 9$

Now use this information to find the area and perimeter.

A = LW	P = 2(L + W)	1. Write formula.
A = (12)(9)	P = 2(12 + 9)	2. Substitute.
A = 108 in²	P = 42 inches	3. Solve.

Example: Two old cars leave a road intersection at the same time. One car traveled due north at 55 mph while the other car traveled due east. After 3 hours, the cars were 180 miles apart. Find the speed of the second car.

Using a right triangle to represent the problem we get the figure:

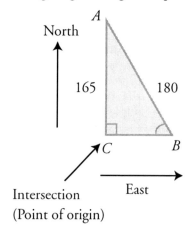

Traveling at 55 mph for 3 hours, the northbound car has driven $(55)(3) = 165$ miles. This is the side AC. The cars are 180 miles apart. This is side AB.

Since ΔABC is a right triangle, then, by the Pythagorean theorem, we get:

$(AB)^2 = (BC)^2 + (AC)^2$ or

$(BC)^2 = (AB)^2 - (AC)^2$

$(BC)^2 = 180^2 + 165^2$

$(BC)^2 = 32400 - 27225$

$(BC)^2 = 5175$

Take the square root of both sides to get:

$$\sqrt{(BC)^2} = \sqrt{5175} \approx 71.935 \text{ miles}$$

Since the east bound car has traveled 71.935 miles in 3 hours, then the average speed is:

$\frac{71.935}{3} \approx 23.97$ mph

SKILL **Identify the location of ordered pairs of integers in all four**
3.3 **quadrants of a coordinate system** *(graph)* **and use the coordinate**
system to apply the concepts of slope and distance to solve
problems

A **COORDINATE PLANE** is a plane with a point selected as an origin, some length selected as a unit of distance, and two perpendicular lines that intersect at the origin, with positive and negative direction selected on each line.

The distance of a point from the lines determines its coordinates and the direction of a point from the origin determines the signs of its coordinates. The standard coordinate plane consists of a plane divided into 4 quadrants by the intersection of two axes, the x-axis (horizontal axis) and the y-axis (vertical axis).

COORDINATE PLANE: a plane with a point selected as an origin, some length selected as a unit of distance, and two perpendicular lines that intersect at the origin, with positive and negative direction selected on each line

Quadrant II
(−, +)
(x, y)

Quadrant I
(+, +)
(x, y)

A (4,2)

B (1,-6)

Quadrant III
(−, −)
(x, y)

Quadrant IV
(+, −)
(x, y)

Traditionally, the lines on a coordinate plane are called x (drawn from left to right, with positive direction to the right of the origin) and y (drawn from bottom to top, with positive direction above the origin).

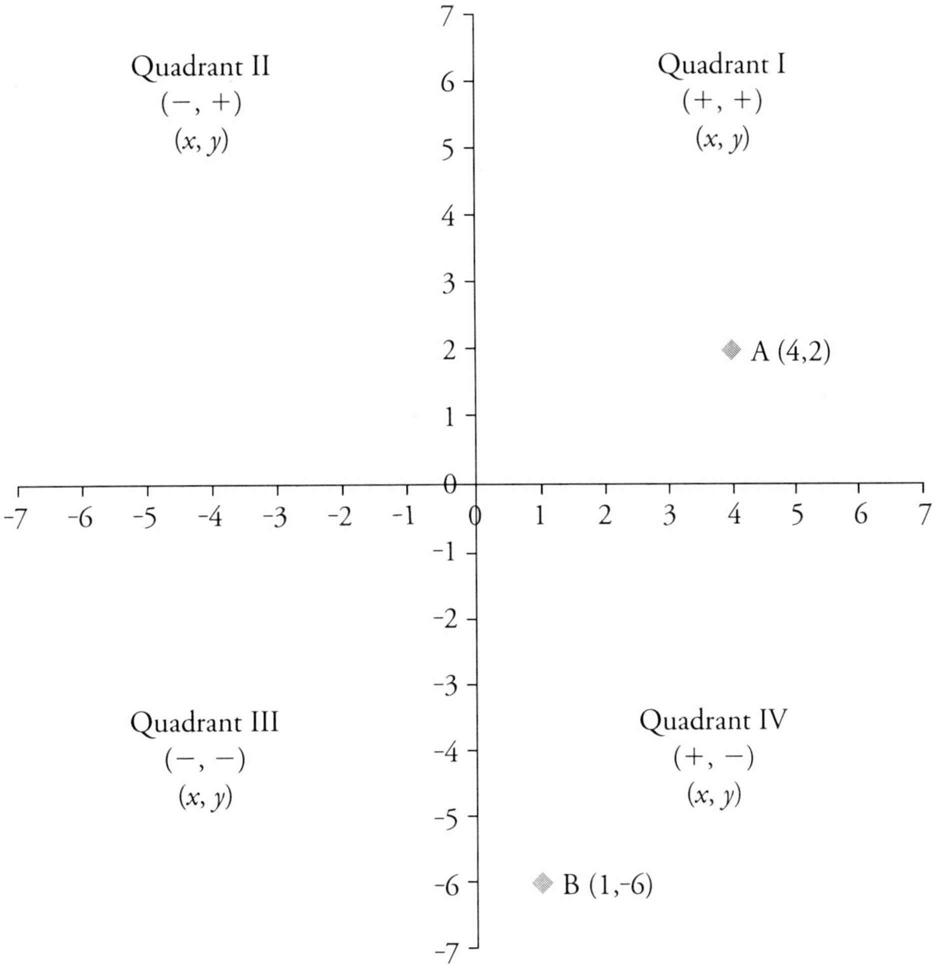

COORDINATES are a unique ordered pair of numbers that identifies a point on the coordinate plane. The first number in the ordered pair identifies the position with regard to the x-axis while the second number identifies the position on the y-axis (x,y).

COORDINATES: unique ordered pair of numbers that identifies a point on the coordinate plane

In the coordinate plane shown above, point A represents the ordered pair (4, 2) and point B represents the ordered pair (1, -6).

The SLOPE of a line is the line's "slant." A downward left-to-right slant represents a negative slope. An upward left-to-right slant represents a positive slope.

SLOPE: the upward or downward direction of a line

The formula for calculating the slope of a line with coordinates (x_1, y_1) and (x_2, y_2) is:

$$slope = \frac{y_2 - y_1}{x_2 - x_1}$$

The top of the fraction, called the RISE, represents the change in the y coordinates.

The bottom of the fraction, called the RUN, represents the change in the x coordinates.

Example: Find the slope of a line with points at (2, 2) and (7, 8).

$\frac{(8) - (2)}{(7) - (2)}$	Plug the values into the formula.
$\frac{6}{5}$	Solve the rise over run.
$= 1.2$	Solve for the slope.

The length of a line segment is the DISTANCE between two different points, A and B.

The formula for the length of a line is:

$$length = \sqrt{(x_1 - x_2)^2 + (y_1 - y_2)^2}$$

Example: Find the length between the points (2, 2) and (7, 8)

$= \sqrt{(2 - 7)^2 + (2 - 8)^2}$	Plug the values into the formula.
$= \sqrt{(-5)^2 + (-6)^2}$	Calculate the x and y differences.
$= \sqrt{25 + 36}$	Square the values.
$= \sqrt{61}$	Add the two values.
$= 7.81$	Calculate the square root.

SKILL 3.4 **Identify real-world examples that represent geometric concepts including perpendicularity, parallelism, tangency, symmetry, and transformations** (e.g., flips, slides, and turns)

PARALLEL LINES or PLANES are lines or planes that do not intersect. Two parallel lines have the same slope.

Sidebar definitions:

The formula for calculating the slope of a line with coordinates (x_1, y_1) and (x_2, y_2) is:

$$slope = \frac{y_2 - y_1}{x_2 - x_1}$$

RISE: the top of the fraction; it represents the change in the y coordinates

RUN: the bottom of the fraction; it represents the change in the x coordinates

DISTANCE: the length of a line segment between two different points, A and B

The formula for the length of a line is:

$$length = \sqrt{(x_1 - x_2)^2 + (y_1 - y_2)^2}$$

PARALLEL LINES OR PLANES: lines or planes that do not intersect

PERPENDICULAR LINES or PLANES are lines or planes that form a 90° angle to one another. Perpendicular lines have slopes that are negative reciprocals.

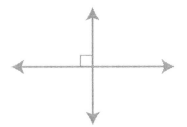

> **PERPENDICULAR LINES OR PLANES:** lines or planes that form a 90° angle to one another

Example: One line passes through the points (-4, -6) and (4, 6); another line passes through the points (-5, -4) and (3, 8). Are these lines parallel, perpendicular, or neither?

Find the slopes.

$$m = \frac{y_2 - y_1}{x_2 - x_1}$$

$$m_1 = \frac{6 - (-6)}{4 - (-4)} = \frac{6 + 6}{4 + 4} = \frac{12}{8} = \frac{3}{2}$$

$$m_2 = \frac{8 - (-4)}{3 - (-5)} = \frac{8 + 4}{3 + 5} = \frac{12}{8} = \frac{3}{2}$$

Since the slopes are the same, the lines are parallel.

Example: One line passes through the points (1, -3) and (0, -6); another line passes through the points (4, 1) and (-2, 3). Are these lines parallel, perpendicular, or neither?

Find the slopes.

$$m = \frac{y_2 - y_1}{x_2 - x_1}$$

$$m_1 = \frac{-6 - (-3)}{0 - 1} = \frac{-6 + 3}{-1} = \frac{-3}{-1} = 3$$

$$m_2 = \frac{3 - 1}{-2 - 4} = \frac{2}{-6} = -\frac{1}{3}$$

The slopes are negative reciprocals, so the lines are perpendicular.

Example: One line passes through the points (-2, 4) and (2, 5); another line passes through the points (-1, 0) and (5, 4). Are these lines parallel, perpendicular, or neither?

Find the slopes.

$$m = \frac{y_2 - y_1}{x_2 - x_1}$$

$$m_1 = \frac{5 - 4}{2 - (-2)} = \frac{1}{2 + 2} = \frac{1}{4}$$

$$m_2 = \frac{4 - 0}{5 - (-1)} = \frac{4}{5 + 1} = \frac{4}{6} = \frac{2}{3}$$

Since the slopes are not the same, the lines are not parallel. Since they are not negative reciprocals, they are not perpendicular either. Therefore, the answer is "neither."

TRANSLATION: a transformation that "slides" an object a fixed distance in a given direction

There are four basic transformational symmetries that can be used: *translation, rotation, reflection,* and *glide reflection.* The transformation of an object is called its image. If the original object was labeled with letters, such as *ABCD*, the image may be labeled with the same letters followed by a prime symbol: *A'B'C'D'*.

A TRANSLATION is a transformation that "slides" an object a fixed distance in a given direction. The original object and its translation have the same shape and size, and they face in the same direction.

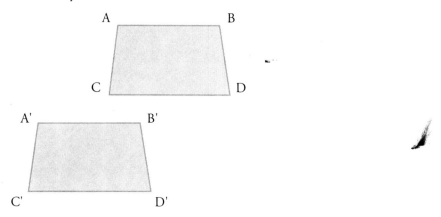

An example of a translation in architecture is stadium seating. The seats are the same size and the same shape, and they face in the same direction.

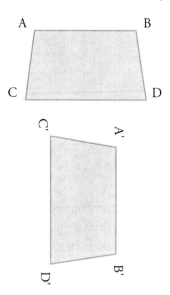

ROTATION: a transformation that turns a figure about a fixed point called the center of rotation

A ROTATION is a transformation that turns a figure about a fixed point called the center of rotation. An object and its rotation are the same shape and size, but the figures may be turned in different directions. Rotations can occur in either a clockwise or a counterclockwise direction.

Rotations can be seen in wallpaper and art; a Ferris wheel is an example of rotation.

An object and its REFLECTION have the same shape and size, but the figures face in opposite directions.

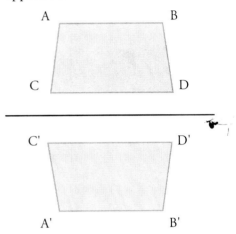

The line (where a mirror may be placed) is called the LINE OF REFLECTION. The distance from a point to the line of reflection is the same as the distance from the point's image to the line of reflection.

A GLIDE REFLECTION is a combination of a reflection and a translation.

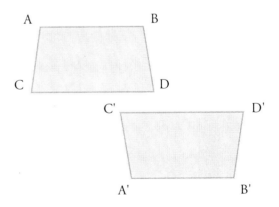

Objects that are TANGENT make contact at a single point or along a line without crossing.

Many types of flooring found in homes are examples of SYMMETRY: Persian carpets, tiling, patterned broadloom, etc. The human body is an example of symmetry, even though that symmetry is not perfect. If you split the torso down the middle, on each half you will find one ear, one eye, one nostril, one shoulder, one arm, one leg, and so on, in approximately the same place.

REFLECTION: when figures have the same shape and size, but they face in opposite directions

LINE OF REFLECTION: the line where a mirror may be placed; the distance from a point to this line is the same as the distance from the points image to this line

GLIDE REFLECTION: a combination of a reflection and a translation

TANGENT: when objects make contact at a single point or along a line without crossing

Understanding tangency is critical in the construction industry, where architects and engineers must figure out how various elements fit together. An example can be demonstrated by building a stair railing. The architect must determine the points of tangency between the banisters, which might even be curved, and the posts supporting the banisters.

SYMMETRY: equal on both sides

COMPETENCY 4
KNOWLEDGE OF ALGEBRAIC THINKING

> **SKILL** **Analyze and generalize patterns including arithmetic and**
> **4.1** **geometric sequences**

Arithmetic Sequences

When given a set of numbers where the common difference between the terms is constant, use the following formula:

$$a_n = a_1 + (n - 1)d$$

where a_1 = the first term

n = the nth term (general term)

d = the common difference between the terms

Example: Find the eighth term of the arithmetic sequence 5, 8, 11, 14, ...

$a_n = a_1 + (n - 1)d$	
$a_n = 5$	Identify the 1st term.
$d = 8 - 5 = 3$	Find d.
$a_n = 5 + (8 - 1)3$	Substitute.
$a_n = 26$	

Example: Given two terms of an arithmetic sequence, find a_1 and d.

$a_4 = 21$	$a_6 = 32$
$a_n = a + (n - 1)d$	$a_4 = 21, n = 4$
$21 = a_1 + (4 - 1)d$	$a_6 = 32, n = 6$
$32 = a_1 + (6 - 1)d$	

$21 = a_1 + 3d$	Solve the system of equations.
$32 = a_1 + 5d$	

$$21 = a_1 + 3d$$
$$\underline{-32 = -a_1 - 5d}$$ Multiply by -1.
$$-11 = \qquad -2d$$ Add the equations.
$$5.5 = d$$

$$21 = a_1 + 3(5.5)$$ Substitute $d = 5.5$, into one of the equations.
$$21 = a_1 + 16.5$$
$$a_1 = 4.5$$

The sequence begins with 4.5 and has a common difference of 5.5 between numbers.

Geometric Sequences

When using geometric sequences, compare consecutive numbers to find the common ratio.

$$r = \frac{a_{n+1}}{a_n}$$

where r = common ratio

a = the nth term

The ratio is then used in the geometric sequence formula:

$$a_n = a_1 r^{n-1}$$

Example: Find the eight term of the geometric sequence 2, 8, 32, 128...

$$r = \frac{a_{n+1}}{a_n}$$ Use the common ratio formula to find the ratio.

$$r = \frac{8}{2}$$ Substitute $a_n = 2$ $a_{n+1} = 8$.

$$r = 4$$

$$a_n = a_1 \times r^{n-1}$$ Use $r = 4$ to solve for the 8th term.

$$a_n = 2 \times 4^{8-1}$$

$$a_n = 32{,}768$$

SKILL 4.2 Interpret algebraic expressions using words, symbols, variables, tables, and graphs

We can use a table, graph, or rule to show a relationship between two quantities. In this example, the rule $y = 9x$ describes the relationship between the total amount earned, y, and the total number of $9 sunglasses sold, x.

A table using these data would appear as:

Number of Sunglasses Sold	1	5	10	15
Total Dollars Earned	9	45	90	135

Each (x, y) relationship between a pair of values is called a coordinate pair and can be plotted on a graph. The coordinate pairs (1, 9), (5, 45), (10, 90), and (15, 135), are plotted on the graph below.

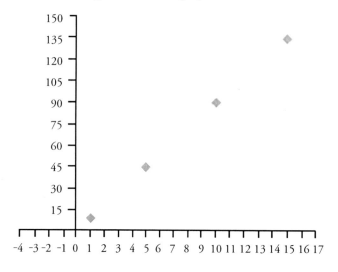

LINEAR RELATIONSHIP: a relationship in which two quantities are proportional to each other

The graph shows a linear relationship. A LINEAR RELATIONSHIP is one in which two quantities are proportional to each other. Doubling x also doubles y. On a graph, a straight line depicts a linear relationship.

We can analyze the function or relationship between two quantities to determine how one quantity depends on the other. For example, the function below shows a relationship between y and x:

$y = 2x + 1$

The function, $y = 2x + 1$, is written as a symbolic rule. The table below shows the same relationship:

x	0	2	3	6	9
y	1	5	7	13	19

We can write this relationship in words by saying "the value of y is equal to 2 times the value of x, plus 1." We can show this relationship on a graph by plotting given points such as the ones shown in the table above.

In real-life situations, we can describe relationships mathematically. We can use the function $y = x + 1$ to represent the idea that people age one year on their birthdays. To describe the relationship in which a person's monthly medical costs are 6 times that person's age, we could write $y = 6x$, where y is the person's monthly medical costs and x is the person's age.

Using this function, we can determine that a 20-year-old person would spend $120 per month on medical costs ($120 = 20 \times 6$). An 80-year-old person would spend $480 per month ($480 = 80 \times 6$). An analysis of this function reveals that a person's medical costs increase $6.00 each year.

<table>
<tr><td>SKILL
4.3</td><td>Solve equations and inequalities graphically or algebraically</td></tr>
</table>

Solving Algebraic Equations

Example: $3(x + 3) = -2x + 4$. Solve for x.

1. Expand to eliminate all parentheses.

   $3x + 9 = -2x + 4$

2. Multiply each term by the LCD to eliminate all denominators.

3. Combine like terms on each side when possible.

4. Use the properties to put all variables on one side and all constants on the other side.

$$\rightarrow 3x + 9 - 9 = -2x + 4 - 9 \qquad \text{Subtract nine from both sides.}$$
$$\rightarrow 3x = -2x - 5$$
$$\rightarrow 3x + 2x = -2x + 2x - 5 \qquad \text{Add } 2x \text{ to both sides.}$$
$$\rightarrow 5x = -5$$
$$\rightarrow \frac{5x}{5} = \frac{-5}{5} \qquad \text{Divide both sides by 5.}$$
$$\rightarrow x = -1$$

Example: Solve: $3(2x + 5) - 4x = 5(x + 9)$

$$6x + 15 - 4x = 5x + 45$$
$$2x + 15 = 5x + 45$$
$$-3x + 15 = 45$$
$$-3x = 30$$
$$x = -10$$

Example: Mark and Mike are twins. Three times Mark's age, plus 4, equals 4 times Mike's age minus 14. How old are the boys?

Because the boys are twins, their ages are the same. "Translate" the English into algebra. Let x = their age.

$$3x + 4 = 4x - 14$$
$$18 = x$$

The boys are each 18 years old.

The **SOLUTION SET OF LINEAR EQUATIONS** is all the ordered pairs of real numbers that satisfy both equations—thus the intersection of the lines. There are two methods for solving linear equations: linear combinations and substitution.

In the **SUBSTITUTION** method, an equation is solved for either variable. That solution is then substituted in the other equation to find the remaining variable.

Example:

1. $2x + 8y = 4$
2. $x - 3y = 5$
2A. $x = 3y + 5$ Solve equation (2) for x.
1A. $2(3y + 5) + 8y = 4$ Substitute for x in equation (1).
     $6y + 10 + 8y = 4$ Solve.
     $14y = -6$
     $y = \frac{-3}{7}$ Solution.
2. $x - 3y = 5$
     $x - 3(\frac{-3}{7}) = 5$ Substitute the value of y.
     $x = \frac{26}{7} = 3\frac{5}{7}$ Solution.

Thus, the solution set of the system of equations is $(3\frac{5}{7}, \frac{-3}{7})$.

In the **LINEAR COMBINATIONS** method, one or both of the equations are replaced with an equivalent equation so that the two equations can be combined (added or subtracted) to eliminate one variable.

Example:

1. $4x + 3y = -2.$
2. $5x - y = 7$
1. $4x + 3y = -2$
2A. $15x - 3y = 2.$ Multiply equation (2) by 3.
     $19x = 19$ Combining (1) and (2a).
     $x = 1$ Solve.

To find y, substitute the value of x in equation 1 (or 2).

1. $4x + 3y = -2$
     $4(1) + 3y = -2$
     $4 + 3y = -2$
     $3y = -6$
     $y = -2$

Thus, the solution is $x = 1$ and $y = -2$ or the ordered pair $(1, -2)$.

Example: Solve for x and y.

$4x + 6y = 340$

$3x + 8y = 360$

To solve by linear combinations:

Multiply the first equation by 4: $4(4x + 6y = 340)$

Multiply the second equation by: -3: $-3(3x + 8y = 360)$

After doing this, the equations can be added to each other to eliminate one variable and solve for the other variable.

$16x + 24y = 1360$

$\underline{-9x - 24y = -1080}$

$7x = 280$

$x = 40$

Solving for y, $y = 30$

Solving Algebraic Inequalities

Use the same procedure used for solving linear equations to solve algebraic inequalities.

Example: Solve the inequality, show its solution using interval form, and graph the solution on the number line.

$\frac{5x}{8} + 3 \geq 2x - 5$

$8\left(\frac{5x}{8}\right) + 8(3) \geq 8(2x) - 5(8)$　　　Multiply by LCD = 8.

$5x + 24 \geq 16x - 40$

$5x + 24 - 24 - 16x \geq 16x - 16x - 40 - 24$

Subtract $16x$ and 24 from both sides of the equation.

$-11x \geq -16$

$\frac{-11x}{-11} \leq \frac{-64}{-11}$

$x \leq \frac{64}{11}$　　；　　$x \leq 5\frac{9}{11}$

Solution in interval form:　$\left(-\infty, 5\frac{9}{11}\right]$

Note: " $]$ " means $5\frac{9}{11}$ is included in the solution.

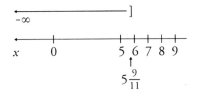

> The answer to an algebraic inequality is represented in interval form or in graphical form on the number line.

Example: Solve the following inequality, and express your answer in both interval and graphical form.

$$3x - 8 < 2(3x - 1)$$
$$3x - 8 < -2 \qquad \text{Distributive property.}$$
$$3x - 6x - 8 + 8 < 6x - 6x - 2 + 8$$

Add 8 and subtract $6x$ from both sides of the equation.

$$-3x < 6$$
$$\frac{-3x}{-3} > \frac{6}{-3} \qquad \text{Note the change in direction of the equality.}$$
$$x > -2$$

Graphical form:

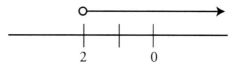

or

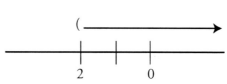

Interval form: $(-2, \infty)$

Recall:

A. Using a parenthesis or an open circle implies that the point is not included in the answer.

B. Using a bracket or a closed circle implies that the point is included in the answer.

Example: Solve:

$$6x + 21 < 8x + 31$$
$$-2x + 21 < 31$$
$$-2x < 10$$
$$x < -5$$

Note that the inequality sign has changed.

Representing Algebraic Expressions Graphically

Slope-intercept form is
$y = mx + b$

A first-degree equation has an equation of the form $ax + by = c$. To find the slope of a line, solve the equation for y. This gets the equation into slope-intercept form, $y = mx + b$. In this equation, m is the line's slope.

The *y* intercept is the coordinate of the point where a line crosses the *y*-axis. To find the *y* intercept, substitute 0 for *x* and solve for *y*. This is the *y* intercept. In slope-intercept form, $y = mx + b$, *b* is the *y* intercept.

To find the *x* intercept, substitute 0 for *y* and solve for *x*. This is the *x* intercept. If the equation solves to $x =$ **any number**, then the graph is a vertical line, because it only has an *x* intercept. Its slope is undefined.

If the equation solves to $y =$ **any number**, then the graph is a horizontal line, because it only has a *y* intercept. Its slope is 0 (zero).

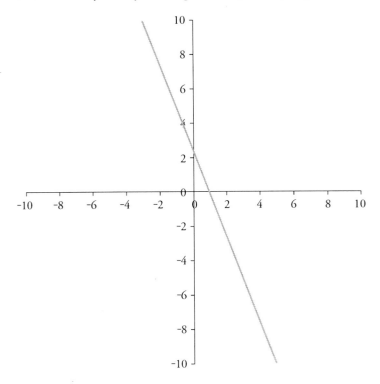

$$5x + 2y = 6$$
$$y = \frac{-5}{2x + 3}$$

The equation of a line can be found from its graph by finding its slope and its intercept. The slope formula looks like this:

$$m = \frac{y_2 - y_1}{x_2 - x_1}$$

The *y* intercept can be found using this equation:

$$Y - y_a = m(X - x_a)$$

(x_a, y_a) can be (x_1, y_1) or (x_2, y_2) If m, the value of the slope, is distributed through the parentheses, the equation can be rewritten into other forms of the equation of a line.

Example: Find the equation of a line through (9, -6) and (-1, 2).

slope $= \dfrac{y_2 - y_1}{x_2 - x_1} = \dfrac{2 - {}^-6}{{}^-1 - 9} = \dfrac{8}{210} = \dfrac{24}{5}$

$Y - y_a = m(X - x_a) \rightarrow Y - 2 = \dfrac{{}^-4}{5(X - {}^-1)} \rightarrow$

$Y - 2 = \dfrac{{}^-4}{5(X + 1)} \rightarrow Y - 2 = \dfrac{{}^-4}{5}X\dfrac{{}^-4}{5}$ This is the slope-intercept form.

$Y = \dfrac{{}^-4}{5}X + \dfrac{6}{5}$

Multiplying by 5 to eliminate fractions, it is:

$5Y = -4X + 6 \rightarrow 4X + 5Y = 6$

Example: Find the slope and intercepts of 3x + 2y = 14.

$3x + 2y = 14$

$2y = -3x + 14$

$y = \dfrac{{}^-3}{2}x + 7$

The slope of the line is $\dfrac{{}^-3}{2}$. The intercept of the line is 7.

The intercepts can also be found by substituting 0 in place of the other variables in the equation.

To find the y-intercept:

Let $x = 0$; $3(0) + 2y = 14$

$0 + 2y = 14$

$2y = 14$

$y = 7$

$(0, 7)$ is the y-intercept.

To find the x-intercept:

Let $y = 0$; $3x + 2(0) = 14$

$3x + 0 = 14$

$3x = 14$

$x = \dfrac{14}{3}$

$(\dfrac{14}{3}, 0)$ is the x-intercept.

Example: Sketch the graph of the line represented by 2x + 3y = 6.

Let $x = 0 \rightarrow 2(0) + 3y = 6$

$\rightarrow 3y = 6$

$\rightarrow y = 2$

$\rightarrow (0, 2)$ is the y-intercept

Let $y = 0 \rightarrow 2x + 3(0) = 6$
  $\rightarrow 2x = 6$
  $\rightarrow x = 3$
  $\rightarrow (3, 0)$ is the x-intercept

Let $x = 1 \rightarrow 2(1) + 3y = 6$
  $\rightarrow 2 + 3y = 6$
  $\rightarrow 3y = 4$
  $\rightarrow y = \frac{4}{3}$
  $\rightarrow \left(1, \frac{4}{3}\right)$ is the third point.

Plotting the three points on the coordinate system, we get the following:

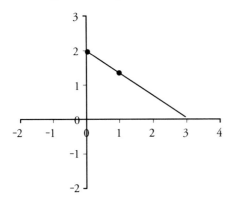

To graph an inequality, solve the inequality for y. This gets the inequality in slope intercept form, (for example: $y < mx + b$). The point $(0, b)$ is the y-intercept and m is the line's slope.

If the inequality solves to $x \geq$ **any number**, then the graph includes a vertical line.

If the inequality solves to $y \leq$ **any number,** then the graph includes a horizontal line.

When graphing a linear inequality, the line will be dotted if the inequality sign is $<$ or $>$. If the inequality signs are either $\geq$ or $\leq$, the line on the graph will be a solid line. Shade above the line when the inequality sign is $\geq$ or $>$. Shade below the line when the inequality sign is $\leq$ or $<$. For inequalities of the forms $x >$ number, $x \leq$ number, $x <$ number, or $x \geq$ number, draw a vertical line (solid or dotted). Shade to the right for $>$ or $\geq$. Shade to the left for $<$ or $\leq$.

Remember: Dividing or multiplying by a negative number will reverse the direction of the inequality sign.

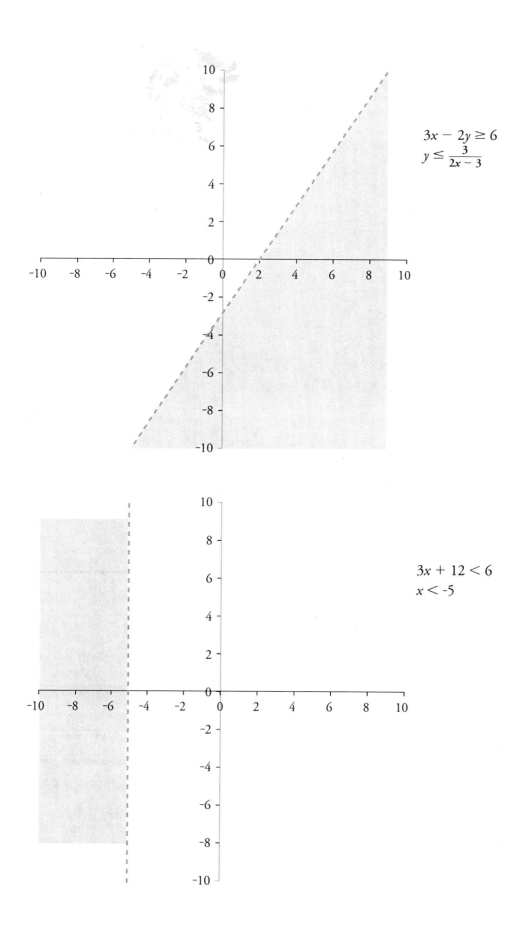

$$3x - 2y \geq 6$$
$$y \leq \frac{3}{2x - 3}$$

$$3x + 12 < 6$$
$$x < -5$$

Example: Solve by graphing.

$x + y \le 6$
$x - 2y \le 6$

Solving the inequalities for y, we find that they become:

$y \le -x + 6$ (y-intercept of 6 and slope $= -1$)
$y \ge \frac{1}{2x - 3}$ (y-intercept of -3 and slope $= \frac{1}{2}$)

A graph with shading is shown below:

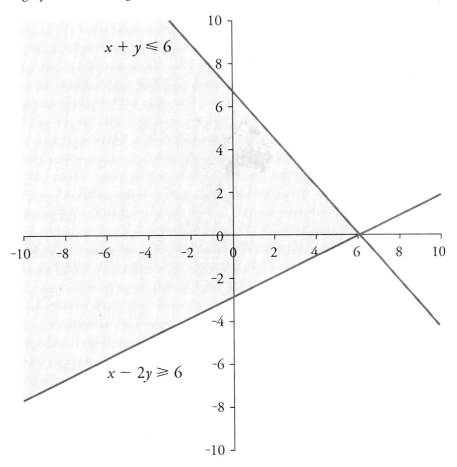

Real-World Example Problems

Example: The YMCA wants to sell raffle tickets to raise at least $32,000. If they must pay $7,250 in expenses and prizes out of the money collected from the tickets, how many $25 tickets must they sell?

Since they want to raise *at least* $32,000, that means they would be happy to get 32,000 *or more*. This requires an inequality.

Let x = number of tickets sold.

Then $25x$ = total amount of money collected for x tickets.

The total amount of money minus expenses is greater than $32,000.

$$25x - 7,250 \geq 32,000$$
$$25x \geq 39,250$$
$$x \geq 1,570$$

If they sell 1,570 tickets or more, they will raise at least $32,000.

Example: The Simpsons went out for dinner. All four of them ordered the aardvark steak dinner. Bert paid for the four meals and included a tip of $12.00 for a total of $84.60. How much was an aardvark steak dinner?

Let x = the price of one aardvark dinner

So $4x$ = the price of four aardvark dinners

$$4x + 12 = 84.60$$
$$4x = 72.60$$
$$x = \$18.50 \text{ for each dinner}$$

Some word problems can be solved using a system, or group, of equations or inequalities. Watch for words like *greater than, less than, at least,* or *no more than,* which indicate the need for inequalities.

Example: Farmer Greenjeans bought 4 cows and 6 sheep for $1,700. Mr. Ziffel bought 3 cows and 12 sheep for $2,400. If all the cows were the same price and all the sheep were another fixed price, find the price charged for a cow and the price charged for a sheep.

Let x = price of a cow

Let y = price of a sheep

Then Farmer Greenjeans's equation would be: $\quad 4x + 6y = 1700$

Mr. Ziffel's equation would be: $\quad 3x + 12y = 2400$

To solve by addition-subtraction:

Multiply the first equation by -2: $\quad -2(4x + 6y = 1700)$

Keep the other equation the same: $\quad (3x + 12y = 2400)$

Now the equations can be added to each other to eliminate one variable, and you can solve for the other variable.

$$-8x - 12y = -3400$$
$$\underline{3x + 12y = \ 2400} \qquad \text{Add these equations.}$$
$$-5x \qquad \ = -1000$$

$x = 200 \ \leftarrow$ the price of a cow was $200.

Solving for y, $y = 150 \ \leftarrow$ the price of a sheep was $150.

To solve by substitution:
Solve one of the equations for a variable. (Try to make an equation without fractions if possible.) Substitute this expression into the equation that you have not yet used. Solve the resulting equation for the value of the remaining variable.

$$4x + 6y = 1700$$
$$3x + 12y = 2400 \leftarrow \text{Solve this equation for } x.$$

It becomes $x = 800 - 4y$. Now substitute $800 - 4y$ in place of x in the *other* equation. $4x + 6y = 1700$ now becomes:

$$4(800 - 4y) + 6y = 1700$$
$$3200 - 16y + 6y = 1700$$
$$3200 - 10y = 1700$$
$$-10y = -1500$$
$$y = 150, \text{ or } \$150 \text{ for a sheep.}$$

Substituting 150 back into an equation for y, find x.

$$4x + 6(150) = 1700$$
$$4x + 900 = 1700$$
$$4x = 800 \text{ so } x = 200, \text{ or } \$200 \text{ for a cow.}$$

Example: Sharon's Bike Shoppe can assemble a three-speed bike in 30 minutes or a ten-speed bike in 60 minutes. The profit on each bike sold is $60 for a three-speed and $75 for a ten-speed bike. How many of each type of bike should the shop assemble during an 8-hour day (480 minutes) to make the maximum profit? Total daily profit must be at least $300.

Let $x =$ number of three-speed bikes.
Let $y =$ number of ten-speed bikes.

Since there are only 480 minutes to use each day, $30x + 60y \leq 480$ is the first inequality.

Since the total daily profit must be at least $300, $60x + 75y \geq 300$ is the second inequality.

$32x + 65y \leq 480$ solves to $y \leq 8 - \frac{1}{2x}$.

$60x + 75y \geq 300$ solves to $y \geq 4 - \frac{4}{5x}$.

Graph these two inequalities:

$$y \leq 8 - \frac{1}{2x}$$
$$y \geq 4 - \frac{4}{5x}$$

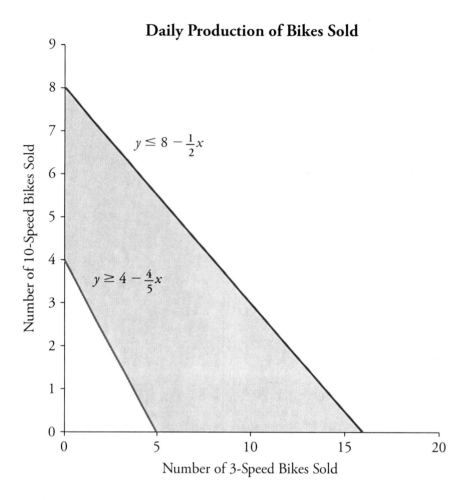

Daily Production of Bikes Sold

Realize that $x \geq 0$ and $y \geq 0$, since the number of bikes assembled cannot be a negative number. Graph these as additional constraints on the problem. The number of bikes assembled must always be an integer value, so points within the shaded area of the graph must have integer values. The maximum profit will occur at or near a corner of the shaded portion of this graph. Those points occur at $(0, 4)$, $(0, 8)$, $(16, 0)$, or $(5, 0)$.

Since profits are \$60/three-speed and \$75/ten-speed, the profits for these four points would be:

$(0, 4)$	$60(0) + 75(4) = 300$
$(0, 8)$	$60(0) + 75(8) = 600$
$(16, 0)$	$60(16) + 75(0) = 960 \leftarrow$ Maximum profit
$(5, 0)$	$60(5) + 75(0) = 300$

The maximum profit will occur if 16 three-speed bikes are made daily.

SKILL **Determine whether a number or ordered pair is among the**

SKILL 4.4 Determine whether a number or ordered pair is among the solutions of given equations or inequalities

If substituting a value for the variable results in the left hand side (LHS) of the equation = the right hand side (RHS) of the equation, or a true statement, then that value is the solution for that equation.

Example: $2x = 6$

(LHS) (RHS)

This statement is only true if we substitute 3 for x.

   $2 \times 3 = 6$ (True)

   Therefore, 3 is a solution of the equation.

Example: Is 2 a solution of $2x - 6 = 6x + 1$?
Substituting 2 for x:

   $2(2) - 6 = 6(2) + 1 \rightarrow 4 - 6 = 12 + 1 \rightarrow -2 = 13$ (False)

   Therefore, 2 is not a solution of this equation.

Example: Is the ordered pair (2, 3) a solution of the linear equation $y = 5x - 3$?
Substituting 2 for x and 3 for y:

   $3 = 5(2) - 3$

   $3 = 10 - 3$

   $3 = 7$

   No, (2, 3) is not among the solutions of the equation.

Example: Is the ordered pair (-4, -2) a solution of the inequality $y \leq 2x + 6$?
Substituting -4 for x and -2 for y.

   $-2 \leq 2(-4) + 6$

   $-2 \leq -8 + 6$

   $-2 \leq -2$

Yes, (-4, -2) is among the solutions of the inequality.

COMPETENCY 5
KNOWLEDGE OF DATA ANALYSIS AND PROBABILITY

> **SKILL** **Analyze data and solve problems using data presented in**
> **5.1** **histograms, bar graphs, circle graphs, pictographs, tables, and**
> **charts**

BAR GRAPH: a graph that compares various quantities

To make a **BAR GRAPH** or a **PICTOGRAPH**, determine the scale to be used for the graph. Then determine the length of each bar on the graph, or determine the number of pictures needed to represent each item of information. Be sure to include, in the legend, an explanation of the scale.

PICTOGRAPHS: a graph that compares quantities using symbols; each symbol represents a number of items

Example: A class had the following grades: 4 As, 9 Bs, 8 Cs, 1 D, and 3 Fs. Graph these on a bar graph and a pictograph.

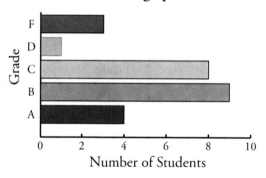

Bar graph

Pictograph

Grade	Number of Students
A	☺☺☺☺
B	☺☺☺☺☺☺☺☺☺
C	☺☺☺☺☺☺☺☺
D	☺
F	☺☺☺

LINE GRAPHS: a graph that shows trends, often over a period of time

To make a **LINE GRAPH**, determine appropriate scales for both the vertical and horizontal axes (based on the information to be graphed). Describe what each axis represents, and mark the scale periodically on each axis. Graph the individual points of the graph, and connect the points on the graph from left to right.

Example: Graph the following information using a line graph.

The number of National Merit Scholarship finalists/school year

	90–91	91–92	92–93	93–94	94–95	95–96
Central	3	5	1	4	6	8
Wilson	4	2	3	2	3	2

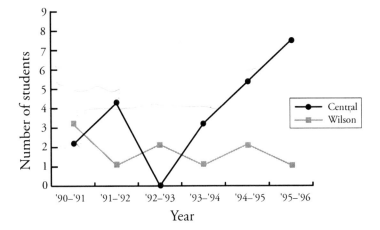

To make a CIRCLE GRAPH, total all the information that is to be included on the graph. Determine the central angle to be used for each sector of the graph using the following formula:

$$\frac{information}{total\ information} \times 360° = degrees\ in\ central\ \sphericalangle$$

Lay out the central angles to these sizes, label each section, and include each section's percent.

> **CIRCLE GRAPH:** also called pie charts, this graph shows quantities in proportional sectors

Example: Graph the following information about monthly expenses on a circle graph:

MONTHLY EXPENSES					
Rent	**Food**	**Utilities**	**Clothes**	**Church**	**Misc.**
$400	$150	$75	$75	$100	$200

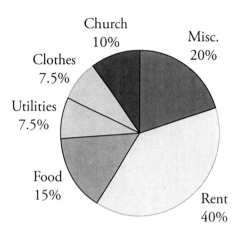

To read a bar graph or a pictograph, read the explanation of the scale that was used in the legend. Compare the length of each bar with the dimensions on the axes, and calculate the value each bar represents. On a pictograph, count the number of pictures used in the chart and calculate the value of all the pictures.

HISTOGRAMS: graphs that summarize information from large sets of data that can be naturally grouped into intervals

To read a circle graph, find the total of the amounts represented on the entire circle graph. To determine the actual amount that each sector of the graph represents, multiply the percent in a sector times the total amount number.

To read a chart, be sure to look at the row and column headings on the table. Use this information to evaluate the information given in the chart.

HISTOGRAMS are used to summarize information from large sets of data that can be naturally grouped into intervals. The vertical axis indicates FREQUENCY (the number of times any particular data value occurs), and the horizontal axis indicates data values or ranges of data values. The number of data values in any interval is the FREQUENCY OF THE INTERVAL.

FREQUENCY: the number of times any particular data value occurs

FREQUENCY OF THE INTERVAL: the number of data values in any interval

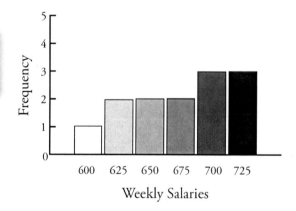

SKILL 5.2 Identify how the presentation of data can lead to different or inappropriate interpretations

Pictographs can be misleading, especially if drawn to represent 3-dimensional objects. If two or more dimensions that reflect ratio are changed, the overall visual effect can be misinterpreted.

Bar and line graphs can be misleading if the scales are changed; for example, if small-scale increments represent large numbers, the differences between sets of information will seem much less than if larger-scale increments are used.

Circle graphs, or pie charts, are excellent for comparing relative amounts. However, they cannot be used to represent absolute amounts and, if interpreted as such, they are misleading.

SKILL 5.3 Calculate range, mean, median, and mode(s) from sets of data and interpret the meaning of the measures of central tendency *(i.e., mean, median, and mode)* and dispersion *(i.e., range and standard deviation)*

The arithmetic MEAN (or average) of a set of numbers is the sum of the numbers divided by the number of items being averaged.

MEAN: the sum of a set of numbers divided by the number of items being averaged; also called the average

Example: Find the mean of the following numbers. Round to the nearest tenth.

24.6, 57.3, 44.1, 39.8, 64.5

The sum is 230.3

The mean is $\frac{230.3}{5}$

$= 46.06$, rounded to 46.1 (nearest tenth)

The MEDIAN of a set of numbers is the middle number when the numbers are arranged in order. To calculate the median, we must arrange the terms in order. If there is an even number of terms, the median is the mean of the two middle terms.

MEDIAN: the middle number when a set of numbers is arranged in order

Example: Find the median.

12, 14, 27, 3, 13, 7, 17, 12, 22, 6, 16

Rearrange the terms from least to greatest.

3, 6, 7, 12, 12, 13,14,16,17, 22, 27

Since there are eleven numbers, the middle would be the sixth number, or 13.

MODE: the number that occurs with the greatest frequency in a set of numbers

The MODE of a set of numbers is the number that occurs with the greatest frequency. A set can have no mode if each term appears exactly one time. Similarly, there can also be more than one mode.

Example: Find the mode.
26, 15, 37, **26**, 35, **26**, 15

  15 appears twice, but 26 appears three times. Therefore, the mode is 26.

RANGE: the difference between the highest and lowest data value in a set of numbers

The RANGE of a set of numbers is the difference between the highest and lowest data value.

Example: Given the ungrouped data below, calculate the mean, range, standard deviation, and variance.

15	22	28	25	34	38
18	25	30	33	19	23

Mean $(\overline{X})$ = 25.8333333
Range: $38 - 15 = 23$
Standard deviation (σ) = 6.699137
Variance (σ^2) = 44.87879

VARIANCE: the sum of the squares of a set of terms divided by the number of items in the set

The VARIANCE is the sum of the squares of a set of terms divided by the number of items in the set. The lower case Greek letter sigma squared (σ^2) represents variance.

$$\frac{Sx^2}{N} = \sigma^2$$

The larger the value of the variance, the larger the spread.

The Greek letter sigma squared (σ^2) represents variance.

  small variation   larger variation

STANDARD DEVIATION: the square root of the variance

STANDARD DEVIATION is the square root of the variance. The lower case Greek letter sigma (σ) is used to represent standard deviation.

$$\sigma = \sqrt{\sigma^2}$$

Most statistical calculators have standard deviation keys and should be used to calculate statistical functions. It is important to become familiar with the calculator and the locations of the necessary keys.

The Greek letter sigma (σ) is used to represent standard deviation.

SKILL 5.4 Identify how the measures of central tendency *(i.e., mean, median, or mode)* can lead to different interpretations

Information can be misleading if the data is not presented appropriately. If a data set contains one very high or one very low value, the mean will not be a good representative of the data set. For example, including the teacher's height in the mean height of a classroom of very young students introduces a comparably high value into the data set and creates a mean that is far greater than it would be without this value.

If the data in a given set clusters around two numbers with a large gap between them, the median will not be representative of the set. For example, the median height of a family with two parents and two small children would be a misleading measure.

Modes are best used with categorical data. For example, a mode of the sale of men's shoe sizes would be helpful to a store when reordering stock of men's shoes. However, finding the mode of men's and women's shoe sizes combined would not be a good indicator of the stock that should be reordered.

Consider this set of test scores from a math class: 0, 16, 19, 65, 65, 65, 68, 69, 70, 72, 73, 73, 75, 78, 80, 85, 88, and 92. The mean of the scores is 64.06 and the median is 71. Because only three of the eighteen scores are less than the mean, the median (71) is a more descriptive measure of how the student scored on the test.

Example: Is the mean, median, or mode the best measure of central tendency for the set 135, 135, 137, and 190?
The mean is 149.25, the median is 136, and the mode is 135. Thus, the median or mode is a better measure than the mean because they are both closer to the majority of the scores.

Example: The yearly salaries of the employees of Company A are $11,000, $12,000, $12,000, $15,000, $20,000, and $25,000. Which measure of central tendency would you use if you were a manager? Which would you use if you were an employee trying to get a raise?
The mean is $15,833. The median is $13,500. The mode is $12,000.

The employee would probably use the mean, since it is the largest amount. The manager would most likely use the mode, since is the smallest.

SKILL 5.5 Calculate the probability of a specified outcome

SAMPLE SPACE: a list of all possible outcomes of an experiment

In probability, the SAMPLE SPACE is a list of all possible outcomes of an experiment. For example, the sample space of tossing two coins is the set {HH, HT, TT, TH}; the sample space of rolling a six-sided die is the set {1, 2, 3, 4, 5, 6}; and the sample space of measuring the height of students in a class is the set of all real numbers {R}.

PROBABILITY: measures the chances that an event will occur

PROBABILITY measures the chances that an event will occur.

$$P(\text{event}) = \frac{\text{number of favorable outcomes}}{\text{number of possible outcomes}}$$

*The probability of an event that must occur, that is, a certain event, is **one**. The probability of an impossible event is **zero**.*

Example: Given one die with faces numbered 1–6, the probability of tossing an even number on one throw of the die is $\frac{3}{6}$ or $\frac{1}{2}$, since there are three favorable outcomes (even faces) and six possible outcomes (faces).

Example: If we roll a fair die:
   A. Find the probability of rolling an even number.
   B. Find the probability of rolling a number less than 3.

   A. The sample space is
      S = {1, 2, 3, 4, 5, 6}, and the event representing even numbers is
      E = {2, 4, 6}.
      Hence, the probability of rolling an even number is

$$p(E) = \frac{n(E)}{n(S)} = \frac{3}{6} = \frac{1}{2} \text{ or } 0.5$$

   B. We represent the event of rolling a number less than 3 by
      A = {1, 2}
      Hence, the probability of rolling a number less than 3 is

$$p(A) = \frac{n(A)}{n(S)} = \frac{2}{6} = \frac{1}{3} \text{ or } 0.33$$

Example: A class has thirty students. Out of the thirty students, twenty-four are males. Assuming all the students have the same chance of being selected, find the probability of selecting a female. (Only one person is selected.)
The number of females in the class is

    30 − 24 = 6

   Hence, the probability of selecting a female is

$$p(\text{female}) = \frac{6}{30} = \frac{1}{5} \text{ or } 0.2$$

Independent Events

If A and B are INDEPENDENT EVENTS, then the outcome of event A does not affect the outcome of event B, and vice versa. We use the multiplication rule to find joint probability.

$$p(A \text{ and } B) = p(A) \times P(B)$$

Example: The probability that a patient is allergic to aspirin is .30. If the probability of a patient having a window in his or her room is .40, find the probability that the patient is allergic to aspirin and has a window in his or her room.

Defining the events:

A = the patient is allergic to aspirin

B = the patient has a window in his or her room

Events A and B are independent; hence

$$p(A \text{ and } B) = p(A) \times p(B)$$
$$= (.30)(.40)$$
$$= .12 \text{ or } 12\%$$

Example: Given a jar containing 10 marbles—3 red, 5 black, and 2 white—what is the probability of drawing a red marble and then a white marble if the marble is returned to the jar after choosing?

$$\frac{3}{10} \times \frac{2}{10} = \frac{6}{100} = \frac{3}{50} \text{ or } .06 \text{ or } 6\%$$

Dependent Events

When the outcome of the first event affects the outcome of the second event, the events are DEPENDENT EVENTS. Any two events that are not independent are dependent. This is also known as conditional probability.

Probability of $(A \text{ and } B) = p(A) \times p(B \text{ given } A)$

Example: Two cards are drawn from a deck of 52 cards without replacement; that is, the first card is not returned to the deck before the second card is drawn. What is the probability of drawing a diamond?

A = drawing a diamond first

B = drawing a diamond second

$p(A)$ = drawing a diamond first

$p(B)$ = drawing a diamond second

$$p(A) = \frac{13}{52} = \frac{1}{4} \qquad p(B) = \frac{12}{52} = \frac{4}{17}$$
$$p(A \text{ and } B) = \frac{1}{4} \times \frac{4}{17} = \frac{7}{34}$$

> **INDEPENDENT EVENTS:** when the outcome of event A does not affect the outcome of event B, and vice versa

> **DEPENDENT EVENTS:** when the outcome of event A affects the outcome of event B

Example: A class of ten students consists of six males and four females. If two students are selected to represent the class, find the probability that:

A. The first is a male and the second is a female
B. The first is a female and the second is a male
C. Both are females
D. Both are males

Define the events:

F = a female is selected to represent the class

M = a male is selected to represent the class

$\frac{F}{M}$ = a female is selected after a male has been selected

$\frac{M}{F}$ = a male is selected after a female has been selected

A. Since F and M are dependent events, it follows that

$$p(\text{M and F}) = p(\text{M}) \times p(\tfrac{F}{M})$$
$$= \frac{6}{10} \times \frac{4}{9} = \frac{3}{5} \times \frac{4}{9} = \frac{12}{45}$$

$p(\frac{F}{M}) = \frac{4}{9}$ instead of $\frac{4}{10}$ because the selection of a male first changed the sample space from ten to nine students.

B. $p(\text{F and M}) = p(\text{F}) \times p(\tfrac{M}{F})$
$$= \frac{4}{10} \times \frac{6}{9} = \frac{2}{5} \times \frac{2}{3} = \frac{4}{15}$$
$p(\text{F and F}) = p(\text{F}) \times p(\tfrac{F}{F})$
$$= \frac{4}{10} \times \frac{3}{9} = \frac{2}{5} \times \frac{1}{3} = \frac{2}{15}$$
$p(\text{both are males}) = p(\text{M and M})$
$$= \frac{6}{10} \times \frac{5}{9} = \frac{30}{90} = \frac{1}{3}$$

ODDS: the ratio of the number of favorable outcomes to the number of unfavorable outcomes

ODDS are the ratio of the number of favorable outcomes to the number of unfavorable outcomes. The sum of the favorable outcomes and the unfavorable outcomes will always equal the total possible outcomes.

For example, given a bag of 12 red and 7 green marbles, compute the odds of randomly selecting a red marble.

Odds of getting red $= \frac{12}{19}$.

Odds of not getting red $= \frac{7}{19}$.

In the case of flipping a coin, it is equally likely that the coin will land on heads or tails. Thus, the odds of tossing a head are 1:1. This is even odds.

> **SKILL 5.6** Solve and interpret real-world problems involving probability using counting procedures, tables, tree diagrams, and the concepts of permutations and combination

Counting Procedures

In all the problems we have seen so far, we were given the sample space for the problem or we could easily obtain it. However, in many real-life situations, the sample space and events within it are very large and difficult to find.

There are three techniques to help find the number of elements in one event or a sample space: the counting principle, permutations, and combinations.

There are three techniques to help find the number of elements in one event or a sample space: the counting principle, permutations, and combinations.

The counting principle

In a sequence of two distinct events where the first one has n number of outcomes or possibilities and the second one has m number of outcomes or possibilities, the total number or possibilities of the sequence is

$n \times m$

Example: A car dealership has three Mazda models and each model comes in a choice of four colors. How many Mazda cars are available at the dealership?

Number of available Mazda cars = $(3)(4) = 12$

Example: If a license plate consists of three digits followed by three letters, find the possible number of licenses if:

A. Repetition of letters and digits is not allowed.
B. Repetition of letters and digits is allowed.

A. Because there are twenty-six letters and ten digits and repetitions are not allowed, by using the counting principle we get:
possible number of licenses = $(26)(25)(24)(10)(9)(8)$
$= 11,232,000$

B. If repetitions are allowed, we get:
possible number of licenses = $(26)(26)(26)(10)(10)(10)$
$= 17,576,000$

The addition principle of counting

If A and B are events, $n(AorB) = n(A) + n(B) - n(A \cap B)$

Example: In how many ways can you select a black card or a Jack from an ordinary deck of playing cards?

Let B denote the set of black cards, and let J denote the set of Jacks.

Then, $n(B) = 26$, $n(J) = 4$, $n(B \cap J) = 2$, and

$n(BorJ) = n(B) + n(J) - n(B \cap A)$

$= 26 + 4 - 2$

$= 28$

The addition principle of counting for mutually exclusive events

If A and B are mutually exclusive events, $n(AorB) = n(A) + n(B)$.

Example: A travel agency offers 40 possible trips: 14 to Asia, 16 to Europe, and 10 to South America. In how many ways can you select a trip to Asia or Europe through this agency?

Let A denote trips to Asia, and let E denote trips to Europe. Then $A \cap E = \varnothing$, and $n(AorE) = 14 + 16 = 30$.

Therefore, the number of ways you can select a trip to Asia or Europe is 30.

The multiplication principle of counting for dependent events

Let A be a set of outcomes of Stage 1 and B a set of outcomes of Stage 2.

The number of ways, $n(AandB)$ that A and B can occur in a two-stage experiment is represented by:

$n(AandE) = n(A)n(B|A)$

where $n(B|A)$ denotes the number of ways B can occur, given that A has already occurred.

Example: How many ways from an ordinary deck of 52 cards can 2 Jacks be drawn in succession if the first card is drawn but not replaced in the deck and then the second card is drawn?

This is a two-stage experiment where we must compute $n(AandB)$, where A is the set of outcomes for which a Jack is obtained on the first draw and B is the set of outcomes for which a Jack is obtained on the second draw.

If the first card drawn is a Jack, then there are only 3 remaining Jacks left to choose from on the second draw. Thus, drawing two cards without replacement means that the events A and B are dependent.

$n(AandB) = n(A)n(B|A) = 4 \times 3 = 12$

The multiplication principle of counting for independent events

Let A be a set of outcomes of Stage 1, and B a set of outcomes of Stage 2. If A and B are independent events, then the number of ways, $n(AandB)$, that A and B can occur in a two-stage experiment is represented by:

$n(AandB) = n(A)n(B)$.

Example: How many six-letter code "words" can be formed if repetition of letters is not allowed?

With code words, a word does not have to look like a word; for example, *abcdef* could be a code word. Since we must choose a first letter and a second letter and a third letter and a fourth letter and a fifth letter and a sixth letter, this experiment has six stages.

Since repetition is not allowed there are twenty-six choices for the first letter, twenty-five for the second, twenty-four for the third, twenty-three for the fourth, twenty-two for the fifth, and twenty-one for the sixth. Therefore, we have:

n (six-letter code words without repetition of letters)

$= 26 \times 25 \times 24 \times 23 \times 22 \times 21$

$= 165{,}765{,}600$

Permutations

In order to understand permutations, we must first address the concept of factorials.

n factorial, written $n!$, is represented by $n! = n(n - 1)(n - 2) \ldots (2)(1)$

$5! = (5)(4)(3)(2)(1) = 120$

$3! = 3(2)(1) = 6$

By definition: $0! = 1$

$1! = 1$

$\frac{6!}{6!} = 1$ but $\frac{6!}{2!} \neq 3!$

$\frac{6!}{6!} = \frac{6 \times 5 \times 4 \times 3 \times 2!}{2!} = 6 \times 5 \times 4 \times 3 = 360$

The number of permutations represents the number of ways we can select r items from n items and arrange them in a specific order.

Write permutations as $_nP_r$ and calculate them using the following relationship:

$$_nP_r = \frac{n!}{(n - r)!}$$

When calculating permutations, order matters. For example, 2, 3, 4 and 4, 3, 2 are counted as two different permutations. Calculating the number of permutations is not valid with experiments where replacement is allowed.

Example: How many different ways can the students in a math class select a president and a vice president if seven students are available?

Because the positions of president and vice president are not equal, this question will have a number of permutations.

$$_7P_2 = \frac{7!}{(7-2)!} = \frac{7!}{5!} = \frac{7 \times 6 \times 5}{5!} = 7 \times 6 = 42$$

This problem can also be solved using the counting principle:

There are seven available students from whom to choose a president. After the math students choose a president, there are six available students from whom to choose a vice president.

Therefore, the number of ways the students can choose a president and a vice president = $7 \times 6 = 42$.

Combinations

COMBINATIONS: an unordered collection of distinct elements

When we are dealing with the number of **COMBINATIONS**, the order in which elements are selected is not important. For instance,

2, 3, 4 and 4, 2, 3 are considered one combination.

The number of combinations represents the number of ways in which r elements can be selected from n elements (in no particular order). The number of combinations is represented by $_nC_r$ and can be calculated using the following relationship.

$$_nC_r = \frac{n!}{(n-r)r!}$$

Example: In how many ways can 2 students be selected from a class of 7 students to represent the class?

Since both representatives have the same position, the order is not important, and we are dealing with the number of combinations.

$$_nC_r = \frac{7!}{(7-2)!2!} = \frac{7 \times 6 \times 5!}{5!2 \times 1} = 21$$

Example: In a club, there are 6 women and 4 men. A committee of 2 women and 1 man is to be selected. How many different committees can be selected?

This problem has a sequence of two events. The first event involves selecting 2 women out of 6 women, and the second event involves selecting 1 man out of 4 men. We use the combination relationship to find the number of ways in events 1 and 2, and we use the counting principle to find the number of ways the sequence can happen.

Number of committees $= {_6}C_2 \times {_4}C_1$

$$\frac{6!}{(6-2)!2!} \times \frac{4!}{(4-1)!1!}$$

$$= \frac{6 \times 5 \times 4!}{4! \times 2 \times 1} \times \frac{4 \times 3!}{3! \times 1}$$

$$= (15) \times (4) = 60$$

Using Tables

Example: The results of a survey of 47 students are summarized in the table below.

	BLACK HAIR	BLONDE HAIR	RED HAIR	TOTAL
Male	10	8	6	24
Female	6	12	5	23
Total	16	20	11	47

Use the table to answer questions A through C.

A. If one student is selected at random, find the probability of selecting a male student.

$$\frac{\text{Number of male students}}{\text{Number of students}} = \frac{24}{47}$$

B. If one student is selected at random, find the probability of selecting a female with red hair.

$$\frac{\text{Number of females with red hair}}{\text{Number of students}} = \frac{5}{47}$$

C. If one student is selected at random, find the probability of selecting a student who does not have red hair.

$$\frac{\text{Number of students with red hair}}{\text{Number of students}} = \frac{11}{47}$$

$$1 - \frac{11}{47} = \frac{36}{45}$$

DOMAIN II
ENGLISH

PERSONALIZED STUDY PLAN

KNOWN MATERIAL/ SKIP IT

COMPETENCY 6
CONCEPTUAL AND ORGANIZATIONAL SKILLS

The organization of written work includes two main elements: the order in which writers choose to present the different parts of the discussion or argument, and the relationships they construct between these parts.

There are many different ways to order a series of ideas, but all aim to lead readers along desired paths to writers' main ideas. These are some of the ways in which paragraphs may be effectively organized:

- Sequence of events: In this type of organization, the details are presented in the order in which they have occurred. Paragraphs that describe a process or procedure, give directions, or outline a given period of time (such as a day or a month) are often arranged as a sequence of events, or CHRONOLOGICALLY.

- Statement support: In this type of organization, the main idea is stated and the rest of the paragraph explains or proves this idea. This type of organization is also referred to as relative importance. There are four ways in which statement support can be organized: most-to-least, least-to-most, most-least-most, and least-most-least.

- Comparison-contrast: The compare-contrast pattern is used to present the differences between or similarities among two or more ideas, actions, events, or things. Usually the topic sentence describes the basic relationship between the ideas or items and the rest of the paragraph explains this relationship.

- Classification: In this type of organization, the paragraph presents grouped information about a topic. The topic sentence usually states the general category, and the rest of the sentences show how various elements of the category have (or to what extent they deviate from) a common base.

- Cause and effect: This pattern describes how two or more events are connected. The main sentence usually states the primary cause(s), the primary effect(s), and the general way in which they are connected. The rest of the sentences explain the connection in more detail.

Written ideas must be presented in a logical order so that readers can follow the information easily and quickly.

CHRONOLOGICALLY: organized as a sequence of events

- Spatial/place: In this type of organization, descriptions are organized according to the location of items in relation to each other and to the larger context. The orderly arrangement guides readers' eyes as they mentally envision the scene or place being described.

TRANSITIONS: words that signal relationships between ideas

Transitions build each sentence on the ideas in the last, and link clearly to the preceding one.

Even if the sentences that make up a given paragraph or passage are arranged in logical order, the document as a whole can still seem choppy and the various ideas disconnected. TRANSITIONS, words that signal relationships between ideas, can improve the flow of a document.

Transitions can help achieve a clear and effective presentation of information by establishing connections between sentences, paragraphs, and whole sections of a document. By signaling how to organize, interpret, and react to information, transitions allow writers to effectively and elegantly explain their ideas.

COMMON TRANSITIONS	
Similarity	also, in the same way, just as … so too, likewise, similarly
Exception/Contrast	but, however, in spite of, on the one hand … on the other hand, nevertheless, nonetheless, notwithstanding, in contrast, on the contrary, still, yet, although
Sequence/Order	first, second, third, … next, then, finally, until
Time	after, afterward, at last, before, currently, during, earlier, immediately, later, meanwhile, now, presently, recently, simultaneously, since, subsequently, then
Example	for example, for instance, namely, specifically, to illustrate
Emphasis	even, indeed, in fact, of course, truly
Place/Position	above, adjacent, below, beyond, here, in front, in back, nearby, there
Cause and Effect	accordingly, consequently, hence, so, therefore, thus, as a result, because, consequently, hence, if…then, in short
Additional Support or Evidence	additionally, again, also, and, as well, besides, equally important, further, furthermore, in addition, moreover, then
Conclusion/ Summary	finally, in a word, in brief, in conclusion, in the end, in the final analysis, on the whole, thus, to conclude, to summarize, in sum, in summary
Statement Support	most important, more significant, primarily, most essential

Continued on next page

Addition	again, also, and, besides, equally important, finally, furthermore, in addition, last, likewise, moreover, too
Clarification	actually, clearly, evidently, in fact, in other words, obviously, of course, indeed

The following example shows good logical order and transitions. The transition words are highlighted in **bold**.

> No one really knows how Valentine's Day started. There are several legends, **however**, which are often told. The **first** attributes Valentine's Day to a Christian priest who lived in Rome during the third century under the rule of Emperor Claudius. Rome was at war and, **apparently**, Claudius felt that married men did not fight as well as bachelors. **Consequently**, Claudius banned marriage for the duration of the war. **But** Valentinus, the priest, risked his life to marry couples secretly in violation of Claudius' law. The **second** legend is **even more** romantic. In this story, Valentinus is a prisoner, having been condemned to death for refusing to worship pagan deities. **While** in jail, he fell in love with his jailer's daughter, who happened to be blind. Daily, he prayed for her sight to return and miraculously, it did. On February 14, the day that he was condemned to die, he was allowed to write the young woman a note. **In this farewell letter**, he promised eternal love and signed at the bottom of the page the now famous words, "Your Valentine."

SKILL 6.2 Identify irrelevant sentences

The main idea of a passage may contain a wide variety of supporting information, but it is important that each sentence be related to the main idea. When a sentence contains information that bears little or no connection to the main idea, it is said to be IRRELEVANT. It is important to continually assess whether or not a sentence contributes to the overall task of supporting the main idea. When a sentence is deemed irrelevant, it is best either to omit it from the passage or to make it relevant by one of the following strategies:

IRRELEVANT: information that bears little or no connection to the main idea

- Adding detail: Sometimes a sentence can seem out of place if it does not contain enough information to link it to the topic. Adding specific information can show how the sentence relates to the main idea.

- **Adding an example:** This is especially important in passages in which information is being argued or compared and contrasted. Examples can support the main idea and give the document credibility.

- **Using diction effectively:** It is important to understand connotation, avoid ambiguity, and avoid too much repetition when selecting words.

- **Adding transitions:** Transitions are extremely helpful for making sentences relevant because they are specifically designed to connect one idea to another. They can also reduce a paragraph's choppiness.

The following passage has several irrelevant sentences, which are highlighted in **bold**:

> The New City Planning Committee is proposing a new capitol building to represent the multicultural face of New City. **The current mayor is a Democrat.** The new capitol building will be on 10th Street across from the grocery store and next to the recreational center. It will be within walking distance to the subway and bus depot, as the designers want to emphasize the importance of public transportation.
>
> Aesthetically, the building will have a contemporary design, featuring a brushed-steel exterior and large, floor-to-ceiling windows. **It is important for employees to have a connection with the outside world even when they are in their offices.** Inside the building, the walls will be moveable. This will not only facilitate a multitude of creative floor plans, but it will also create a focus on open communication and flow of information. **It sounds a bit gimmicky to me.** Finally, the capitol will feature a large outdoor courtyard full of lush greenery and serene fountains. **Work will now seem like Club Med to those who work at the New City capitol building!**

COMPETENCY 7
WORD CHOICE SKILLS

SKILL **Choose the appropriate word or expression in context**
7.1

Practice Exercise: Word Choice I

Choose the most effective word or phrase within the context suggested by the sentences.

1. The defendant was accused of _____ money from his employer.

   A. stealing

   B. borrowing

   C. robbing

   D.

2. Many tourists are attracted to the Paradise Island because of its _____ climate.

   A. friendly

   B. peaceful

   C. balmy

3. The woman was angry because the tomato juice left an _____ stain on her brand new carpet.

   A. unsightly

   B. ugly

   C. unpleasant

4. After disobeying orders, the army private was _____ by his superior officer.

   A. degraded

   B. attacked

   C. reprimanded

5. Sharon's critical evaluation of the student's book report left the student feeling _____, which caused him to want to quit school.

   A. surprised

   B. depressed

   C. discouraged

Practice Exercise: Word Choice I (cont.)

Choose the most effective word or phrase within the context suggested by the sentences.

6. The life-saving medication created by the scientist had a _____ impact on further developments in the treatment of cancer.

   A. beneficial

   B. fortunate

   C. miraculous

7. *The Phantom of the Opera* is one of Andrew Lloyd Webber's most successful musicals, largely because of its _____ themes.

   A. romantic

   B. melodramatic

   C. imaginary

8. The massive Fourth of July fireworks display _____ the partygoers with lots of colored lights and sound.

   A. disgusted

   B. captivated

   C. captured

9. Many of the residents of Grand Forks, North Dakota, were forced to _____ their homes because of the flood.

   A. escape

   B. evacuate

   C. exit

Answer Key

1.	A	6.	A
2.	C	7.	A
3.	A	8.	B
4.	C	9.	B
5.	C		

Practice Exercises: Word Choice II

Choose the sentence that expresses the thought most clearly and most effectively and that is structurally correct in grammar and syntax.

1. A. The movie was three hours in length, featuring interesting characters, and moved at a fast pace.

    B. The movie was three hours long, featured interesting characters, and moved at a fast pace.

    C. Moving at a fast pace, the movie was three hours long and featured interesting characters.

2. A. We were so offended by the waiter's demeanor that we left the restaurant without paying the check.

    B. The waiter's demeanor offended us so much that without paying the check, we left the restaurant.

    C. We left the restaurant without paying the check because we were offended by the waiter's demeanor.

3. A. In today's society, information about our lives is provided to us by computers.

    B. We rely on computers in today's society to provide us information about our lives.

    C. In today's society, we rely on computers to provide us with information about our lives.

4. A. Folding the sides of the tent carefully, Jack made sure to be quiet so none of the other campers would be woken up.

    B. So none of the other campers would be woken up, Jack made sure to be quiet by folding the sides of the tent carefully.

    C. Folding the sides of the tent carefully, so none of the other campers would wake up, Jack made sure to be quiet.

Answer Key: Word Choice II

1. B
2. A
3. C
4. A

Practice Exercises: Word Choice III

Choose the most effective word or phrase within the context suggested by the sentence(s).

1. The six hundred employees of General Electric were _____ by the company due to budgetary cutbacks.

   A. released

   B. terminated

   C. downsized

2. The force of the tornado _____ the many residents of the town of Russell, Kansas.

   A. intimidated

   B. repulsed

   C. frightened

3. Even though his new car was easy to drive, Fred _____ to walk to work every day because he liked the exercise.

   A. needed

   B. preferred

   C. considered

4. June's parents were very upset over the school board's decision to suspend her from Adams High for a week. Before they filed a lawsuit against the board, they _____ with a lawyer to help them make a decision.

   A. consulted

   B. debated

   C. conversed

5. The race car driver's _____ in handling the automobile was a key factor in his victory.

   A. patience

   B. precision

   C. determination

6. After impressing the judges with her talent and charm, the beauty contestant _____ more popularity by singing an aria from *La Bohème*.

   A. captured

   B. scored

   C. gained

7. The stained-glass window was _____ when a large brick flew through it during the riot.

   A. damaged

   B. cracked

   C. shattered

8. The class didn't know what happened to the professor until the principal _____ why the professor quit his job.

   A. informed

   B. discovered

   C. explained

Practice Exercises: Word Choice III

Choose the most effective word or phrase within the context suggested by the sentence(s).

9. The giant penthouse at the top of the building enables the billionaire industrialist _____ the citizens on the street.

    A. to view from above

    B. the chance to see

    C. to glance at

10. Sally's parents _____ her to attend the dance after she promised to return by midnight.

    A. prohibited

    B. permitted

    C. asked

Answer Key

1.	C	5.	B	9.	C
2.	C	6.	C	10.	B
3.	B	7.	C		
4.	A	8.	C		

SKILL 7.2 Recognize commonly confused or misused words or phrases

HOMONYM: a word that is spelled and pronounced just like another word but that has a different meaning

Students frequently encounter problems with homonyms. Strictly speaking, a HOMONYM is a word that is spelled and pronounced just like another word but that has a different meaning. An example is the word *mean*, which can be a verb—"to intend"; an adjective—"unkind"; or a noun or adjective—"average."

HOMOGRAPHS are words that share the same spelling, regardless of how they are pronounced, and have different meanings. Words that are pronounced the same but may or may not have different spellings are called HOMOPHONES.

HOMOGRAPHS: words that share the same spelling, regardless of how they are pronounced, and have different meanings

HOMOPHONES: words that are pronounced the same but may or may not have different spellings

HETERONYMS: (sometimes called heterophones) share the same spelling but have different pronunciations and meanings

CAPITONYMS: words that are spelled the same but have different meanings when capitalized

HETERONYMS (sometimes called heterophones) share the same spelling but have different pronunciations and meanings. For example, the homographs *desert* (abandon) and *desert* (arid region) are heteronyms (pronounced differently), but the homographs *mean* (intend) and *mean* (average) are homophones because they are pronounced the same (they are also homonyms).

CAPITONYMS are words that are spelled the same but have different meanings when capitalized. A capitonym may or may not have different pronunciations; for example, *polish* (to make shiny) and *Polish* (from Poland).

Some of the most troubling homophones are those that are spelled differently but that sound the same. Some examples include its (third person singular neuter pronoun) and *it's* ("it is"); *there* (a location), *their* (third person plural pronoun), and *they're* ("they are"). Another common example is *to*, *too*, and *two*.

Some homonyms/homographs are particularly intriguing. *Fluke*, for instance, refers to a fish, a flatworm, the end parts of an anchor, the fins on a whale's tail, and a stroke of luck.

COMMONLY MISUSED WORDS		
Accept is a verb meaning "to receive or to tolerate"	**Except** is usually a preposition meaning "excluding"	**Except** is also a verb meaning "to exclude"
Advice is a noun meaning "recommendation"	**Advise** is a verb meaning "to recommend"	
Affect is usually a verb meaning "to influence"	**Effect** is usually a noun meaning "result." Effect can also be a verb meaning "to bring about"	
An **allusion** is "an indirect reference"	An **illusion** is "a misconception or false impression"	
Add is a verb meaning "to put together"	**Ad** is a noun that is the abbreviation for the word "advertisement"	
Ain't is a common, nonstandard contraction for the contraction "aren't"		
Allot is a verb meaning "to distribute"	**A lot** can act as an adverb that means "often," "to a great degree," or "a large quantity" (example: She shops a lot)	

Continued on next page

Allowed is used as an adjective that means "permitted"	**Aloud** is an adverb that means "audible"	
Bare is an adjective that means "naked" or "exposed"; it can also indicate a minimum	As a noun, **bear** is a large mammal	As a verb, **bear** means "to carry a heavy burden"
Capital refers to a city; capitol to "a building where lawmakers meet"	**Capital** also refers to "wealth" or "resources"	
A **chord** is a noun that refers to "a group of musical notes"	**Cord** is a noun meaning "rope" or "a long electrical line"	
Compliment is a noun meaning "a praising or flattering remark"	**Complement** is a noun that means "something that completes or makes perfect"	
Climactic is derived from climax, "the point of greatest intensity in a series or progression of events"	**Climatic** is derived from climate; it refers to meteorological conditions	
Discreet is an adjective that means "tactful" or "diplomatic"	**Discrete** is an adjective that means "separate" or "distinct"	
Dye is a noun or verb used to indicate artificial coloring	**Die** is a verb that means "to pass away"	**Die** is also a noun that means "a cube-shaped game piece"
Effect is a noun that means "outcome"	**Affect** is a verb that means "to influence"	
Elicit is a verb meaning "to bring out" or "to evoke"	**Illicit** is an adjective meaning "unlawful"	
Emigrate means "to leave one country or region to settle in another"	**Immigrate** means "to enter another country and reside there"	
Gorilla is a noun meaning "a large great ape"	**Guerrilla** is "a member of a band of irregular soldiers"	
Hoard is a verb that means "to accumulate" or "store up"	A **horde** is "a large group"	
Lead is a verb that means "to guide" or "to serve as the head of"; it is also a noun that is a type of metal		

Continued on next page

Medal is a noun that means "an award that is strung round the neck"	**Meddle** is a verb that means "to involve oneself in a matter without right or invitation"	**Metal** is "an element such as silver or gold"; **mettle** is a noun meaning "toughness" or "courage"
Morning is a noun indicating "the time between midnight and midday"	**Mourning** is a verb or noun pertaining to "the period of grieving after a death"	
Past is a noun meaning "a time before now" (past, present, and future)	**Passed** is the past tense of the verb "to pass"	
Piece is a noun meaning "portion"	**Peace** is a noun meaning "the opposite of war, or serenity"	
Peak is a noun meaning "the tip" or "height to reach the highest point"	**Peek** is a verb that means "to take a brief look"	**Pique** is a verb meaning "to incite or raise interest"
Principal is a noun most commonly meaning "the chief or head"; it also means "a capital sum of money"	**Principle** is a noun meaning "a basic truth or law"	
Rite is a noun meaning "a special ceremony"	**Right** is an adjective meaning "correct" or "the opposite direction of left"	**Write** is a verb meaning "to compose in writing"
Than is a conjunction used in comparisons (that pizza is more *than* I can eat);	**Then** is an adverb denoting time (Tom laughed, and *then* we recognized him)	To remember the correct use of these words, you can use the following: **Than** is used to *compare*; both words have the letter a in them **Then** tells *when*; both words are spelled the same, except for the first letter
There is an adverb specifying place (Sylvia is lying *there* unconscious); it is also an expletive (*there* are two plums left)	**Their** is a possessive pronoun	**They're** is a contraction of "they are": Fred and Jane finally washed *their* car, or *they're* later than usual today.
To is a preposition	**Too** is an adverb	**Two** is a number
Your is a possessive pronoun	**You're** is a contraction of "you are"	

To help students master these difficult distinctions, practice using these words in sentences. Context is useful in understanding differences, and drill is necessary to overcome misuses.

Denotative and Connotative Language

To effectively teach language, it is necessary to understand that as human beings acquire language, they realize that words have denotative and connotative meanings. Generally, denotative words point to things, and connotative words deal with the mental suggestions that the words convey.

*The word **skunk** has a denotative meaning if the speaker intends the word to identify the animal. **Skunk** has connotative meaning depending upon the tone of delivery, the socially acceptable attitudes about the animal, and the speaker's personal feelings about the animal.*

PROBLEM PHRASES	
CORRECT	**INCORRECT**
Supposed to	Suppose to
Used to	Use to
Toward	Towards
Anyway	Anyways
Couldn't care less	Could care less
For all intents and purposes	For all intensive purposes
Come to see me	Come and see me
En route	In route
Regardless	Irregardless
Second, Third	Secondly, Thirdly

Other Confusing Words

Lie is an intransitive verb meaning to recline or rest on a surface. Its principal parts are *lie, lay,* and *lain*. **Lay** is a transitive verb meaning "to put or place." Its principal parts are *lay, laid,* and *laid*.

Birds lay eggs.
I lie down for bed around 10 p.m.

Set is a transitive verb meaning "to put or to place." Its principal parts are *set, set,* and *set*. **Sit** is an intransitive verb meaning "to be seated." Its principal parts are *sit, sat,* and *sat*.

> I set my backpack down near the front door.
>
> They sat in the park until the sun went down.

Among is a preposition to be used with three or more items. **Between** is to be used with two items.

> Between you and me, I cannot tell the difference among those three Johnson sisters.

As is a subordinating conjunction used to introduce a subordinating clause. **Like** is a preposition and is followed by a noun or a noun phrase.

> As I walked to the lab, I realized that the recent experiment findings were much like those we found last year.

Can is a verb that means "to be able." **May** is a verb that means "to have permission." "Can" and "may" are only interchangeable in cases of possibility.

> I can lift 250 pounds.
>
> May I go to Alex's house?

SKILL 7.3 Recognize diction and tone appropriate to a given audience

Determining the appropriate language for a particular audience hinges on two things: word choice and formality/informality.

Tailoring language for a particular audience is an important skill. Writing intended to be read by a business associate will surely sound different from writing intended to be read by a young child. Not only are the vocabularies different, but the formality of the discourse needs to be adjusted as well.

Determining the appropriate language for a particular audience hinges on two things: word choice and formality/informality. The most formal language does not use contractions or slang. The most informal language will probably feature a more casual use of common sayings and anecdotes. Formal language will use longer sentences and will not sound like a conversation. The most informal language will use shorter sentences—not necessarily simple sentences, but shorter constructions—and may sound like a conversation.

In both formal and informal writing, there exists a TONE—the writer's attitude toward the material and/or reader. The tone may be playful, formal, intimate, angry, serious, ironic, outraged, baffled, tender, serene, depressed, and so on. Both the subject matter and the audience dictate the overall tone of a piece of writing. Tone is also related to the actual words that make up the document, since we attach affective meanings, called connotations, to words. Gaining conscious control over language makes it possible for the writer to use language appropriately in various situations. By evoking the proper responses from readers/listeners, the writer can prompt them to take action.

> **TONE:** the author's attitude toward the material and/or the reader

The following questions are an excellent way to help the writer choose the appropriate audience and tone for a piece of writing.

1. Who is your audience? (friend, teacher, businessperson, etc.)

2. How much does this person know about you and/or your topic?

3. What is your purpose? (to prove an argument, to persuade, to amuse, to register a complaint, to ask for a raise, etc.)

4. What emotions do you have about the topic? (nervousness, happiness, confidence, anger, sadness, no feelings at all)

5. What emotions do you want to register with your audience? (anger, nervousness, happiness, boredom, interest)

6. What persona do you need to create in order to achieve your purpose?

7. What choice of language is best suited to achieving your purpose with your particular subject? (slang, friendly but respectful, formal)

8. What emotional quality do you want to transmit to achieve your purpose? (matter-of-fact, informative, authoritative, inquisitive, sympathetic, or angry) To what degree do you want to express this tone?

COMPETENCY 8
SENTENCE STRUCTURE SKILLS

SKILL 8.1 Recognize correct placement of modifiers

Phrases that are not placed near the word they modify often result in misplaced modifiers. Phrases that do not relate to the subject being modified result in dangling modifiers.

Error: *Weighing the options carefully, a decision was made regarding the punishment of the convicted murderer.*

Problem: Who is weighing the options? No one capable of weighing is named in the sentence; thus, the participle phrase *weighing the options carefully* dangles. This problem can be corrected by adding a subject to the sentence who is capable of doing the action.

Correction: *Weighing the options carefully, the judge made a decision regarding the punishment of the convicted murderer.*

Error: *Returning to my favorite watering hole brought back many fond memories.*

Problem: The person who returned is never indicated, and the participle phrase dangles. This problem can be corrected by creating a dependent clause from the modifying phrase.

Correction: *When I returned to my favorite watering hole, many fond memories came back to me.*

Error: *One damaged house stood only to remind townspeople of the hurricane.*

Problem: The placement of the modifier only suggests that the sole reason the house remained was to serve as a reminder. The misplaced modifier creates ambiguity. This problem can be corrected by moving the modifier.

Correction: *Only one damaged house stood, reminding townspeople of the hurricane.*

Error: *Recovered from the five-mile hike, the obstacle course was a piece of cake for the Boy Scout troop.*

Problem: The obstacle course is not recovered from the five-mile hike, so the modifying phrase must be placed closer to the word that it modifies, troop.

Correction: *The obstacle course was a piece of cake for the Boy Scout troop, which had just recovered from a five-mile hike.*

Practice Exercise: Misplaced and Dangling Modifiers

Choose the sentence that expresses the thought most clearly and effectively and that has no error in structure.

1. A. Attempting to remove the dog from the well, the paramedic tripped and fell in also.

    B. As the paramedic attempted to remove the dog from the well, he tripped and fell in also.

    C. The paramedic tripped and fell in also attempting to remove the dog from the well.

2. A. To save the wounded child, a powerful explosion ripped through the operating room as the doctors worked.

    B. In the operating room, as the wounded child was being saved, a powerful explosion ripped through.

    C. To save the wounded child, the doctors worked as an explosion ripped through the operating room.

3. A. One hot July morning, a herd of giraffes screamed wildly in the jungle next to the wildlife habitat.

    B. One hot July morning, a herd of giraffes screamed in the jungle wildly next to the wildlife habitat.

    C. One hot July morning, a herd of giraffes screamed in the jungle next to the wildlife habitat, wildly.

4. A. Looking through the file cabinets in the office, the photographs of the crime scene revealed a new suspect in the investigation.

    B. Looking through the file cabinets in the office, the detective discovered photographs of the crime scene that revealed a new suspect in the investigation.

    C. A new suspect in the investigation was revealed in photographs of the crime scene that were discovered while looking through the file cabinets in the office.

5. A. In the grand ballroom, the tables and chairs were moved off to the side to make room for the dancers.

    B. To make room for the dancers, the tables and chairs were moved off to the side in the grand ballroom.

    C. To make room for the dancers, we moved the tables and chairs off to the side in the grand ballroom.

Answer Key: Misplaced and Dangling Modifiers

1. B

   Option B corrects the dangling participle *attempting to remove the dog from the well* by creating a dependent clause introducing the main clause. In Option A, the introductory participle phrase *Attempting . . . well* does not refer to a paramedic, the subject of the main clause. The word *also* in Option C incorrectly implies that the paramedic was doing something besides trying to remove the dog.

2. C

   Option C corrects the dangling modifier *to save the wounded child by* adding the concrete clause *doctors worked*. Option A infers that an explosion was working to save the wounded child. Option B never tells who was trying to save the wounded child.

3. A

   Option A places the adverb *wildly* closest to the verb *screamed*, which it modifies. Both Options B and C incorrectly place the modifier away from the verb.

4. B

   Option B corrects the modifier *looking* through the file cabinets in the *office* by placing it next to the detective who is doing the looking. Option A sounds as though the photographs were looking; Option C has no one doing the looking.

5. C

   Option C corrects the dangling modifier *to make room for the dancers* by adding the concrete subject *we moved the tables and chairs off to the side*. In Option A, the modifier *to make room for the dancers* has no word to refer to in the sentence. Option B puts the modifier *to make room* at the beginning of the sentence, but it still has no referent.

SKILL 8.2 Recognize parallelism, including parallel expressions for parallel ideas

Faulty Parallelism

Two or more elements stated in a single clause should be expressed with the same (or parallel) structure.

Two or more elements stated in a single clause should be expressed with the same (or parallel) structure. For example, the elements could all be adjectives, verb forms, or nouns. When the elements are verbs, the tense should be consistent.

Error: *She needed to be beautiful, successful, and have fame.*

Problem: The phrase *to be* is followed by two different structures: *beautiful* and *successful* are adjectives, and *have fame* is a verb phrase.

Correction: *She needed to be <u>beautiful</u>, <u>successful</u>, and <u>famous</u>.*
                      (adjective) (adjective)   (adjective)

             -OR-
             She needed <u>beauty</u>, <u>success</u>, and <u>fame</u>.
                  (noun) (noun)   (noun)

Error: *I plan either to sell my car during the spring or during the summer.*

Problem: Paired conjunctions (also called *correlative conjunctions*, such as *either-or, both-and, neither-nor,* and *not only-but also*) need to be followed with similar structures. In the sentence above, *either* is followed by *to sell my car during the spring*, while *or* is followed only by the phrase *during the summe*r.

Correction: *I plan to sell my car during either the spring or the summer.*

Error: *The President pledged to lower taxes and that he would cut spending to lower the national debt.*

Problem: Since the phrase *to lower taxes* follows the verb *pledged*, a similar structure of *to* is needed with the phrase *cut spending*.

Correction: *The President pledged to lower taxes and to cut spending to lower the national debt.*
             -OR-
             The President pledged that he would lower taxes and cut spending to lower the national debt.

Practice Exercise: Parallelism

Choose the sentence that expresses the thought most clearly and effectively and that has no error in structure.

1. A. Andy found the family tree, researches the Irish descendents, and he was compiling a book for everyone to read.

    B. Andy found the family tree, researched the Irish descendents, and compiled a book for everyone to read.

    C. Andy finds the family tree, researched the Irish descendents, and compiled a book for everyone to read.

2. A. In the last ten years, computer technology has advanced so quickly that workers have had difficulty keeping up with the new equipment and the increased number of functions.

    B. Computer technology has advanced so quickly in the last ten years that workers have had difficulty to keep up with the new equipment and by increasing number of functions.

    C. In the last ten years, computer technology has advanced so quickly that workers have had difficulty keeping up with the new equipment, and the number of functions are increasing.

3. A. The History Museum contains exhibits honoring famous residents, a video presentation about the state's history, an art gallery featuring paintings and sculptures, and they even display a replica of the State House.

    B. The State History Museum contains exhibits honoring famous residents, a video presentation about the state's history, an art gallery featuring paintings and sculptures, and even a replica of the State House.

    C. The State History Museum contains exhibits honoring famous residents, a video presentation about the state's history, an art gallery featuring paintings and sculptures, and there is even a replica of the State House.

Answer Key: Parallelism

1. **B**

   Option B uses parallelism by presenting a series of past tense verbs: *found, researched, and compiled.* Option A interrupts the parallel structure of past tense verbs: found, researches, and *he was compiling.* Option C uses present tense verbs and then shifts to past tense: *finds, researched, and compiled.*

2. **A**

   Option A uses parallel structure at the end of the sentence: *the new equipment and the increased number of functions.* Option B creates a faulty structure with *to keep up with the new equipment and by increasing number of functions.* Option C creates faulty parallelism with *the number of functions are increasing* (and uses a plural verb for a singular noun).

3. **B**

   Option B uses parallelism by presenting a series of noun phrases acting as objects of the verb *contains.* Option A interrupts that parallelism by inserting *they even display*, and Option C interrupts the parallelism with the addition of *there is.*

4. **C**

   In the either-or parallel construction, look for a balance on both sides. Option C creates that balanced parallel structure: *either had ... or had.* Options A and B do not create the balance. In Option A, the structure is *Either the criminal justice students ... or too much.* In Option B, the structure is *either had ... or too much.*

5. **A**

   Option A uses parallelism by presenting a series of verbs with objects: *hires the cast and crew, chooses locations for filming, supervises the actual production, and guides the editing.* The structure of Option B incorrectly suggests that filmmaking chooses locations, supervises the actual production, and guides the editing. Option C interrupts the series of present tense verbs by inserting the participle *guided* instead of the present tense *guides.*

SKILL 8.3 Recognize fragments, comma splices, and run-on sentences

Fragments occur when word groups standing alone are missing either a subject or a verb, or when word groups containing a subject and verb and standing alone are made dependent through the use of subordinating conjunctions or relative pronouns.

Error:	*The teacher waiting for the class to complete the assignment.*
Problem:	This sentence is not complete because an *-ing* word alone does not function as a verb. When a helping verb is added (for example, *was waiting*), the fragment becomes a sentence.
Correction:	*The teacher was waiting for the class to complete the assignment.*

Error:	*Until the last toy was removed from the floor.*
Problem:	Words such as *until, because, although, when,* and *if* make a clause dependent and thus incapable of standing alone. An independent clause must be added to make the sentence complete.
Correction:	*Until the last toy was removed from the floor, the kids could not go outside to play.*

Error:	*The city will close the public library. Because of a shortage of funds.*
Problem:	The problem is the same as above. The dependent clause must be joined to the independent clause.
Correction:	*The city will close the public library because of a shortage of funds.*

Error:	*Anyone planning to go on the trip should bring the necessary items. Such as a backpack, boots, a canteen, and bug spray.*
Problem:	The second word group is a phrase and cannot stand alone because there is neither a subject nor a verb. The fragment can be corrected by adding the phrase to the sentence.
Correction:	*Anyone planning to go on the trip should bring the necessary items, such as a backpack, boots, a canteen, and bug spray.*

Practice Exercise: Fragments

Choose the option that corrects an error in the underlined portion(s). If no error exists, choose "No change is necessary."

1. Despite the lack of funds in the <u>budget it</u> was necessary to rebuild the roads that were damaged from the recent floods.

    A. budget: it

    B. budget, it

    C. budget; it

    D. No change is necessary

2. After determining that the fire was caused by faulty <u>wiring, the</u> building inspector said the construction company should be fined.

    A. wiring. The

    B. wiring the

    C. wiring; the

    D. No change is necessary

3. Many years after buying a grand <u>piano Henry</u> decided he'd rather play the violin instead.

    A. piano: Henry

    B. piano, Henry

    C. piano; Henry

    D. No change is necessary

Answer Key: Fragments

1. **B**

   The clause that begins with *despite* is introductory and must be separated from the clause that follows by a comma. Option A is incorrect because a colon is used to set off a list or to emphasize what follows. In Option B, a comma incorrectly suggests that the two clauses are dependent.

2. **D**

   A comma correctly separates the dependent clause *After...wiring* at the beginning of the sentence from the independent clause that follows. Option A incorrectly breaks the two clauses into separate sentences, Option B omits the comma, and Option C incorrectly suggests that the phrase is an independent clause.

3. **B**

   The phrase *Henry decided... instead* must be joined to the independent clause. Option A incorrectly puts a colon before *Henry decided*, and Option C incorrectly separates the phrase as if it were an independent clause.

4. **A**

   The second clause *because... information* is dependent and must be joined to the first independent clause. Option B is incorrect because, as the dependent clause comes at the end of the sentence rather than at the beginning, a comma is not necessary. In Option C, a semicolon incorrectly suggests that the two clauses are independent.

5. **A**

   The second clause to *keep...guests* is dependent and must be joined to the first independent clause. Option B is incorrect because, as the dependent clause comes at the end of the sentence rather than at the beginning, a comma is not necessary. In Option C, a semicolon incorrectly suggests that the two clauses are independent.

Comma splices appear when a comma joins two sentences. Fused sentences appear when two sentences are run together with no punctuation at all.

Comma splices appear when a comma joins two sentences. Fused sentences appear when two sentences are run together with no punctuation at all.

Error: *Dr. Sanders is a brilliant scientist, his research on genetic disorders won him a Nobel Prize.*

Problem: A comma alone cannot join two independent clauses (complete sentences). The two clauses can be joined by a semicolon, joined by a conjunction and a comma, or separated into two sentences by a period.

Correction: *Dr. Sanders is a brilliant scientist; his research on genetic disorders won him a Nobel Prize.*
-OR-
Dr. Sanders is a brilliant scientist. His research on genetic disorders won him a Nobel Prize.
-OR-
Dr. Sanders is a brilliant scientist, and his research on genetic disorders won him a Nobel Prize.

Error: *Paradise Island is noted for its beaches they are long, sandy, and beautiful.*

Problem: The first independent clause ends with the word *beaches*, and the second independent clause is fused to the first. The fused sentence error can be corrected in several ways:

1. One clause may be made dependent on another by inserting a subordinating conjunction or a relative pronoun

2. A semicolon may be used to combine two equally important ideas

3. The two independent clauses may be separated by a period

4. The independent clauses may be joined by a conjunction and a comma

Correction: *Paradise Island is noted for its beaches, which are long, sandy, and beautiful.*
-OR-
Paradise Island is noted for its beaches; they are long, sandy, and beautiful.
-OR -
Paradise Island is noted for its beaches. They are long, sandy, and beautiful.
-OR-
Paradise Island is noted for its beaches, for they are long, sandy, and beautiful.

Error: *The number of hotels has increased, however, the number of visitors has grown also.*

Problem: The first sentence ends with the word increased, and a comma is not strong enough to connect it to the second sentence. The adverbial transition *however* does not function in the same way as a coordinating conjunction and cannot be used with commas to link two sentences. Several different corrections are available.

Correction: *The number of hotels has increased; however, the number of visitors has grown also.*

[Two separate but closely related sentences are created with the use of the semicolon.]

-OR-

The number of hotels has increased. However, the number of visitors has grown also.

[Two separate sentences are created.]

-OR-

Although the number of hotels has increased, the number of visitors has grown also.

[One idea is made subordinate to the other and separated with a comma.]

-OR-

The number of hotels has increased, but the number of visitors has grown also.

[The comma before the coordinating conjunction *but* is appropriate. The adverbial transition *however* does not function in the same way as the coordinating conjunction *but*.]

Practice Exercise: Fused Sentences and Comma Splices

Choose the option that corrects an error in the underlined portion(s). If no error exists, choose "No change is necessary."

1. Scientists are excited at the ability to clone a <u>sheep: however,</u> it is not yet known if the same can be done to humans.

   A. sheep, however,

   B. sheep. However,

   C. sheep, however;

   D. No change is necessary

2. Because of the rising cost of college <u>tuition the</u> federal government now offers special financial <u>assistance, such as loans,</u> to students.

   A. tuition, the

   B. tuition; the

   C. such as loans

   D. No change is necessary

3. As the number of homeless people continues to <u>rise, the major cities</u> such as <u>New York and Chicago,</u> are now investing millions of dollars in low-income housing.

   A. rise. The major cities

   B. rise; the major cities

   C. New York and Chicago

   D. No change is necessary

4. Unlike in <u>the 1950s, in most</u> households the husband and wife work full-time to make <u>ends meet in many</u> different career fields.

   A. the 1950s; in most

   B. the 1950s in most

   C. ends meet, in many

   D. No change is necessary

Answer Key: Fused Sentences and Comma Splices

1. B

   Option B correctly separates two independent clauses. The comma in Option A after the word *sheep* creates a run-on sentence. The semicolon in Option C does not separate the two clauses because it occurs at an inappropriate point.

2. A

   The comma in Option A correctly separates the independent clause and the dependent clause. The semicolon in Option B is incorrect because one of the clauses is independent. Option C requires a comma to prevent a run-on sentence.

3. C

   Option C is correct because a comma creates a run-on sentence. Option A is incorrect because the first clause is dependent. The semicolon in Option B incorrectly separates the dependent clause from the independent clause.

4. D

   Option D correctly separates the two clauses with a comma. Option A incorrectly uses a semicolon to separate the clauses. The lack of a comma in Option B creates a run-on sentence. Option C puts a comma in an inappropriate place.

COMPETENCY 9
GRAMMAR, SPELLING, CAPITALIZATION, AND PUNCTUATION SKILLS

SKILL Identify standard verb forms
9.1

Past Tense and Past Participles

Both regular and irregular verbs must appear in their standard forms for each tense.

> **Note:** The -ed or -d ending is added to regular verbs in the past tense and to past participles.

REGULAR VERB FORMS		
Infinitive	**Past Tense**	**Past Participle**
bake	baked	baked

IRREGULAR VERB FORMS		
Infinitive	**Past Tense**	**Past Participle**
be	was/were	been
become	became	become
break	broke	broken
bring	brought	brought
choose	chose	chosen
come	came	come
do	did	done
draw	drew	drawn

Continued on next page

Infinitive	Past Tense	Past Participle
eat	ate	eaten
fall	fell	fallen
forget	forgot	forgotten
freeze	froze	frozen
give	gave	given
go	went	gone
grow	grew	grown
have/has	had	had
hide	hid	hidden
know	knew	known
lay	laid	laid
lie	lay	lain
ride	rode	ridden
rise	rose	risen
run	ran	run
see	saw	seen
steal	stole	stolen
take	took	taken
tell	told	told
throw	threw	thrown
wear	wore	worn
write	wrote	written

Error: *She should have went to her doctor's appointment at the scheduled time.*

Problem: The past participle of the verb *to go* is *gone. Went* expresses the simple past tense.

Correction: *She should have gone to her doctor's appointment at the scheduled time.*

Error: *My train is suppose to arrive before two o'clock.*

Problem: The verb following *train* is a present tense passive construction, which requires the present tense verb *to be* and the past participle.

Correction: *My train is supposed to arrive before two o'clock.*

Error: *Linda should of known that the car wouldn't start after leaving it out in the cold all night.*

Problem: *Should of* is a nonstandard expression. *Of* is not a verb.

Correction: *Linda should have known that the car wouldn't start after leaving it out in the cold all night.*

Practice Exercise: Standard Verb Forms

Choose the option that corrects an error in the underlined portion(s). If no error exists, choose "No change is necessary."

1. My professor <u>had knew</u> all along that we would pass his course.

   A. know

   B. had known

   C. knowing

   D. No change is necessary

2. Kevin was asked to erase the vulgar words he <u>had wrote</u>.

   A. writes

   B. has write

   C. had written

   D. No change is necessary

Practice Exercise: Standard Verb Forms (cont.)

Choose the option that corrects an error in the underlined portion(s). If no error exists, choose "No change is necessary."

3. Melanie <u>had forget</u> to tell her parents that she left the cat in the closet.

   A. had forgotten

   B. forgot

   C. forget

   D. No change is necessary

4. Craig always <u>leave</u> the house a mess when his parents aren't there.

   A. left

   B. leaves

   C. leaving

   D. No change is necessary

5. The store manager accused Kathy of <u>having stole</u> more than five hundred dollars from the safe.

   A. has stolen

   B. having stolen

   C. stole

   D. No change is necessary

Answer Key: Standard Verb Forms

1. B

   Option B is correct because the past participle needs the helping verb *had*. Option A is incorrect because *it* is in the infinitive tense. Option C incorrectly uses the present participle.

2. C

   Option C is correct because the past participle follows the helping verb *had*. Option A uses the verb in the present tense. Option B is an incorrect use of the verb.

3. A

   Option A is correct because the past participle uses the helping verb *had*. Option B uses the wrong form of the verb. Option C uses the wrong form of the verb.

4. B

   Option B correctly uses the present tense of the verb. Option A uses the verb in an incorrect way. Option C uses the verb without a helping verb such as *is*.

5. B

   Option B is correct because it is the past participle. Options A and C use the verb incorrectly.

SKILL 9.2 Identify inappropriate shifts in verb tense

Unless a change in time is required, verb tenses within a sentence must consistently refer to the same time period.

Error: *Despite the increased number of students attending school this year, overall attendance is higher last year at the sporting events.*

Problem: The verb *is* represents an inconsistent shift to the present tense when the action refers to a past occurrence.

Correction: *Despite the increased number of students attending school this year, overall attendance was higher last year at sporting events.*

Error: *My friend Lou, who just competed in the marathon, ran since he was twelve years old.*

Problem: Because Lou continues to run, the present perfect tense is needed.

Correction: *My friend Lou, who just competed in the marathon, has run since he was twelve years old.*

Error: *The mayor congratulated Wallace Mangham, who renovates the city hall last year.*

Problem: Although the speaker is talking in the present, the action of renovating the city hall was in the past.

Correction: *The mayor congratulated Wallace Mangham, who renovated the city hall last year.*

Practice Exercise: Shifts in Tense

Choose the option that corrects an error in the underlined portion(s). If no error exists, choose "No change is necessary."

1. After we <u>washed</u> the fruit that had <u>growing</u> in the garden, we knew there <u>was</u> a store that would buy the fruit.

   A. washing

   B. grown

   C. is

   D. No change is necessary

2. The tourists <u>used</u> to visit the Atlantic City boardwalk whenever they <u>vacationed</u> during the summer. Unfortunately, their numbers have <u>diminished</u> every year.

   A. use

   B. vacation

   C. diminish

   D. No change is necessary

3. When the temperature <u>drops</u> to below thirty-two degrees Fahrenheit, the water on the lake <u>freezes</u>, which <u>allowed</u> children to skate across it.

   A. dropped

   B. froze

   C. allows

   D. No change is necessary

4. The artists were <u>hired</u> to <u>create</u> a monument that would pay tribute to the men who were <u>killed</u> in World War II.

   A. hiring

   B. created

   C. killing

   D. No change is necessary

5. Emergency medical personnel rushed to the scene of the shooting, where many injured people <u>waiting</u> for treatment.

   A. wait

   B. waited

   C. waits

   D. No change is necessary

Answer Key: Shifts in Tense

1. B

    The past participle *grown* is needed instead of *growing*, which is the progressive tense. Option A is incorrect because the past participle *washed* takes the *-ed*. Option C incorrectly replaces the past participle *was* with the present tense *is*.

2. D

    Option A is incorrect because *use* is the present tense. Option B incorrectly uses the present tense of the verb *vacation*. Option C incorrectly uses the present tense *diminish* instead of the past tense *diminished*.

3. C

    The present tense *allows* is necessary in the context of the sentence. Option A is incorrect because *dropped* is a past participle. Option B is incorrect because *froze* is also a past participle.

4. D

    Option A is incorrect because *hiring* is the present tense. Option B is incorrect because *created* is a past participle. In Option C, *killing* does not fit into the context of the sentence.

5. B

    In Option B, *waited* corresponds with the past tense *rushed*. In Option A, *wait* is incorrect because it is present tense. In Option C, *waits* is incorrect because the noun *people* is plural and requires the singular form of the verb.

SKILL 9.3 Identify agreement between subject and verb

A verb must correspond in the singular or plural form with the simple subject; interfering elements do not affect it.

Note: *A simple subject is never found in a prepositional phrase (that is, a phrase beginning with a word such as of, by, over, through, until).*

PRESENT TENSE VERB FORM		
	Singular	**Plural**
1st person (talking about oneself)	I do	We do
2nd person (talking to another)	You do	You do
3rd person (talking about someone or something)	He does She does It does	They do

Error: *Sally, as well as her sister, plan to go into nursing.*

Problem: The subject of the sentence is *Sally* and does not include the word *sister*. Therefore, the verb must be singular.

Correction: *Sally, as well as her sister, plans to go into nursing.*

Error: *There has been many car accidents lately on that street.*

Problem: The subject *accidents* in this sentence is plural; the verb must be plural also, even though it comes before the subject.

Correction: *There have been many car accidents lately on that street.*

Error: *Every one of us have a reason to attend the school musical.*

Problem: The simple subject is the phrase *every one*, not the *us* in the prepositional phrase. Therefore, the verb must be singular also.

Correction: *Every one of us has a reason to attend the school musical.*

Error: *Either the police captain or his officers is going to the convention.*

Problem: In either/or and neither/nor constructions, the verb agrees with the subject closer to it.

Correction: *Either the police captain or his officers are going to the convention.*

Practice Exercise: Subject-Verb Agreement

Choose the option that corrects an error in the underlined portion(s). If no error exists, choose "No change is necessary."

1. Every year, the store <u>stays</u> open late while shoppers desperately <u>try</u> to purchase Christmas presents as they <u>prepare</u> for the holiday.

   A. stay

   B. tries

   C. prepared

   D. No change is necessary

2. Paul McCartney, together with George Harrison and Ringo Starr, <u>sing</u> classic Beatles songs on a special greatest-hits CD.

   A. singing

   B. sings

   C. sung

   D. No change is necessary

Practice Exercise: Subject-Verb Agreement (cont.)

Choose the option that corrects an error in the underlined portion(s). If no error exists, choose "No change is necessary."

3. My friend's cocker spaniel, while <u>chasing</u> cats across the street, always <u>manages</u> to <u>knock</u> over the trash cans.

   A. chased

   B. manage

   C. knocks

   D. No change is necessary

4. Some of the ice on the driveway <u>have melted</u>.

   A. having melted

   B. has melted

   C. has melt

   D. No change is necessary

5. Neither the criminal forensics expert nor the DNA blood evidence <u>provide</u> enough support for that verdict.

   A. provides

   B. were providing

   C. are providing

   D. No change is necessary

Answer Key: Subject-Verb Agreement

1. D

   Option D is correct because *store* is third person singular and requires the third person singular verb *stays*. Option B is incorrect because the plural noun *shoppers* requires a plural verb *try*. In Option C, there is no reason to shift to the past tense *prepared*.

2. B

   Option B is correct because the subject, Paul McCartney, is singular and requires the singular verb *sings*. Option A is incorrect because the present participle *singing* does not stand alone as a verb. Option C is incorrect because the past participle *sung* cannot function as the verb in this sentence.

3. D

   Option D is the correct answer because the subject *cocker spaniel* is singular and requires the singular verb *manages*. Options A, B, and C do not work structurally with the sentence.

4. B

   The subject of the sentence is *some*, which requires a third-person, singular verb: *has melted*. Option A incorrectly uses the present participle *having*, which does not act as a helping verb. Option C does not work structurally with the sentence.

5. A

   In Option A, the singular subject *evidence* is closer to the verb and thus requires the singular in the neither/nor construction. Both Options B and C are plural forms with the helping verb and the present participle.

SKILL 9.4 Identify agreements between pronoun and antecedent

A pronoun must correspond to its antecedent in number (singular or plural), person (first, second, or third person), and gender (male, female, or neutral). A pronoun must refer clearly to a single word, not to a complete idea.

A PRONOUN SHIFT is a grammatical error in which the author starts a sentence, paragraph, or section of a paper using one particular type of pronoun and then suddenly shifts to another. This often confuses the reader.

A pronoun must correspond to its antecedent in number (singular or plural), person (first, second, or third person), and gender (male, female, or neutral).

PRONOUN SHIFT: a grammatical error in which the author starts a sentence, paragraph, or section of a paper using one particular type of pronoun and then suddenly shifts to another

Error: *A teacher should treat all their students fairly.*

Problem: Because *teacher* is singular, the pronoun referring to it must also be singular. Otherwise, the noun has to be made plural.

Correction: *Teachers should treat all their students fairly.*

Error: *When an actor is rehearsing for a play, it often helps if you can memorize the lines in advance.*

Problem: *Actor* is a third-person word; that is, the writer is talking about the subject. The pronoun *you* is in the second person, which means the writer is talking to the subject.

Correction: *When actors are rehearsing for plays, it helps if they can memorize the lines in advance.*

Error: *The workers in the factory were upset when his or her paychecks didn't arrive on time.*

Problem: *Workers* is a plural form, while *his or her* refers to one person.

Correction: *The workers in the factory were upset when their paychecks didn't arrive on time.*

Error: *The charity auction was highly successful, which pleased everyone.*

Problem: In this sentence, the pronoun *which* refers to the idea of the auction's success. In fact, *which* has no antecedent in the sentence; the word *success* is not stated.

Correction: *Everyone was pleased at the success of the auction.*

Error: *Lana told Melanie that she would like aerobics.*

Problem: The person that *she* refers to is unclear; *she* could be either Lana or Melanie.

Correction: *Lana said that Melanie would like aerobics.*
    -OR-
Lana told Melanie that she, Melanie, would like aerobics.

Error: *I dislike accounting even though my brother is one.*

Problem: A person's occupation is not the same as a field, and the pronoun *one* is thus incorrect. Note that the word *accountant* is not used in the sentence, so *one* has no antecedent.

Correction: *I dislike accounting even though my brother is an accountant.*

Practice Exercise: Pronoun/Antecedent Agreement

Choose the option that corrects an error in the underlined portion(s). If no error exists, choose "No change is necessary."

1. <u>You</u> can get to Martha's Vineyard by driving from Boston to Woods Hole. Once there, you can travel on a ship, but <u>you</u> may find traveling by <u>airplane</u> to be an exciting experience.

   A. They

   B. visitors

   C. it

   D. No change is necessary

2. Both the city leader and the <u>journalist</u> are worried about the new interstate; <u>she fears the new roadway</u> will destroy precious farmland.

   A. journalist herself

   B. they fear

   C. it

   D. No change is necessary

3. When <u>hunters</u> are looking for deer in <u>the woods</u>, <u>you</u> must remain quiet for long periods of time.

   A. you

   B. it

   C. they

   D. No change is necessary

Practice Exercise: Pronoun/Antecedent Agreement (cont.)

Choose the option that corrects an error in the underlined portion(s). If no error exists, choose "No change is necessary."

4. The strong economy is based on the importance of the citrus industry. <u>Producing</u> orange juice for most of the country.

    A. They produce

    B. Who produce

    C. Farmers there produce

    D. No change is necessary

5. Dr. Kennedy told Paul Elliot, <u>his</u> assistant, that <u>he</u> would have to finish grading the tests before going home, no matter how long <u>it</u> took.

    A. their

    B. he, Paul,

    C. they

    D. No change is necessary

Answer Key: Pronoun/Antecedent Agreement

1. D

    Pronouns must be consistent. As *you* is used throughout the sentence, the shift to *visitors* is incorrect. Option A, *They*, is vague and unclear. Option C, *it*, is also unclear.

2. B

    The plural pronoun *they* is necessary to agree with the two nouns *leader* and *journalist*. There is no need for the reflexive pronoun *herself* in Option A. In Option C, *it* is vague.

3. C

    The shift to *you* is unnecessary. The plural pronoun *they* is necessary to agree with the noun *hunters*. The word *it* in Option B is vague; the reader does not know to what the word *it* refers. *It* has no antecedent.

4. C

    The noun *farmers* is needed for clarification because *producing* alone creates a fragment. Option A is incorrect because *they produce* is vague. Option B is incorrect because *who* has no antecedent and creates a fragment.

5. B

    The repetition of the name *Paul* is necessary to clarify who the pronoun *he* refers to. (*He* could be Dr. Kennedy.) Option A is incorrect because the singular pronoun *his* is needed, not the plural pronoun *their*. Option C is incorrect because the pronoun *it* refers to the grading of the tests, not the tests themselves.

SKILL 9.5 Identify inappropriate pronoun shifts

See Skill 9.4

SKILL 9.6 Identify clear pronoun references

Rules for Clearly Identifying Pronoun Reference

Make sure that the antecedent reference is clear and cannot refer to something else

A "distant relative" is a relative pronoun or a relative clause that has been placed too far away from the antecedent to which it refers. It is a common error to place a verb between the relative pronoun and its antecedent.

Error:	*Return the books to the library that are overdue.*
Problem:	The relative clause *that are overdue* refers to the books and should be placed immediately after the antecedent.
Correction:	*Return the books that are overdue to the library.* *-OR-* *Return the overdue books to the library.*

A pronoun should not refer to adjectives or possessive nouns

Adjectives, nouns, or possessive pronouns should not be used as antecedents. This will create ambiguity in sentences.

Error:	*In Todd's letter, he told his mom he'd broken the priceless vase.*
Problem:	In this sentence, the pronoun *he* seems to refer to the noun phrase *Todd's letter*, though it is probably meant to refer to the possessive noun *Todd's*.
Correction:	*In his letter, Todd told his mom that he had broken the priceless vase.*

A pronoun should not refer to an implied idea

A pronoun must refer to a specific antecedent rather than an implied antecedent. When an antecedent is not stated specifically, the reader has to guess or assume the meaning of a sentence. Pronouns that do not have antecedents are called EXPLETIVES. "It" and "there" are the most common expletives, though other pronouns can become expletives as well.

Error: *She said that it is important to floss every day.*

Problem: The pronoun *it* refers to an implied idea.

Correction: *She said that flossing every day is important.*

Error: *Milt and Bette returned the books because they had missing pages.*

Problem: The pronoun *they* does not refer to the antecedent.

Correction: *The customers returned the books with missing pages.*

> **EXPLETIVE:** a pronoun that does not have an antecedent

> *In informal conversation, expletives allow for casual presentation of ideas without supporting evidence. However, in more formal writing, it is best to be more precise.*

Using Who, That, and Which

Who, whom, and *whose* refer to human beings and can introduce either essential or nonessential clauses. *That* refers to things other than humans and is used to introduce essential clauses. *Which* refers to things other than humans and is used to introduce nonessential clauses.

Error: *The doctor that performed the surgery said the patient would recover fully.*

Problem: Since the relative pronoun is referring to a human, *who* should be used.

Correction: *The doctor who performed the surgery said the patient would recover fully.*

Error: *That ice cream cone that you just ate looked delicious.*

Problem: *That* has already been used, so you must use *which* to introduce the next clause, whether it is essential or nonessential.

Correction: *That ice cream cone, which you just ate, looked delicious.*

SKILL 9.7 Identify proper case forms

Pronouns, unlike nouns, change case forms.

Pronouns must be in the subjective, objective, or possessive form, according to their function in the sentence.

PERSONAL PRONOUNS						
SUBJECTIVE (NOMINATIVE)		POSSESSIVE		OBJECTIVE	
	Singular	Plural	Singular	Plural	Singular	Plural
1st person	I	We	My	Our Ours	Me	Us
2nd person	You	You	Your Yours	Your Yours	You	You
3rd person	He She It	They	His Her/ Hers Its	Their Theirs	Him Her It	Them

RELATIVE PRONOUNS	
Who	Subjective/Nominative
Whom	Objective
Whose	Possessive

Error: *Tom and me have reserved seats for next week's baseball game.*

Problem: The pronoun *me* is the subject of the verb *have reserved* and should be in the subjective form.

Correction: *Tom and I have reserved seats for next week's baseball game.*

Error: *Mr. Green showed all of we students how to make paper hats.*

Problem: The pronoun *we* is the object of the preposition *of.* It should be in the objective form, us.

Correction: *Mr. Green showed all of us students how to make paper hats.*

Error: *Who's coat is this?*

Problem: The interrogative possessive pronoun is *whose*; *who's* is the contraction for *who is*.

Correction: *Whose coat is this?*

Practice Exercise: Pronoun Case

Choose the option that corrects an error in the underlined portion(s). If no error exists, choose "No change is necessary."

1. Even though Sheila and <u>he</u> had planned to be alone at the diner, <u>they</u> were joined by three friends of <u>their's</u> instead.

    A. him

    B. him and her

    C. theirs

    D. No change is necessary

2. Uncle Walter promised to give his car to <u>whomever</u> would guarantee to drive it safely.

    A. whom

    B. whoever

    C. them

    D. No change is necessary

3. Eddie and <u>him</u> gently laid <u>the body</u> on the ground next to <u>the sign</u>.

    A. he

    B. them

    C. it

    D. No change is necessary

4. Mary, <u>who</u> is competing in the chess tournament, is a better player than <u>me</u>.

    A. whose

    B. whom

    C. I

    D. No change is necessary

5. <u>We ourselves</u> have decided not to buy property in that development; however, our friends have already bought <u>themselves</u> some land.

    A. We, ourself,

    B. their selves

    C. their self

    D. No change is necessary

Answer Key: Pronoun Case

1. **C**

   The possessive pronoun *theirs* does not need an apostrophe. Option A is incorrect because the subjective pronoun *he* is needed in this sentence. Option B is incorrect because the subjective pronoun *they*, not the objective pronouns *him* and *her*, is needed.

2. **B**

   The subjective case *whoever*—not the objective case *whomever*—is the subject of the relative clause *whoever would guarantee to drive it safely*. Option A is incorrect because *whom* is an objective pronoun. Option C is incorrect because *car* is singular and takes the pronoun *it*.

3. **A**

   The subjective pronoun *he* is needed as the subject of the verb *laid*. Option B is incorrect because *them* is vague; the noun *body* is needed to clarify *it*. Option C is incorrect because *it* is vague, and the noun *sign* is necessary for clarification.

4. **C**

   The subjective pronoun *I* is needed because the comparison is understood. Option A incorrectly uses the possessive *whose*. Option B is incorrect because the subjective pronoun *who*, and not the objective *whom*, is needed.

5. **D**

   The reflexive pronoun *themselves* refers to the plural *friends*. Option A is incorrect because the plural *we* requires the reflexive *ourselves*. Option C is incorrect because the possessive pronoun *their* is never joined with either *self* or *selves*.

SKILL 9.8 Identify the correct use of adjectives and adverbs

ADJECTIVES: words that modify or describe nouns or pronouns

ADVERBS: words that modify verbs, adjectives, or other adverbs

ADJECTIVES are words that modify or describe nouns or pronouns. Adjectives usually precede the words they modify but not always; for example, an adjective may occur after a linking verb.

ADVERBS are words that modify verbs, adjectives, or other adverbs. They cannot modify nouns. Adverbs answer such questions as how, why, when, where, how much, or how often. Many adverbs are formed by adding *-ly*.

Error: *The birthday cake tasted sweetly.*

Problem: *Tasted* is a linking verb; the modifier that follows should be an adjective, not an adverb.

Correction: *The birthday cake tasted sweet.*

> Many adverbs are formed by adding the suffix –ly to the end of adjectives.

Error: *You have done good with this project.*

Problem: *Good* is an adjective and cannot be used to modify a verb phrase such as *have done.*

Correction: *You have done well with this project.*

Error: *The coach was positive happy about the team's chance of winning.*

Problem: The adjective positive cannot be used to modify another adjective, *happy.* An adverb is needed instead.

Correction: *The coach was positively happy about the team's chance of winning.*

Error: *The fireman acted quick and brave to save the child from the burning building.*

Problem: *Quick* and *brave* are adjectives and cannot be used to describe a verb. Adverbs are needed instead.

Correction: *The fireman acted quickly and bravely to save the child from the burning building.*

Practice Exercise: Adjectives and Adverbs

Choose the option that corrects an error in the underlined portion(s). If no error exists, choose "No change is necessary."

1. Moving <u>quick</u> throughout the house, the burglar <u>removed</u> several priceless antiques before <u>carelessly</u> dropping his wallet.

   A. quickly

   B. remove

   C. careless

   D. No change is necessary

2. The car <u>crashed</u> <u>loudly</u> into the retaining wall before spinning <u>wildly</u> on the sidewalk.

   A. crashes

   B. loudly

   C. wild

   D. No change is necessary

Practice Exercise: Adjectives and Adverbs (cont.)

Choose the option that corrects an error in the underlined portion(s). If no error exists, choose "No change is necessary."

3. The airplane <u>landed</u> <u>safe</u> on the runway after <u>nearly</u> colliding with a helicopter.

   A. land

   B. safely

   C. near

   D. No change is necessary

4. The <u>horribly bad</u> special effects in the movie disappointed us <u>great</u>.

   A. horrible

   B. badly

   C. greatly

   D. No change is necessary

5. The man promised to obey <u>faithfully</u> the rules of the social club.

   A. faithful

   B. faithfulness

   C. faith

   D. No change is necessary

Answer Key: Adjectives and Adverbs

1. A.

   The adverb *quickly* is needed to modify *moving*. Option B is incorrect because it uses the wrong form of the verb. Option C is incorrect because the adverb *carelessly*, not the adjective *careless*, is needed before the verb *dropping*.

2. D.

   The sentence is correct as it is written. The adverbs *loudly* and *wildly* are needed to modify *crashed* and *spinning*. Option A incorrectly uses the verb *crashes* instead of the participle *crashing*, which acts as an adjective.

3. B.

   The adverb *safely* is needed to modify the verb *landed*. Option A is incorrect because *land* is a noun. Option C is incorrect because *near* is an adjective, not an adverb.

4. C.

   The adverb *greatly* is needed to modify the verb *disappointed*. Option A is incorrect because *horrible* is an adjective, not an adverb. Option B is incorrect because the adverb *horribly* needs to modify the adjective *bad*.

5. D.

   The adverb *faithfully* is the correct modifier of the verb *promised*. Option A is an adjective used to modify nouns. Neither Option B nor Option C, both of which are nouns, is a modifier.

**SKILL Identify appropriate comparative and superlative degree forms
9.9**

Comparative and Superlative Forms

When comparisons are made, the correct form of the adjective or adverb must be used. The COMPARATIVE FORM is used for two items. The SUPERLATIVE FORM is used for more than two items.

	Comparative	Superlative
slow	slower	slowest
young	younger	youngest
tall	taller	tallest

COMPARATIVE FORM:
used to compare two items

SUPERLATIVE FORM:
used to compare more
than two items

With some words, *more* and *most* are used to make comparisons instead of *-er* and *-est*.

	Comparative	Superlative
energetic	more energetic	most energetic
quick	more quickly	most quickly

Comparisons must be made between similar structures or items. In the sentence "My house is similar in color to Steve's," one house is being compared to another house, as understood by the use of the possessive *Steve's*.

On the other hand, if the sentence reads "My house is similar in color to Steve," the comparison would be faulty because it would be comparing the house to Steve, not to Steve's house.

Error: *Last year's rides at the carnival were bigger than this year.*

Problem: In the sentence as it is worded, the rides at the carnival are being compared to this year, not to this year's rides.

Correction: *Last year's rides at the carnival were bigger than this year's.*

Practice Exercise: Logical Comparisons

Choose the sentence that logically and correctly expresses the comparison.

1. A. This year's standards are higher than last year.

    B. This year's standards are more high than last year.

    C. This year's standards are higher than last year's.

2. A. Tom's attitudes are very different from his father's.

    B. Toms attitudes are very different from his father.

    C. Tom's attitudes are very different from his father.

3. A. John is the stronger member of the gymnastics team.

    B. John is the strongest member of the gymnastics team.

    C. John is the most strong member of the gymnastics team.

4. A. Tracy's book report was longer than Tony's.

    B. Tracy's book report was more long than Tony's.

    C. Tracy's book report was longer than Tony.

5. A. Becoming a lawyer is as difficult as, if not more difficult than, becoming a doctor.

    B. Becoming a lawyer is as difficult, if not more difficult than, becoming a doctor.

    C. Becoming a lawyer is difficult, if not more difficult than, becoming a doctor.

6. A. Better than any movie of the modern era, *Schindler's List* portrays the destructiveness of hate.

    B. More better than any movie of the modern era, *Schindler's List* portrays the destructiveness of hate.

    C. Better than any other movie of the modern era, *Schindler's List* portrays the destructiveness of hate.

Answer Key: Logical Comparisons

1. C

    Option C is correct because the comparison is between this year's standards and last year's (*standards* is understood). Option A compares the standards to last year. In Option B, the faulty comparative *more high* should be *higher*.

2. A

    Option A is correct because Tom's attitudes are compared to his father's (*attitudes* is understood). Option B deletes the apostrophe that is necessary to show possession (*Tom's*), and the comparison is faulty because *attitudes* is compared to *father*. While Option C uses the correct possessive, it retains the faulty comparison shown in Option B.

3. B

    In Option B, John is correctly the strongest member of a team that consists of more than two people. Option A uses the comparative *stronger* (comparison of two items) rather than the superlative *strongest* (comparison of more than two items). Option C uses a faulty superlative, *most strong*.

4. A

    Option A is correct because the comparison is between Tracy's book report and Tony's (book report). Option B uses the faulty comparative *more long* instead of *longer*. Option C wrongly compares Tracy's book report to Tony.

5. A

    In Option A, the dual comparison is correctly stated: *as difficult as, if not more difficult than*. Remember to test the dual comparison by taking out the intervening comparison. Option B deletes the necessary *as* after the first *difficult*. Option C deletes the *as* before and after the first *difficult*.

6. C

    Option C includes the necessary word *other* in the comparison *better than any other movie*. The comparison in Option A is not complete, and Option B uses the faulty comparative *more better*.

SKILL 9.10 Identify standard spelling

Spelling correctly is not always easy because English not only utilizes an often inconsistent spelling system, but also uses many words derived from other languages.

Common Misspellings

The following is a list of the most often misspelled words in the English language:

COMMONLY MISSPELLED WORDS			
commitment	patience	height	guarantee
succeed	obstinate	leisurely	tropical
necessary	achievement	shield	misfortune
connected	responsibility	foreign	particular
opportunity	prejudice	innovative	yield
embarrassed	familiar	similar	possession
occasionally	hindrance	proceed	accumulate
receive	controversial	contemporary	hospitality
their	publicity	beneficial	judgment
accelerate	prescription	attachment	conscious

Spelling Plurals and Possessives

Most plurals of nouns that end in hard consonants or in hard consonant sounds followed by a silent *e* are made by adding *-s*. Plurals of some words ending in vowels are formed by adding only *-s*.

fingers, numerals, banks, bugs, riots, homes, gates, radios, bananas

Good spelling is important because incorrect spelling damages the physical appearance of writing and can puzzle readers.

Spelling errors resulting from the multiplicity and complexity of spelling rules based on phonics, letter doubling, and exceptions can be avoided by consulting a good dictionary. Learning to use a dictionary and thesaurus effectively is more efficient than attempting to master the bewildering forest of rules.

For nouns that end in soft consonant sounds—*s, j, x, z, ch,* and *sh*—the plurals are formed by adding *-es.* Plurals of some nouns ending in *o* are formed by adding *-es.*

dresses, waxes, churches, brushes, tomatoes

For nouns ending in *y* preceded by a vowel, just add *-s.*

boys, alleys

For nouns ending in *y* preceded by a consonant, change the *y* to *i* and add *-es.*

babies, corollaries, frugalities, poppies

Irregular plurals

Some nouns' plurals are formed irregularly or remain the same.

sheep, deer, children, leaves, oxen

Some nouns derived from foreign words, especially Latin words, are made plural in two different ways. Sometimes the meanings are the same; other times the two plural forms are used in slightly different contexts. It is always wise to consult the dictionary.

appendices, appendixes   *criterion, criteria*

indexes, indices   *crisis, crises*

Make the plurals of closed (solid) compound words in the usual way.

timelines, hairpins

cupfuls, handfuls

Make the plurals of open or hyphenated compounds by adding the change in inflection to the word that changes in number.

fathers-in-law, courts-martial, masters of art, doctors of medicine

Make the plurals of letters, numbers, and abbreviations by adding *-s.*

fives and tens, IBMs, 1990s, ps and qs *(note that letters are italicized.)*

I BEFORE E	
i before e	grieve, fiend, niece, friend
except after c	receive, conceive, receipt
or when sounded like "a"	as in reindeer, weight, and reign
Exceptions:	weird, foreign, seize, leisure

Practice Exercise: EI/IE WORDS

Circle the correct spelling of the word in each parenthesis.

1. The (sheild, shield) protected the gladiator from serious injury.

2. Tony (received, recieved) an award for his science project.

3. Our (neighbors, nieghbors), the Thomsons, are in the Witness Protection Program.

4. Janet's (friend, freind), Olivia, broke her leg while running the marathon.

5. She was unable to (conceive, concieve) a child after her miscarriage.

6. "Rudolph the Red-Nosed (Riendeer, Reindeer)" is my favorite Christmas song.

7. The farmer spent all day plowing his (feild, field).

8. Kat's (wieght, weight) loss plan failed, and she gained twenty pounds!

9. They couldn't (beleive, believe) how many people showed up for the concert.

10. Ruby's (niece, neice) was disappointed when the movie was sold out.

Answer Key: EI/IE WORDS

1. shield
2. received
3. neighbors
4. friend
5. conceive
6. reindeer
7. field
8. weight
9. believe
10. niece

Commas

COMMAS are used to indicate a brief pause. They are used to set off dependent clauses and long introductory word groups, to separate words in a series, to set off unimportant material that interrupts the flow of the sentence, and to separate independent clauses joined by conjunctions.

COMMA: used to indicate a brief pause

Error:	*After I finish my master's thesis I plan to work in Chicago.*
Problem:	A comma is needed after an introductory dependent word group containing a subject and verb.
Correction:	*After I finish my master's thesis, I plan to work in Chicago.*

Error:	*I washed waxed and vacuumed my car today.*
Problem:	Commas should separate nouns, phrases, or clauses in a list, as well as two or more coordinate adjectives that modify one word. Although the word *and* is sometimes considered optional, it is often necessary to clarify the meaning.
Correction:	*I washed, waxed, and vacuumed my car today.*

Error:	*She was a talented dancer but she is mostly remembered for her singing ability.*
Problem:	A comma is needed before a conjunction that joins two independent clauses (complete sentences).
Correction:	*She was a talented dancer, but she is mostly remembered for her singing ability.*

Error:	*This incident is I think typical of what can happen when the community remains so divided.*
Problem:	Commas are needed between nonessential words or words that interrupt the main clause.
Correction:	*This incident is, I think, typical of what can happen when the community remains so divided.*

Semicolons and Colons

SEMICOLONS are needed to separate two or more closely related independent clauses when a transitional adverb introduces the second clause. (These clauses may also be written as separate sentences, preferably by placing the adverb within the second sentence.)

Error:	*I climbed to the top of the mountain, it took me three hours.*
Problem:	A comma alone cannot separate two independent clauses. Instead, a semicolon is needed to separate two related sentences.
Correction:	*I climbed to the top of the mountain; it took me three hours.*

Error:	*In the movie, asteroids destroyed Dallas, Texas, Kansas City, Missouri, and Boston, Massachusetts.*
Problem:	Semicolons are needed to separate items in a series that already contain internal punctuation.
Correction:	*In the movie, asteroids destroyed Dallas, Texas; Kansas City, Missouri; and Boston, Massachusetts.*

COLONS are used to introduce lists and to emphasize what follows.

Error:	*Essays will receive the following grades, A for excellent, B for good, C for average, and D for unsatisfactory.*
Problem:	A colon is needed to emphasize the information or list that follows.
Correction:	*Essays will receive the following grades: A for excellent, B for good, C for average, and D for unsatisfactory.*

Error:	*The school carnival included: amusement rides, clowns, food booths, and a variety of games.*
Problem:	The material preceding the colon and the list that follows are not complete sentences. Do not separate a verb (or preposition) from the object.
Correction:	*The school carnival included amusement rides, clowns, food booths, and a variety of games.*

Apostrophes

APOSTROPHES are used to show contractions or possession.

Error: *She shouldnt be permitted to smoke cigarettes in the building.*

Problem: An apostrophe is needed in a contraction in place of the missing letter.

Correction: *She shouldn't be permitted to smoke cigarettes in the building.*

Error: *My cousins motorcycle was stolen from his driveway.*

Problem: An apostrophe is needed to show possession.

Correction: *My cousin's motorcycle was stolen from his driveway. (Note: The use of the apostrophe before the letter "s" means that there is just one cousin. The plural form would read as follows: My cousins' motorcycle was stolen from their driveway.)*

Error: *The childrens new kindergarten teacher was also a singer.*

Problem: An apostrophe is needed to show possession.

Correction: *The children's new kindergarten teacher was also a singer.*

Error: *Children screams could be heard for miles.*

Problem: An apostrophe and the letter *s* are needed in the sentence to show who is screaming.

Correction: *Children's screams could he heard for miles. (Note: Because the word children is already plural, the apostrophe and -s must be added afterward to show ownership.)*

Quotation Marks

In a quoted statement that is either declarative or imperative, place the period inside the closing quotation marks.

"The airplane crashed on the runway during takeoff."

If other words in the sentence follow the quotation, place a comma inside the closing quotations marks and a period at the end of the sentence.

> "The airplane crashed on the runway during takeoff," said the announcer.

Usually, when a quoted title or expression occurs at the end of a sentence, the period is placed before the single or double quotation marks.

> "The middle school readers were unprepared to understand Bryant's poem 'Thanatopsis.'"
>
> Early book-length adventure stories such as Don Quixote and The Three Musketeers were known as "picaresque novels."

The final quotation mark precedes the period if the content of the sentence is about a speech or quote.

> The first thing out of his mouth was "Hi, I'm home."
>
> -BUT-
>
> The first line of his speech began: "I arrived home to an empty house".

In interrogatory or exclamatory sentences, the question mark or exclamation point should be positioned outside the closing quotation marks if the quote itself is a statement, command, or cited title.

> Who decided to lead us in the recitation of the "Pledge of Allegiance"?
>
> Why was Tillie shaking as she began her recitation, "Once upon a midnight dreary. . ."?
>
> I was embarrassed when Mrs. White said, "Your slip is showing"!

In declarative sentences, where the quotation is a question or an exclamation, place the question mark or exclamation point inside the quotation marks.

> The hall monitor yelled, "Fire! Fire!"
>
> "Fire! Fire!" yelled the hall monitor.
>
> Cory shrieked, "Is there a mouse in the room?" (In this instance, the question supersedes the exclamation.)

Quotations—whether words, phrases, or clauses—should be punctuated according to the rules of the grammatical function they serve in the sentence.

The works of Shakespeare, "the Bard of Avon," have been contested as originating with other authors.

"You'll get my money," the old man warned, "when 'hell freezes over'."

Sheila cited the passage that began "Four score and seven years ago . . . ." (Note the ellipsis followed by an enclosed period.)

"Old Ironsides" inspired the preservation of the U.S.S. Constitution.

Use quotation marks to enclose the titles of shorter works: songs, short poems, short stories, essays, and chapters of books. (See "Dashes and Italics" for rules on punctuating longer titles.)

"The Tell-Tale Heart" "Casey at the Bat" "America the Beautiful"

Dashes and Italics

Place EM DASHES to denote sudden breaks in thought.

Some periods in literature—the Romantic Age, for example—spanned different periods in different countries.

Use dashes instead of commas if commas are already used elsewhere in the sentence for amplification or explanation.

The Fireside Poets included three Brahmans—James Russell Lowell, Henry David Wadsworth, and Oliver Wendell Holmes.

Use ITALICS to punctuate the titles of long works of literature, names of periodical publications, musical scores, works of art, and motion picture, television, and radio programs. (If italic type is unavailable, students should be instructed to use underlining where italics would be appropriate.)

The Idylls of the King	*Hiawatha*	*The Sound and the Fury*
Mary Poppins	*Newsweek*	*The Nutcracker Suite*

EM DASHES: used to denote sudden breaks in thought or if commas are already used in the sentence for amplification or explanation

ITALICS: used to punctuate the titles of long works of literature, names of periodical publications, musical scores, works of art, and motion picture, television, and radio programs

SKILL 9.12 Identify standard capitalization

Capitalize all proper names of persons (including specific organizations or agencies of government), places (countries, states, cities, parks, and specific geographical areas), things (political parties, structures, historical and cultural terms, and calendar and time designations), and religious terms (deities, revered persons or groups, and sacred writings).

> *Percy Bysshe Shelley, Argentina, Mount Rainier National Park, Grand Canyon, League of Nations, the Sears Tower, Birmingham, Lyric Theater, Americans, Midwesterners, Democrats, Renaissance, Boy Scouts of America, Easter, God, Bible, Dead Sea Scrolls, Koran*

Capitalize proper adjectives and titles used with proper names.

> *California gold rush, President John Adams, French fries, Homeric epic, Romanesque architecture, Senator John Glenn*

Capitalize all main words in titles of works of literature, art, and music.

Note: Some words that represent titles and offices are not capitalized unless used with a proper name.

Capitalized	Not Capitalized
Congressman McKay	the congressman from Hawaii
Commander Alger	the commander of the Pacific Fleet
Queen Elizabeth	the queen of England

Error: *Emma went to Dr. Peters for treatment because her own Doctor was on vacation.*

Problem: The use of capital letters with *Emma* and *Dr. Peters* is correct because they are specific (proper) names; the title *Dr.* is also capitalized. However, the word *doctor* is not a specific name and should not be capitalized.

Correction: *Emma went to Dr. Peters for treatment because her own doctor was on vacation.*

Error: *Our Winter break does not start until next wednesday.*

Problem: Days of the week are capitalized, but seasons are not capitalized.

Correction: *Our winter break does not start until next Wednesday.*

Error: *The exchange student from Israel, who came to study biochemistry, spoke spanish very well.*

Problem: Languages and the names of countries are always capitalized. Courses are capitalized when one is referring to a specific course; courses in general are not capitalized.

Correction: *The exchange student from Israel, who came to study biochemistry, spoke Spanish very well.*

Practice Exercise: Capitalization and Punctualization

Choose the option that corrects an error in the underlined portion(s). If no error exists, choose "No change is necessary."

1. <u>Greenpeace</u> is an <u>Organization</u> that works to preserve the <u>world's</u> environment.

   A. greenpeace
   B. organization
   C. worlds
   D. No change is necessary

2. When our class travels to <u>France</u> next <u>year, we</u> will see the <u>country's</u> many famous landmarks.

   A. france
   B. year; we
   C. countries
   D. No change is necessary

3. <u>New York City</u>, the most heavily populated city <u>in America has</u> more than eight million people living there <u>every day</u>.

   A. new york city
   B. in America, has
   C. Everyday
   D. No change is necessary

4. The <u>television</u> show *Lost* gained a huge <u>following because</u> it focused on paranormal phenomena, time travel, and the frailties of <u>human existence</u>.

   A. Television
   B. following, because
   C. Human existence
   D. No change is necessary

5. Being a <u>Policeman</u> requires having many <u>qualities</u>: physical <u>agility</u>, good reflexes, and the ability to make quick decisions.

   A. policeman
   B. qualities;
   C. agility:
   D. No change is necessary

6. "'Tis <u>better to have loved and lost, than never to have loved at all</u>," wrote Tennyson, the poet <u>who</u> demonstrates the value of love in a <u>mans</u> life.

   A. Better to have loved and lost than never to have loved at all
   B. Tennyson who
   C. man's
   D. No change is necessary

7. The <u>Boston Americans</u> won the first <u>world series</u> championship by defeating the Pittsburgh Pirates in <u>October 1903</u>.

   A. Boston americans
   B. World Series
   C. October, 1903
   D. No change is necessary

Answer Key: Capitalization and Punctualization

1. **B**

   In the sentence, the word *organization* does not need to be capitalized because it is a general noun. In Option A, the name of the organization should be capitalized. In Option C, an apostrophe is needed to show that one world is being protected, not more than one.

2. **D**

   In Option A, *France* must be capitalized because it is the name of a country. In Option B, a comma, not a semicolon, should separate the dependent clause from the main clause. In Option C, an apostrophe and an -s are needed to indicate that only one country is being visited.

3. **B**

   In Option A, New York City must be capitalized because it is the name of a place. In Option B, a comma is needed to separate the adjective clause ending with *America* from the verb **has**. In Option C, *every day* needs no capitalization and should not be joined as a compound word. (The word *everyday* is an adjective meaning *routine.*)

4. **D**

   In Option A, *television* does not need to be capitalized because it is a common noun. In Option B, a comma is only necessary to separate an independent clause from the main clause. In Option C, *human existence* is a general term that does not need capitalization.

5. **A**

   In Option A, *policeman* does not need capitalization because it is a common noun. In Option B, a colon, not a semicolon, is needed because the rest of the sentence is related to the main clause. In Option C, a comma, not a colon, is needed to separate the adjectives.

6. **C**

   In Option A, a comma is needed to break the quote into distinct parts that give it greater clarity. In Option B, a comma is needed to separate the subject of the sentence from the relative clause. In Option C, an apostrophe is needed to show possession.

7. **B**

   In Option A, *Americans* must be capitalized because it is the name of a team. In Option B, *World Series* is capitalized because it is the title of a sporting event. In Option C, no comma is needed because month and year need no distinction; they are general terms.

DOMAIN III
READING

PERSONALIZED STUDY PLAN

KNOWN MATERIAL/ SKIP IT

COMPETENCY 10
KNOWLEDGE OF LITERAL COMPREHENSION

SKILL 10.1 Recognize main ideas

The **MAIN IDEA** of a passage or paragraph is the basic message, idea, point, concept, or meaning that the author wants to convey to the reader. Understanding the main idea of a passage or paragraph is the key to understanding the more subtle components of the author's message. The main idea is what is being said about a topic or subject. Once you have identified the basic message, you will have an easier time answering other questions that test critical skills.

Main ideas are either stated or implied. A stated main idea is explicit: it is directly expressed in a sentence or two in the paragraph or passage. An implied main idea is suggested by the overall reading selection. In the first case, you need not pull information from various points in the paragraph or passage in order to form the main idea because the author already states it. If a main idea is implied, however, you must formulate—in your own words—a main idea statement by condensing the overall message contained in the material itself.

> **MAIN IDEA:** the basic message, idea, point, concept, or meaning that the author wants to convey to the reader

> Once you have identified the basic message, you will have an easier time answering other questions that test critical skills.

Sample Passage

Sometimes too much of a good thing can become a very bad thing indeed. In an earnest attempt to consume a healthy diet, dietary supplement enthusiasts have been known to overdose. Vitamin C, for example, long thought to help people ward off cold viruses, is currently being studied for its possible role in warding off cancer and other diseases that cause tissue degeneration. Unfortunately, an overdose of vitamin C—more than 10,000 mg—on a daily basis can cause nausea and diarrhea. Calcium supplements, commonly taken by women, are helpful in warding off osteoporosis. More than just a few grams a day, however, can lead to stomach upset and even kidney and bladder stones. Niacin, proven useful in reducing cholesterol levels, can be dangerous in large doses to those who suffer from heart problems, asthma, or ulcers.

The main idea expressed in this paragraph is:

A. Supplements taken in excess can be a bad thing indeed

B. Dietary supplement enthusiasts have been known to overdose

C. Vitamins can cause nausea, diarrhea, and kidney or bladder stones

D. People who take supplements are preoccupied with their health

Answer A is a paraphrase of the first sentence and provides a general framework for the rest of the paragraph: excess supplement intake is bad. The rest of the paragraph discusses the consequences of taking too many vitamins. Options B and C refer to major details, and Option D introduces the idea of preoccupation, which is not included in this paragraph.

SKILL 10.2 Identify supporting details

Supporting details are specific examples, facts, ideas, illustrations, cases, and anecdotes writers use to explain, expand upon, and develop the main idea. A writer's choice of supporting materials is determined by the nature of the topic being covered and the purpose for writing the selection.

For example, an advertisement writer seeking to persuade the reader to buy a particular running shoe will emphasize only the positive characteristics of the shoe for advertisement copy. A columnist for a running magazine, on the other hand, might list the good and bad points about the same shoe in an article recommending appropriate shoes for different kinds of runners. Both major details (those that directly support the main idea) and minor details (those that provide interesting, but not always essential, information) help create a well-written and fluid passage.

> *Both major details (those that directly support the main idea), and minor details (those that provide interesting but not always essential, information) help create a well-written and fluid passage.*

In the following paragraph, the sentences in **bold** print provide a skeleton of a paragraph on the benefits of recycling. The sentences in bold are generalizations that, by themselves, do not explain the need to recycle. The sentences in *italics* add details to SHOW the general points in bold. Notice how the supporting details help you understand the necessity of recycling.

> ***While one day recycling may become mandatory in all states, right now it is voluntary in many communities.*** *Those of us who participate in recycling are amazed by how much material is recycled.* ***For many communities, the blue-box recycling program has had an immediate effect.*** *By just recycling glass, aluminum cans, and plastic bottles, we have reduced the volume of disposable trash by one-third, thus extending the useful life of local landfills by over a decade. Imagine the difference if those dramatic results were achieved nationwide.* ***The number of reusable items we thoughtlessly dispose of is staggering.*** *For example, Americans dispose of enough steel every day to supply Detroit car manufacturers for three months. Additionally, we dispose of enough aluminum annually to rebuild the nation's air fleet. These statistics, available from the Environmental Protection Agency (EPA), should encourage all of us to watch what we throw away.* ***Clearly, recycling in our homes and in our communities directly improves the environment.***

Notice how the author's supporting examples enhance the message of the paragraph and relate to the author's thesis noted above. If you only read the boldface sentences, you have a glimpse of the topic. This paragraph of illustration, however, is developed through numerous details creating specific images: *reduced the volume of disposable trash by one-third; extended the useful life of local landfills by over a decade; enough steel every day to supply Detroit car manufacturers for three months; enough aluminum to rebuild the nation's air fleet.* If the writer had merely written a few general sentences, as those shown in bold, you would not fully understand the vast amount of trash involved in recycling or the positive results of current recycling efforts.

Concluding paragraph

End your essay with a brief, straightforward concluding paragraph that ties together the essay's content and leaves the reader with a sense of its completion. The conclusion should reinforce the main points and offer some insight into the topic, provide a sense of unity by relating the essay to the thesis, and signal clear closure of the essay.

SKILL 10.3 Determine meaning of words in context

CONTEXT CLUES help readers determine the meanings of words with which they are not familiar. The CONTEXT of a word is the sentence or sentences that surround the word.

Read the following sentences and attempt to determine the meanings of the words in **bold** print.

> The **luminosity** of the room was so incredible that there was no need for lights.

If there was no need for lights, then one must assume that the word luminosity has something to do with giving off light. The definition of luminosity is "the emission of light."

> Jamie could not understand Joe's feelings. His mood swings made understanding him somewhat of an **enigma**.

The fact that he could not be understood made him somewhat of a puzzle. The definition of enigma is "a mystery or puzzle."

CONTEXT CLUES: help readers determine the meanings of words with which they are not familiar

CONTEXT: the sentence or sentences that surround a word

ROOTS: the basic elements of words

PREFIXES: affixes that are added to the fronts of words to form derivative words.

Familiarity with terms ROOTS (the basic elements of words) and PREFIXES (affixes that are added to the fronts of words to form derivative words) can help you determine the meanings of unknown words.

Following are some common roots and prefixes.

COMMON ROOTS AND THEIR MEANINGS		
Root	**Meaning**	**Example**
aqua	water	aqualung
astro	stars	astrology
bio	life	biology
carn	meat	carnivorous
circum	around	circumnavigate
geo	earth	geology
herb	plant	herbivorous
mal	bad	malicious
neo	new	neonatal
tele	distant	telescope

COMMON PREFIXES AND THEIR MEANINGS		
Prefix	**Meaning**	**Example**
un-	not	unnamed
re-	again	reenter
il-	not	illegible
pre-	before	preset
mis-	incorrectly	misstate
in-	not	informal

Continued on next page

anti-	against	antiwar
de-	opposite	derail
post-	after	postwar
ir-	not	irresponsible

Word Forms

Sometimes a very familiar word can appear as a different part of speech.

You may have heard that *fraud* involves a criminal misrepresentation, so when it appears as the adjective form *fraudulent* ("He was suspected of fraudulent activities"), you can make an educated guess about its meaning.

You probably know that something out of date is *obsolete*; therefore, when you read about "built-in *obsolescence*," you can detect the meaning of the unfamiliar word.

Practice Questions: Word Forms

Read the following sentences and attempt to determine the meanings of the underlined words.

1. Farmer John got a two-horse plow and went to work. Straight <u>furrows</u> stretched out behind him.

   The word <u>furrows</u> means:

   A. Long cuts made by plow

   B. Vast, open fields

   C. Rows of corn

   D. Pairs of hitched horses

2. The survivors struggled ahead, <u>shambling</u> through the terrible cold, doing their best not to fall.

   The word <u>shambling</u> means:

   A. Frozen in place

   B. Running

   C. Shivering uncontrollably

   D. Walking awkwardly

Answer Key: Word Forms

1. A.

    The words "straight" and the expression "stretched out behind him" are your clues.

2. D.

    The words "ahead" and "through" are your clues.

Context clues can appear within the sentence itself, within the preceding and/or following sentence(s), or in the passage as a whole.

Context clues can appear within the sentence itself, within the preceding and/or following sentence(s), or in the passage as a whole.

Sentence Clues

Often, a writer will actually define a difficult or particularly important word for you the first time it appears in a passage. Phrases like *that is, such as, which is,* or *is called* might announce the writer's intention to give just the definition you need. Occasionally, a writer will simply use a synonym (a word that means the same thing) or near-synonym joined by the word or. Look at the following examples:

> *Nothing would <u>assuage</u> or lessen the child's grief.*
>
> *The <u>credibility</u>, that is to say the believability, of the witness was called into question by evidence of previous perjury.*

Punctuation at the sentence level is often a clue to the meaning of a word. Commas, parentheses, quotation marks, and dashes tell the reader that a definition is being offered by the writer.

> *A tendency toward <u>hyperbole</u>, extravagant exaggeration, is a common flaw among persuasive writers.*
>
> *Political <u>apathy</u>—lack of interest—can lead to the death of the state.*

A writer might simply give an explanation in other words that you can understand, in the same sentence:

> *The <u>xenophobic</u> townspeople were suspicious of every foreigner.*

Writers also explain a word in terms of its opposite at the sentence level:

> *His <u>incarceration</u> was ended, and he was elated to be out of jail.*

Adjacent Sentence Clues

The context for a word goes beyond the sentence in which it appears. At times, the writer uses adjacent (adjoining) sentences to present an explanation or definition:

> The $200 for the car repair would have to come out of the <u>contingency</u> fund. Fortunately, Angela's father had taught her to keep some money set aside for just such emergencies.

The second sentence offers a clue to the definition of *contingency* as used in this sentence: "emergencies." Therefore, a fund for contingencies would be money tucked away for unforeseen and/or urgent events.

Entire Passage Clues

On occasion, you must look at an entire paragraph or passage to figure out the definition of a word or term. In the following paragraph, notice how the word *nostalgia* undergoes a form of extended definition throughout the selection rather than in just one sentence.

> The word <u>nostalgia</u> links Greek words for "away from home" and "pain." If you're feeling <u>nostalgic</u>, then, you are probably in some physical distress or discomfort, suffering from a feeling of alienation and separation from loved ones or loved places. <u>Nostalgia</u> is that awful feeling you remember you felt the first time you went away to camp or spent the weekend with a friend's family—homesickness, or some condition even more painful than that. But in common use, <u>nostalgia</u> has come to have more sentimental associations. A few years back, for example, a <u>nostalgia</u> craze had to do with the 1950s. We resurrected poodle skirts and saddle shoes, built new restaurants to look like old ones, and tried to make chicken a la king just as mother probably never made it. In TV situation comedies, we recreated a pleasant world that probably never existed and relished our <u>nostalgia</u>, longing for a homey, comfortable lost time.

COMPETENCY 11
KNOWLEDGE OF INFERENTIAL COMPREHENSION

SKILL Determine purpose
11.1

ESSAY: an extended discussion of a writer's point of view about a particular topic

A good essay is clear, coherent, well-organized, and fully developed.

An **ESSAY** is an extended discussion of a writer's point of view about a particular topic. This point of view may be supported by using such writing modes as examples, argument and persuasion, analysis, or comparison/contrast. In any case, a good essay is clear, coherent, well organized, and fully developed.

When an author sets out to write a passage, he or she usually has a purpose for doing so. That purpose may be simply to give information that might be interesting or useful to the reader; it may be to persuade the reader to a point of view or to move the reader to act in a particular way; it may be to tell a story; or it may be to describe an experience in such a way that it becomes available to the reader through one of the five senses. Following are the primary devices for expressing a particular purpose in a piece of writing:

- Basic expository writing gives information not previously known about a topic or is used to explain or define one. Facts, examples, statistics, cause and effect, direct tone, objective rather than subjective delivery, and non-emotional information are presented in a formal manner.

- Descriptive writing centers on a person, place, or object. Descriptive writing uses concrete and sensory words to create a mood or impression, arranging details in a chronological or spatial sequence.

- Narrative writing is developed using an incident, an anecdote, or a related series of events. Chronology, the five Ws, a topic sentence, and a conclusion are essential ingredients.

- Persuasive writing implies the writer's ability to select vocabulary and arrange facts and opinions in such a way as to direct the beliefs or actions of the listener/reader. Persuasive writing may incorporate exposition and narration to illustrate the main idea.

- Journalistic writing is theoretically free of author bias. It is essential, when relaying information about an event, a person, or a thing, that the information be factual and objective. Provide students with an opportunity to

To teach about journalistic writing, provide students with an opportunity to examine newspapers and create their own. Many newspapers have educational programs that offer free subscriptions to schools.

examine newspapers and create their own newspaper. Many newspapers have educational programs that are offered free to schools.

See also Skill 7.3

SKILL 11.2 Identify overall organizational pattern

See Skill 6.1

SKILL 11.3 Distinguish between fact and opinion

FACTS are verifiable statements. OPINIONS are statements that must be supported in order to be accepted, such as beliefs, values, judgments, or feelings. Facts are objective statements used to support subjective opinions. For example, "Jane is a bad girl" is an opinion. However, "Jane hit her sister with a baseball bat" is a fact upon which the opinion is based. JUDGMENTS are opinions, decisions, or declarations based on observation or reasoning that express approval or disapproval. Facts report what has happened or what exists and come from observation, measurement, or calculation. Facts can be tested and verified, whereas opinions and judgments cannot. They can only be supported with facts.

Most statements cannot be so clearly distinguished. "I believe that Jane is a bad girl" is a fact. The speaker knows what he or she believes. However, it obviously includes a judgment that could be disputed by another person who might believe otherwise. Judgments are not usually so firm. They are, rather, plausible opinions that provoke thought or lead to factual development.

> *Mickey Mantle replaced Joe DiMaggio, a Yankees centerfielder, in 1952.*

This is a fact. If necessary, evidence can be produced to support this statement.

> *First-year players are more ambitious than seasoned players are.*

This is an opinion. There is no proof to support that everyone feels this way.

FACTS: verifiable statements that report what has happened or what exists

OPINIONS: statements that must be supported in order to be accepted, such as beliefs, values, judgments, or feelings

JUDGMENTS: opinions, decisions, or declarations based on observation or reasoning that express approval or disapproval

Practice Questions: Fact and Opinion

1. The Inca were a group of Indians who ruled an empire in South America.

   A. Fact

   B. Opinion

2. The Inca were clever.

   A. Fact

   B. Opinion

3. The Inca built very complex systems of bridges.

   A. Fact

   B. Opinion

Answer Key: Fact and Opinion

1. A

   Research can prove this statement true.

2. B

   It is doubtful that all people who have studied the Inca agree with this statement. Therefore, no proof is available.

3. A

   As with question number one, research can prove this statement true.

SKILL 11.4 Recognize bias

BIAS: an opinion, feeling or influence that strongly favors one side of an argument

BIAS is an opinion, feeling, or influence that strongly favors one side of an argument. A statement or passage is biased if an author attempts to influence a reader without presenting information about both sides of an argument.

Practice Questions: Bias

Read the following statements and determine if they are biased.

1. Using a calculator cannot help a student understand the process of graphing, so using one is a waste of time.

2. There are teachers who feel that computer programs are useful in helping students grasp certain math concepts. There are also those who disagree with this feeling. It is up to each individual math teacher to decide if computer programs benefit the teacher's particular group of students.

Answer Key: Bias

1. Since it is clear that the author does not favor the use of a calculator in graphing problems, the answer is yes, there is evidence of bias. This statement is an opinion without supporting evidence.

2. Since the author presents both sides of the argument about the usefulness of computers to teach math skills, this passage is not biased.

SKILL 11.5 Recognize tone

TONE: the author's attitude toward the subject matter

The TONE of a written passage is the author's attitude toward the subject matter. The tone (mood, feeling) is revealed through the qualities of the writing itself and is a direct product of such stylistic elements as language and sentence structure. The tone of the written passage is much like a speaker's voice; instead of being spoken, however, it is the product of words on a page.

The tone of a written passage is much like a speaker's voice.

Often, writers have an emotional stake in their subjects, and their purpose, either explicitly or implicitly, is to convey those feelings to the reader. In such cases, the writing is generally subjective; that is, it stems from opinions, judgments, values, ideas, and feelings. Both sentence structure (syntax) and word choice (diction) are instrumental tools in creating tone.

Tone may be thought of generally as positive, negative, or neutral. Below is a statement about snakes that demonstrates this.

> Many species of snakes live here. Some of those species, both poisonous and nonpoisonous, have habitats that coincide with those of human residents of the state.

The voice of the writer in this statement is neutral. The sentences are declarative (not exclamations, fragments, or questions). The adjectives are few and nondescript—*many, some, poisonous* (balanced with *nonpoisonous*). Nothing much in this brief paragraph would alert the reader to the feelings of the writer about snakes. The paragraph has a neutral, objective, detached, impartial tone.

If the writer's attitude toward snakes involved admiration, or even affection, the tone would generally be positive:

> These snakes are a tenacious bunch. When they find their habitats invaded by humans, they cling to their home territories as long as they can, as if vainly attempting to fight off the onslaught of the human hordes.

An additional message emerges in this paragraph—the writer quite clearly favors snakes over people. The writer uses adjectives such as tenacious to describe his or her feelings about snakes. The writer also humanizes the reptiles, making them brave, beleaguered creatures. Obviously, the writer is more sympathetic to snakes than to people in this paragraph.

If the writer's attitude toward snakes involved active dislike and fear, then the tone would also reflect that attitude by being negative:

> Countless species of snakes, some more dangerous than others, still lurk on the urban fringes of towns and cities. They will often invade domestic spaces, terrorizing people and their pets.

Here, obviously, the snakes are the villains. They *lurk*, they *invade*, and they *terrorize*. The tone of this paragraph might be defined as *distressed*.

In the same manner, a writer can use language to portray characters as good or bad. A writer uses positive and negative adjectives to convey the manner of a character.

SKILL 11.6 Determine relationships between sentences

Most sentences cannot meaningfully stand alone. To read a passage without recognizing how each sentence is linked to those around it is to lose the passage's meaning.

Sentences can be connected to one another in many ways.

HOW SENTENCES ARE CONNECTED	
Addition	One sentence is "tacked on" to another without making one sentence depend upon the other. Both are equally important. *Joanna recently purchased a new stereo system, computer, and home alarm system. She **also** put a down payment on a new automobile.*
Clarification	One sentence restates the point of an earlier one but in different terms. *The national debt is growing continually. **In fact**, by next year it may be ten trillion dollars.*
Comparison/Contrast	Connection is one of similarity or difference. *Shelley's strained relationship with his father led the poet to a life of rebellion. **Likewise**, Byron's Bohemian lifestyle may be traced to his ambivalence toward authority.*
Example	One sentence works to make another more concrete or specific. *Sarah has always been an optimistic person. She believes that when she graduates from college, she will get the job of her choice. (implicit)*
Location/Spatial Order	The relationship between sentences shows the placement of objects or items relative to each other in space. *The park was darkened by the school building's shadow. However, the sun still splashed the front window with light. (implicit)*
Cause/Effect	One event (cause) brings about the second event (effect). *General Hooker failed to anticipate General Lee's bold maneuver. **As a result**, Hooker's army was nearly routed by a smaller force.*

Continued on next page

Summary	A summary sentence surveys and captures the most important points of the previous sentence(s).
	Every Fourth of July, Ralph brings his whole family to the local parade; every Memorial Day, he displays the flag; and every November 4, he votes. **Overall**, *he is a patriotic American.*
Time	The relationship describes the passage of time or various states of completion of events.
	The car slid down the embankment. **Shortly thereafter**, *curious onlookers had backed up traffic five miles.*

SKILL 11.7 Analyze the validity of arguments

On the certification test, the terms valid and invalid have special meaning. If an argument is valid, it is reasonable. It is objective (not biased) and can be supported by evidence. If an argument is invalid, it is not reasonable and it is not objective. In other words, one can find evidence of bias.

Read the following passage:

> *Most dentists agree that Bright Smile Toothpaste is the best for fighting cavities. It tastes good and leaves your mouth minty fresh.*

Is this a valid or an invalid argument?

It is invalid. It mentions that most dentists agree. What about those who do not agree? The author is clearly exhibiting bias in leaving out those who disagree.

Read the following passage:

> *It is difficult to decide who will make the best presidential candidate, Senator Johnson or Senator Keeley. They have both been involved in scandals and have both gone through messy divorces while in office.*

Is this argument valid or invalid?

The argument is valid. The author appears to be listing facts. She does not seem to favor one candidate over the other.

SKILL 11.8 Draw logical inferences and conclusions

An **INFERENCE** is sometimes called an "educated guess" because it requires going beyond the strictly obvious to create additional meaning by taking the text one logical step further. Inferences and conclusions are based on the content of the passage—that is, on what the passage says or how the writer says it—and are derived by reasoning.

> **INFERENCE:** an educated guess based on given facts and premises

Inference is an essential and automatic component of most reading. Examples include making educated guesses about the meaning of unknown words, the author's main idea, or the existence of bias. Such is the essence of inference. You use your own ability to reason in order to figure out what the writer is implying.

Consider the following example. Assume you are an employer, and you are reading over the letters of reference submitted by a prospective employee for the position of clerk/typist in your real estate office. The position requires the applicant to be neat, careful, trustworthy, and punctual. You come across this letter of reference submitted by an applicant:

> *To Whom It May Concern:*
>
> *Todd Finley has asked me to write a letter of reference for him. I am well qualified to do so because he worked for me for three months last year. His duties included answering the phone, greeting the public, and producing some simple memos and notices on the computer. Although Todd initially had few computer skills and little knowledge of telephone etiquette, he did acquire some during his stay with us. Todd's manner of speaking, both on the telephone and with the clients who came to my establishment, could be described as casual. He was particularly effective when communicating with peers. Please contact me by telephone if you wish to have further information about my experience with Todd.*

Here the writer implies, rather than openly states, the main idea. This letter calls attention to itself because there is a problem with its tone. A truly positive letter would say something such as, "I have the distinct honor of recommending Todd Finley." Here, however, the letter simply verifies that Todd worked in the office. Second, the praise is obviously lukewarm. For example, the writer says that Todd "was particularly effective when communicating with peers." An educated guess translates that statement into a nice way of saying Todd was not serious about his communication with clients.

Here the writer implies, rather than openly states, his opinion about Todd Finley. A positive letter of reference would include a direct recommendation, for example: "I highly recommend Todd Finley for this position." Instead, this letter simply verifies that Todd worked in the office.

While not explicitly critical of Todd's work, the writer provides only backhanded compliments, like the fact that Todd did acquire some computer skills while in the position and communicated well with his peers. A prospective employer can easily infer that Todd is not a good candidate for the position.

In order to draw inferences and make conclusions, a reader must use prior knowledge and apply it to the current situation. A conclusion or inference is never stated. The reader must rely on common sense.

Practice Questions: Inferences and Conclusions

Read the following passages and select an answer.

1. Tim Sullivan had just turned fifteen. As a birthday present, his parents had given him a guitar and a certificate for ten guitar lessons. He had always shown a love of music and a desire to learn an instrument. Tim began his lessons and, before long, he was making up his own songs. At the music studio, Tim met Josh, who played the piano, and Roger, whose instrument was the saxophone. They all shared the same dream—to start a band—and each was praised by his teacher as having real talent.

   From this passage, one can infer that:

   A. Tim, Roger, and Josh are going to start their own band

   B. Tim is going to give up his guitar lessons

   C. Tim, Josh, and Roger will no longer be friends

   D. Josh and Roger are going to start their own band

2. The Smith family waited patiently around carousel number 7 for their luggage to arrive. They were exhausted after their five-hour trip and were anxious to get to their hotel. After about an hour, they realized that they no longer recognized any of the other passengers' faces. Mrs. Smith asked the person who appeared to be in charge if they were at the right carousel. The man replied, "Yes, this is it, but we finished unloading that baggage almost half an hour ago."

   From the man's response, we can infer that:

   A. The Smiths were ready to go to their hotel

   B. The Smiths' luggage was lost

   C. The man had the Smiths' luggage

   D. The Smiths were at the wrong carousel

Answer Key: Inferences and Conclusions

1. A

   Given the facts that Tim wanted to be a musician and start his own band, after he met others who shared the same dreams, we can infer that the friends joined in an attempt to make their dreams become a reality.

2. B

   Because the Smiths were still waiting for their luggage, we know that they were not yet ready to go to their hotel. From the man's response, we know that they were not at the wrong carousel and that he did not have their luggage. Therefore, though not directly stated, it appears that their luggage was lost.

Writers can use inductive or deductive reasoning when developing their ideas. Inductive reasoning moves from specific pieces of information to general conclusions. The following selection illustrates inductive reasoning:

> *I tasted a green apple from my grandfather's yard when I was five years old, and it was sour. I also tasted a green apple that my friend brought to school in his lunchbox when I was eight years old, and it was sour. I was in Browns' Roadside Market and bought some green Granny Smith apples last week, and they were sour.*

From these specific examples, the reader might draw a conclusion—a generalization—all apples are sour, a conclusion reached through inductive reasoning.

The same simple theme developed deductively would begin with the generalization that all green apples are sour. This generalization would be followed by specific examples to support it: the sour green apple I tasted in my grandfather's orchard, the sour green apple in my friend's lunchbox, and the Granny Smith apples from the market.

Sometimes writers use generalizations with the assumption that they are commonly accepted and do not need to be supported. However, on closer examination, generalizations are often complex issues with no clear-cut answers. The following two statements are good examples of the complexity of generalization. Are these statements commonly accepted, needing no support?

> *Providing healthcare for all citizens is the responsibility of the government.*
>
> *All true patriots will support any war the government declares.*

DOMAIN IV
ESSAY

PERSONALIZED STUDY PLAN

The General Knowledge Essay subtest requires that the examinee select from two topics and organize and compose an original essay about one of them in 50 minutes.

The intent of the essay test component is to show that you can, in the time allotted, compose and write an original essay that addresses the topic in an effective, well-organized manner with good grammar and spelling.

An examinee is absolutely not permitted to memorize an essay from another source and present it as an original essay. Doing so is considered cheating, and if the essay is identified as being preprepared, all tests taken that day will be invalidated and no scores will be received. In addition, the incident will be reported to the Department's Bureau of Professional Practices Services.

GENERAL STRATEGIES FOR WRITING THE ESSAY	
Watch the time	Use all the time wisely. You should neither run out of time before you are done, nor write an incomplete essay because you did not use all the time allowed.
Read the instructions carefully and select one of the topics	Determine what the topic is asking. Think of how the topic relates to what you know, what you have learned, and what experiences you have had so that you can provide concrete details rather than vague generalities.
Take a few minutes to prewrite	Jot down your first ideas. Sketch a quick outline or group your ideas together with arrows or numbers.
Write a thesis statement that provides a clear focus for your essay	In your thesis, state a point of view that guides the purpose and scope of your essay. Consider the larger point you're trying to convey to the reader and what you want the reader to understand about the topic. Avoid a thesis statement framed as a fact statement, a question, or an announcement.
Develop the essay while considering your purpose	Develop paragraphs fully and give examples and reasons that support your thesis. Indent each new paragraph. Note that a good essay may be longer or shorter than the basic five-paragraph format of some short essays. The key is to *develop* a topic by using concrete, informative details.
Tie your main ideas together with a brief conclusion	Provide a concluding paragraph that ties together the essay's points and offers insights about the topic. Avoid a conclusion that merely restates the thesis and repeats the supporting details.
Revise/proofread the essay so that it conforms to standard American English	Look for particular errors you tend to make. Mark errors, then correct them. You will never be penalized for clearly crossing out errors. Look for words, sentences, or even paragraphs that need changing. Write legibly so that the reader knows what you have written.

SKILL 12.1 Determine the purpose for writing

Topic Analysis

Even before you select a topic, determine what each prompt is asking you to discuss. This first decision is crucial. If you pick a topic that you do not understand well or about which you have little to say, you will have difficulty developing your essay. Take a few moments to analyze each topic carefully before you chose a topic and begin to write.

Topic A: A modern invention that can be considered a wonder of the world

In general, the topic prompts have two parts:

1. The SUBJECT of the topic

2. An ASSERTION about the subject

The subject is a modern invention. In this prompt, the word modern indicates you should discuss something invented recently, at least in this century. The word invention indicates you should write about something created by humans (not natural phenomena such as mountains or volcanoes). You may discuss an invention that has potential for harm, such as chemical weapons or the atomic bomb, or you may discuss an invention that has the potential for good, such as the computer, DNA testing, television, or antibiotics.

> **ASSERTION:** a statement of point of view

The ASSERTION is that the invention has such powerful or amazing qualities that it should be considered a wonder of the world. The assertion states your point of view about the subject and it limits the range of possible discussion. In this essay, you should discuss particular qualities or uses of the invention you choose, not just how it was invented or whether it should have been invented at all.

Note also that this particular topic encourages you to use examples to show the reader that a particular invention is a modern wonder. Some topic prompts lend themselves to essays with an argumentative edge, one in which you take a stand on a particular issue and persuasively prove your point. In this case, you undoubtedly could offer examples or illustrations of the many "wonders" and uses of the particular invention you chose.

> *Some topic prompts lend themselves to essays with an argumentative edge, one in which you take a stand on a particular issue and persuasively prove your point.*

Be aware that misreading or misinterpreting the topic prompt can lead to serious problems. If you misread or misinterpret words, or read the topic too quickly, you may write an essay that does not address the topic. Misreading can also lead to an essay that addresses only part of the topic prompt rather than the entire topic.

See also Skill 11.1

SKILL Formulate a thesis or statement of main idea
12.2

To develop a complete essay, spend a few minutes planning. Jot down your ideas and quickly sketch an outline. Although you may feel under pressure to begin writing, you will write more effectively if you plan your major points.

Prewriting

Before actually writing, you will need to generate content and develop a writing plan. Three prewriting techniques can be helpful.

Brainstorming

When brainstorming, quickly create a list of words and ideas that are connected to the topic. Let your mind roam free to generate as many relevant ideas as possible in a few minutes. For example, on the topic of computers you may write:

computer—modern invention

types—personal computers, microchips in calculators and watches

wonder—acts like an electronic brain

uses—science, medicine, offices, homes, schools

problems—too much reliance; the machines are not perfect

This list could help you focus on the topic, and it states the points you could develop in the body paragraphs. The brainstorming list keeps you on track and is well worth the few minutes it takes to jot down the ideas. While you have not yet ordered the ideas, seeing them on paper is an important step.

Questioning

Questioning helps you focus as you mentally ask a series of exploratory questions about the topic. You may use the most basic questions: who, what, where, when, why, and how.

*"**What** is my subject?"*
[computers]

*"**What** types of computers are there?"*
[personal computers, microchip computers]

*"**Why** have computers been a positive invention?"*
[act as an electronic brain in machinery and equipment; help solve complex scientific problems]

*"**How** have computers been a positive invention?"*
[used to make improvements in:
• *Science (space exploration, moon landings)*
• *Medicine (MRIs, CT scans, surgical tools, research models)*
• *Business (PCs, FAX, telephone equipment)*
• *Education (computer programs for math, languages, science, social studies)*
• *Personal tasks (family budgets, tax programs, healthy diet plans)]*

*"**How** can I show that computers are good?"*
[cite numerous examples]

*"**What** problems do I see with computers?"*
[too much reliance; not yet perfect]

*"**What** personal experiences would help me develop examples to respond to this topic?*
[my own experiences using computers]

Of course, you may not have time to write out the questions completely. You might just write the words *who*, *what*, *where*, *when*, *why*, and *how* and the major points next to each. An abbreviated list might look like this:

*   **What:** *computers/modern wonder/making life better*
    How: *through technological improvements: lasers, calculators, CT scans, MRIs*
    Where: *in science and space exploration, medicine, schools, offices*

In a few moments, your questions should help you focus on the topic and generate interesting ideas and points to make in the essay. Later in the writing process, you can look back at the list to be sure you have made your key points.

Clustering

Some visual thinkers find clustering an effective prewriting method. When clustering, you draw a box in the center of your paper and write your topic within that box. Then, you draw lines from the center box connecting it to small satellite boxes that contain related ideas. Note the cluster below on computers:

Sample Cluster

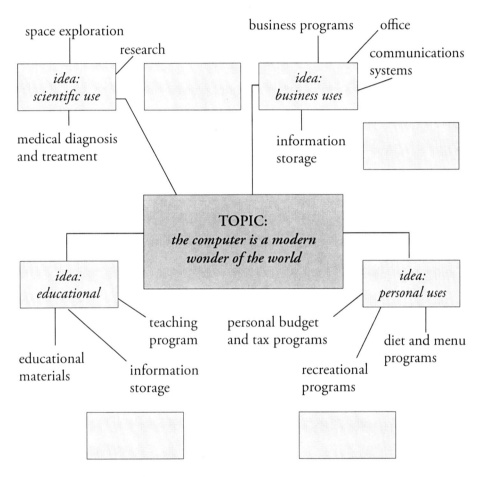

Writing the Thesis

After focusing on the topic and generating your ideas, you will form your THESIS, the controlling idea of your essay. The thesis is your general statement to the reader that expresses your point of view and guides your essay's purpose and scope. A strong thesis will enable you either to explain your subject or to take an arguable position about it. A good thesis statement is neither too narrow nor too broad.

> **THESIS:** the controlling idea of an essay

Subject and Assertion of the Thesis

From the statement of the general topic, you analyzed the topic in terms of its two parts: subject and assertion. On the teacher certification exam, your thesis or viewpoint on a particular topic is stated in two important points:

✗

1. The *subject* of the paper.

2. The *assertion* about the subject

SUBJECT OF THE THESIS: relates directly to the topic prompt but expresses the specific area you have chosen to discuss

The **SUBJECT OF THE THESIS** relates directly to the topic prompt but expresses the specific area you have chosen to discuss. (Remember, the exam topic will be general and will allow you to choose a particular subject related to the topic.) For example, the computer is one of many modern inventions you might choose to write about.

ASSERTION OF THE THESIS: your viewpoint, or opinion, about the subject

The **ASSERTION OF THE THESIS** is your viewpoint, or opinion, about the subject. The assertion provides the motive or purpose for your essay, and it may be an arguable point or one that explains or illustrates a point of view.

For example, you may present an argument for or against a particular issue. You may contrast two people, objects, or methods to show that one is better than the other. You may analyze a situation in all aspects and make recommendations for improvement. You may assert that a law or policy should be adopted, changed, or abandoned. You may also explain to your reader, as in the computer example, that a situation or condition exists; rather than argue a viewpoint, you would use examples to illustrate your assertion about the essay's subject.

Specifically, the subject of Topic A *is the computer.* The assertion is that *it is a modern wonder that has improved our lives*, and *we rely on it.* Now you quickly have created a workable thesis in a few moments:

> *The computer is a modern wonder of the world that has improved our lives and that we have come to rely on.*

Guidelines for Writing Thesis Statements

The following guidelines are not a formula for writing thesis statements, but rather are general strategies for making your thesis statement clear and effective.

1. State a particular point of view about the topic with both a subject and an assertion. The thesis should give the essay purpose and scope and thus provide the reader a guide. If the thesis is vague, your essay may be undeveloped because you do not have an idea to assert or a point to explain. Weak thesis statements are often framed as facts, questions, or announcements:

The thesis should give the essay purpose and scope and thus provide readers a guide.

A. Avoid a fact statement as a thesis. While a fact statement may provide a subject, it generally does not include a point of view about the subject that provides the basis for an extended discussion. Example: *Recycling saved our community over $10,000 last year.* This fact statement provides a detail, not a point of view. Such a detail might be found within an essay, but it does not state a point of view.

B. Avoid framing the thesis as a vague question. In many cases, rhetorical questions do not provide a clear point of view for an extended essay. Example: *How do people recycle?* This question neither asserts a point of view nor helpfully guides the reader to understand the essay's purpose and scope.

C. Avoid the "announcer" topic sentence that merely states the topic you will discuss. Example: *I will discuss ways to recycle.* This sentence states the subject, but the scope of the essay is only suggested. Again, this statement does not assert a viewpoint that guides the essay's purpose. It merely "announces" that the writer will write about the topic.

2. Start with a workable thesis. You might revise your thesis as you begin writing and discover your own point of view.

3. If feasible and appropriate, perhaps state the thesis in multipoint form, expressing the scope of the essay. By stating the points in parallel form, you clearly lay out the essay's plan for the reader. Example: *To improve the environment, we can recycle our trash, elect politicians who see the environment as a priority, and support lobbying groups that work for environmental protection.*

4. Because of the exam time limit, place your thesis in the first paragraph to key the reader to the essay's main idea.

SKILL 12.3 Organize ideas and details effectively

Creating a Working Outline

A good thesis gives structure to your essay and helps focus your thoughts. When forming your thesis, look at your prewriting strategy—clustering, questioning, or brainstorming. Then, decide quickly which two or three major areas you will discuss. Remember, you must limit the scope of the paper because of the time factor.

The OUTLINE lists the main points as topics for each paragraph. Looking at the prewriting cluster on computers, you might choose several areas in which computers help us; for example, in science and medicine, business, and education. You might also consider people's reliance on this "wonder" and include at least one paragraph about this reliance. A formal outline for this essay might look like the one below:

OUTLINE: a list of the main points of a thesis that will be used as topics for each paragraph

I. Introduction and thesis

II. Computers used in science and medicine

III. Computers used in business

IV. Computers used in education

V. People's reliance on computers

VI. Conclusion

Under time pressure, however, you may use a shorter organizational plan, such as abbreviated key words in a list. For example:

1. *intro: wonders of the computer* -OR-	a. *intro: wonders of computers—science*
2. *science*	b. *in the space industry*
3. *med*	c. *in medical technology*
4. *schools*	d. *conclusion*
5. *business*	
6. *conclusion*	

Developing the Essay

With a working thesis and an outline, you can begin writing the essay. The essay should be divided into three main sections:

1. The introduction sets up the essay and leads to the thesis statement

2. The body paragraphs are developed with concrete information leading from the topic sentences

3. The conclusion ties the essay together

Introduction

Put your thesis statement into a clear, coherent opening paragraph. One effective device is to use a funnel approach, in which you begin with a brief description of the broader issue and then move to a clearly focused, specific thesis statement.

Consider the following possible introductions to the essay on computers. The length of each is obviously different. Read each, and consider the other differences.

Does each introduce the subject generally?

Does each lead to a stated thesis?

Does each relate to the topic prompt?

Introduction 1: *Computers are used every day. They have many uses. Some people who use them are workers, teachers, and doctors.*

Analysis: This introduction does give the general topic—computers are used every day—but it does not explain what those uses are. This introduction does not offer a point of view in a clearly stated thesis, nor does it convey the idea that computers are a modern wonder.

Introduction 2: *Computers are used just about everywhere these days. I don't think there's an office around that doesn't use computers, and we use them a lot in all kinds of jobs. Computers are great for making life easier and work better. I don't think we'd get along without the computer.*

Analysis: This introduction gives the general topic as computers and mentions one area that uses computers. The thesis states that people could not get along without computers, but it does not state the specific areas the essay will discuss. Note, too, that the meaning is not helped by vague diction, such as *a lot* and *great*.

Introduction 3: *Each day, we either use computers or see them being used around us. We wake to the sound of a digital alarm operated by a microchip. Our cars run by computerized machinery. We use computers to help us learn. We receive phone calls and letters transferred from computers across continents. Our astronauts walked on the moon and returned safely, all because of computer technology. The computer is a wonderful electronic brain that we have come to rely on, and it has changed our world through advances in science, business, and education.*

Analysis: This introduction is the most thorough and fluent because it provides interest in the general topic and offers specific information about computers as a modern wonder. It also leads to a thesis that directs the reader to the scope of the discussion—advances in science, business, and education.

Topic sentences

Just as the essay must have an overall focus reflected in the thesis statement, each paragraph must have a central idea reflected in the topic sentence. A good topic sentence provides transition from the previous paragraph and relates to the essay's thesis. Good topic sentences, therefore, provide unity throughout the essay.

Consider the following potential topic sentences. Determine whether each provides transition and clearly states the subject of the paragraph.

Just as the essay must have an overall focus that is reflected in the thesis statement, each paragraph must have a central idea reflected in the topic sentence.

Topic Sentence 1: *Computers are used in science.*

Analysis: This sentence simply states the topic: Computers are used in science. It does not relate to the thesis nor provide transition from the introduction. The reader still does not know how computers are used in science.

Topic Sentence 2: *Now I will talk about computers used in science.*

Analysis: Like the faulty "announcer" thesis statement, this "announcer" topic sentence is vague and merely names the topic.

Topic Sentence 3: *First, computers used in science have improved our lives.*

Analysis: The transition word *First* helps link the introduction and this paragraph. It adds unity to the essay. It does not, however, give specifics about the improvements computers have made in our lives.

Topic Sentence 4: *First used in scientific research and spaceflights, computers are now used extensively in the diagnosis and treatment of disease.*

Analysis: This sentence is the most thorough and fluent. It provides specific areas that will be discussed in the paragraph and it offers more than an announcement of the topic. The writer gives concrete information about the content of the paragraph that will follow.

SUMMARY GUIDELINES FOR WRITING TOPIC SENTENCES
Specifically relate the topic to the thesis statement
State clearly and concretely the subject of the paragraph
Provide some transition from the previous paragraph
Avoid topic sentences that are facts, questions, or announcements

SKILL 12.4 Provide adequate, relevant supporting material

See Skill 10.2

SKILL 12.5 Use effective transitions

See Skill 6.1

SKILL 12.6 Demonstrate a mature command of language

See Competency 7

SKILL 12.7 Avoid inappropriate use of slang, jargon, and clichés

SLANG is defined as very informal usage of vocabulary and idiom that is characteristically more metaphorical, playful, elliptical, vivid, and ephemeral than ordinary language. The phrase *to hit the road*, meaning to leave, is a good example of slang. Slang is fine in conversation between friends, but it is extremely inappropriate in formal writing.

Slang is often specific to a social group or geographic region. Because it is so colloquial, slang can be easily misunderstood. Moreover, using slang can affect how seriously readers regard your writing. The only time that slang may be appropriate in formal writing is when it is being used in a quote or dialogue.

JARGON is defined as the language, especially the vocabulary, peculiar to a particular trade, profession, or group, for instance, *medical jargon*. Because jargon pertains to the vocabulary used by a limited or specialized group of people, using jargon can hinder clear and effective communication to a general reading public.

Jargon, like slang, has its own time and place. If you are writing for a specialized audience, specialized language will communicate meaning effectively and show the audience that you are familiar with the terms associated with that specialized field. If, however, you are writing for a more general audience, jargon will be unintelligible gibberish and, perhaps, even offensive. If readers feel that an author is being pretentious or boastful, they may find the jargon distasteful.

A CLICHÉ is defined as a trite, stereotyped expression that has lost originality, ingenuity, and impact by long overuse. The sayings *older but wiser* and *strong as an ox*

> **SLANG:** informal usage of vocabulary and idiom that is characteristically more metaphorical, playful, elliptical, vivid, and ephemeral than ordinary language

> *The phrase* to hit the road, *meaning to leave, is a good example of slang.*

> **JARGON:** language, especially the vocabulary, peculiar to a particular trade, profession, or group

> **CLICHÉ:** a trite, stereotyped expression

are examples of clichés. The use of clichés weakens writing due to lack of creativity, thoughtfulness, and personal perspective. Clichés are boring and sometimes even offensive, and they are best avoided when one is writing an original piece. Rather than using tired expressions to convey an idea, rethink the idea that is being conveyed and reword it with correct vocabulary and specific details.

> *The sayings* older but wiser *and* strong as an ox *are examples of clichés.*

SKILL 12.8 Use a variety of sentence patterns effectively

See Competency 8

SKILL 12.9 Maintain consistent point of view

Point of view defines the focus a writer assumes in relation to a given topic. It is extremely important to maintain a consistent point of view in order to create coherent paragraphs. Point of view is related to matters of person, tense, tone, and number.

- Person: A shift in the form that indicates whether a person is speaking (first), is being spoken to (second), or is being spoken about (third) can disrupt the continuity of a passage. In your essay, it is recommended that you write in the third person because it is often considered to be the most formal of the modes of person. If you do decide to use the more informal first or second person (I, you, we) in your essay, be careful not to shift between first, second, and third person from sentence to sentence or paragraph to paragraph.

- Tense: Verbs tenses indicate the time of an action or state of being: the past, present, or future. It is important, usually, to stick to a selected tense, though this may not always be the case. For instance, in an essay about the history of environmental protection, it might be necessary to include a paragraph about past environmental catastrophes or a paragraph about the future benefits or consequences of protecting the Earth.

- Tone: The tone of an essay varies greatly with the purpose, subject, and audience. It is best to assume a formal tone for this essay.

- **Number:** Words change when their meanings are singular or plural. Make sure that you do not shift number needlessly; if a meaning is singular in one sentence, do not make it plural in a subsequent sentence.

SKILL 12.10 Observe the conventions of standard American English

See Competencies 6 through 9

ESSAY

SAMPLE TEST

SAMPLE TEST

Mathematics

(Easy) (Skill 1.1)

1. 0.74 =

    A. $\frac{74}{100}$

    B. 7.4%

    C. $\frac{33}{50}$

    D. $\frac{74}{10}$

(Easy) (Skill 1.1)

2. Identify the missing term in the following harmonic sequence: $\frac{1}{3}, \frac{1}{6}, \frac{1}{9}, \frac{1}{12}, \frac{1}{15}$, ?

    A. $\frac{1}{16}$

    B. $\frac{1}{17}$

    C. $\frac{1}{18}$

    D. 18

(Average) (Skill 1.1)

3. Choose the set in which the members are not equivalent.

    A. $\frac{1}{2}$, 0.5, 50%

    B. $\frac{10}{5}$, 2.0, 200%

    C. $\frac{3}{8}$, 0.385, 38.5%

    D. $\frac{7}{10}$, 0.7, 70%

(Easy) (Skill 1.2)

4. 303 is what percent of 600?

    A. 0.505%

    B. 5.05%

    C. 505%

    D. 50.5%

(Average) (Skill 1.2)

5. $\left(\frac{-4}{9}\right) + \left(\frac{-7}{10}\right) =$

    A. $\frac{23}{90}$

    B. $\frac{-23}{90}$

    C. $\frac{103}{90}$

    D. $\frac{-103}{90}$

(Average) (Skill 1.2)

6. (5.6) × (-0.11) =

    A. -0.616

    B. 0.616

    C. -6.110

    D. 6.110

(Average) (Skill 1.2)

7. An item that sells for $375 is put on sale for $120. What is the percent of discount?

    A. 25%

    B. 28%

    C. 68%

    D. 34%

(Average) (Skill 1.2)

8. Two mathematics classes have a total of 410 students. The 8:00 am class has 40 more than the 10:00 am class. How many students are in the 10:00 am class?

    A. 123.3

    B. 370

    C. 185

    D. 330

(Average) (Skill 1.2)

9. A restaurant employs 465 people. There are 280 waiters and 185 cooks. If 168 waiters and 85 cooks receive pay raises, what percent of the waiters receive a pay raise?

A. 36.13%

B. 60%

C. 60.22%

D. 40%

(Average) (Skill 1.2)

10. $\frac{7}{9} + \frac{1}{3} \div \frac{2}{3} =$

A. $\frac{5}{3}$

B. $\frac{3}{2}$

C. 2

D. $\frac{23}{18}$

(Average) (Skill 1.2)

11. The price of gas is $3.27 per gallon. Your tank holds 15 gallons of fuel. You are using two tanks of gas a week. Approximately how much will you save each week if the price of gas goes down to $2.30 per gallon?

A. $26.00

B. $29.00

C. $15.00

D. $17.00

(Average) (Skill 1.2)

12. Choose the statement that is true for all real numbers.

A. $a = 0, b \neq 0$, then $\frac{b}{a}$ = undefined

B. $-(a + (-a)) = 2a$

C. $2(ab) = -(2a)b$

D. $-a(b + 1) = ab - a$

(Rigorous) (Skill 1.2)

13. In a sample of 40 full-time employees at a particular company, 35 are also working a part-time job requiring at least 10 hours per week. If this proportion holds true for the entire company of 25,000 employees, how many full-time employees at this company are also working a part-time job at least 10 hours per week?

A. 714

B. 625

C. 21,875

D. 28,571

(Rigorous) (Skill 1.2)

14. $4\frac{2}{9} \times \frac{7}{10} =$

A. $4\frac{9}{10}$

B. $\frac{266}{90}$

C. $2\frac{43}{45}$

D. $2\frac{6}{20}$

(Easy) (Skill 1.3)

15. What is the greatest common factor of 16, 28, and 36?

A. 2

B. 4

C. 8

D. 16

(Rigorous) (Skill 1.3)

16. $(-2.1 \times 10^4)(4.2 \times 10^{-5}) =$

A. 8.82

B. -8.82

C. -0.882

D. 0.882

(Rigorous) (Skill 1.3)

17. $\frac{2^{10}}{2^5} =$

    A. 2^2

    B. 2^5

    C. 2^{50}

    D. $2^{\frac{1}{2}}$

(Average) (Skill 1.4)

18. Choose the expression that is *not* equivalent to $5x + 3y + 15z$:

    A. $5(x + 3z) + 3y$

    B. $3(x + y + 5z)$

    C. $3y + 5(x + 3z)$

    D. $5x + 3(y + 5z)$

(Average) (Skill 1.4)

19. A sofa sells for $520. If the retailer makes a 30% profit, what is the wholesale price?

    A. $400

    B. $676

    C. $490

    D. $364

(Rigorous) (Skill 1.4)

20. $(3 \times 9)^4 =$

    A. $(3 \times 9)(3 \times 9)(27 \times 27)$

    B. $(3 \times 9) + (3 \times 9)$

    C. (12×36)

    D. $(3 \times 9) + (3 \times 9) + (3 \times 9) + (3 \times 9)$

(Rigorous) (Skill 1.4)

21. Choose the equation that is equivalent to the following: $\frac{3x}{5} - 5 = 5x$

    A. $3x - 25 = 25x$

    B. $x - \frac{25}{3} = 25x$

    C. $6x - 50 = 75x$

    D. $x + 25 = 25x$

(Easy) (Skill 2.1)

22. What unit of measurement could we use to record the distance traveled walking around a track?

    A. Degrees

    B. Square meters

    C. Kilometers

    D. Cubic feet

(Average) (Skill 2.1)

23. What is the area of a square with a side measuring 13 feet?

    A. 169 feet

    B. 169 square feet

    C. 52 feet

    D. 52 square feet

(Average) (Skill 2.1)

24. What is the circumference of a circle with a diameter of 4 meters?

    A. 6.28 m

    B. 25.12 m

    C. 12.56 m

    D. None of the above

(Rigorous) (Skill 2.1)

25. What is the area of this triangle?

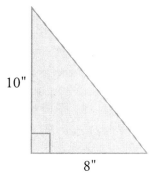

10"

8"

A. 80 square inches

B. 20 square inches

C. 40 square inches

D. 30 square inches

(Rigorous) (Skill 2.1)

26. The trunk of a tree has a 2.1 meter radius. What is its circumference?

A. 2.1π square meters

B. 4.2π meters

C. 2.1π meters

(Rigorous) (Skill 2.1)

27. The figure below shows a running track and the shape of an inscribed rectangle with semicircles at each end.

Calculate the distance around the track.

A. $6\pi y + 14x$

B. $3\pi y + 7x$

C. $6\pi y + 7x$

D. $3\pi y + 14x$

(Average) (Skill 2.2)

28. What unit of measurement could be used to describe the spread of a forest fire in a unit time?

A. 10 square yards per second

B. 10 yards per minute

C. 10 feet per hour

D. 10 cubit feet per hour

(Average) (Skill 2.2)

29. Given the formula $d = rt$, (where $d =$ distance, $r =$ rate, and $t =$ time), calculate the time required for a vehicle to travel 585 miles at a rate of 65 miles per hour.

A. 8.5 hours

B. 6.5 hours

C. 9.5 hours

D. 9 hours

(Easy) (Skill 2.4)

30. A teacher spends 45 minutes per day reading and replying to email messages. How many hours does the teacher devote to email correspondence during a five-day workweek?

A. 4.25 hours

B. 3.25 hours

C. 3.75 hours

D. 3.50 hours

(Easy) (Skill 2.5)

31. Round $1\frac{13}{16}$ of an inch to the nearest quarter of an inch.

    A. $1\frac{1}{4}$ inch

    B. $1\frac{5}{8}$ inch

    C. $1\frac{3}{4}$ inch

    D. 2 inches

(Average) (Skill 2.5)

32. A car gets 25.36 miles per gallon. The car has been driven 83,310 miles. What is a reasonable estimate of the total number of gallons of gas the car has used?

    A. 2,087 gallons

    B. 3,000 gallons

    C. 1,800 gallons

    D. 164 gallons

(Average) (Skill 2.5)

33. Estimate $5,743 - 318$ by front-end estimation.

    A. 5,430

    B. 5,420

    C. 5,425

    D. 5,400

(Rigorous) (Skill 2.5)

34. The owner of a rectangular piece of land 40 yards in length and 30 yards in width wants to divide it into two parts. She plans to join two opposite corners with a fence as shown in the diagram below. The cost of the fence will be approximately $25 per linear foot. What is the estimated total cost for the fence?

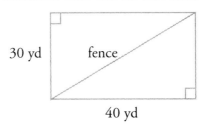

    A. $1,250

    B. $62,500

    C. $5,250

    D. $3,750

(Average) (Skill 3.1)

35. What type of triangle is △ ABC?

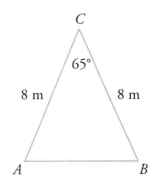

    A. Right

    B. Equilateral

    C. Scalene

    D. Isosceles

(Average) (Skill 3.1)

36. Consider the following statements:

    I. All parallelograms are rectangles

    II. Some rhombi are squares

    A. Both statements are correct

    B. Both statements are incorrect

    C. Only statement II is correct

    D. Only statement I is correct

(Rigorous) (Skill 3.1)

37. Study figures A through D. Select the letter in which all triangles are similar.

    A.

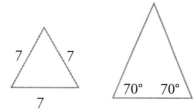

    B.

    C.

    D.

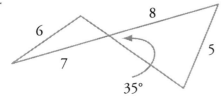

(Average) (Skill 3.2)

38. At the lake, the ratio is 16 ducks to 9 geese. Suppose there are 192 ducks. How many geese are there?

    A. 21

    B. 108

    C. 7

    D. 1,728

(Rigorous) (Skill 3.2)

39. Which formula would you use to find the length of the hypotenuse in the figure shown below?

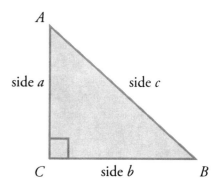

    A. $(\frac{1}{2})bh$

    B. $c^2 = a^2 + b^2$

    C. $\frac{1}{2}h(b_1 + b_2)$

    D. None of the above

(Average) (Skill 3.3)

40. Find the slope of a line with points at (5, 3) and (8, 9).

    A. $\frac{12}{13}$

    B. 2.0

    C. $\frac{27}{13}$

    D. −2.0

(Rigorous) (Skill 3.3)

41. What is the equation that expresses the relationship between x and y in the table below?

x	-2	-1	0	1	2
y	4	1	-2	-5	-8

A. $y = -x - 2$

B. $y = -3x - 2$

C. $y = 3x - 2$

D. $y = \frac{1}{3}x - 1$

(Average) (Skill 4.3)

42. If $4x - (3 - x) = 7(x - 3) + 10$, then:

A. $x = 8$

B. $x = -8$

C. $x = 4$

D. $x = -4$

(Average) (Skill 4.3)

43. Solve for x: $3(5 + 3x) - 8 = 88$

A. 30

B. 9

C. 4.5

D. 27

(Rigorous) (Skill 4.3)

44. $3x - \frac{2}{3} = \frac{5x}{2} + 2$. Solve for x.

A. $5\frac{1}{3}$

B. $\frac{17}{3}$

C. 2

D. $\frac{16}{2}$

(Rigorous) (Skill 4.3)

45. What is the x-intercept of the line represented by $4x + 2y = 12$?

A. $(0, 6)$

B. $(3, 0)$

C. $(0, 3)$

D. $(0, 8)$

(Rigorous) (Skill 4.4)

46. For each of the statements below, determine whether $x = \frac{1}{6}$ is a solution.

   I. $6x \leq\ = 4x^2 + 2$

   II. $10x + 1 = 3(4x - 3)$

   III. $|x - 1| = x$

A. I, II, and III

B. I and III only

C. I only

D. III only

(Easy) (Skill 5.1)

47. The following chart shows the yearly average number of international tourists visiting Palm Beach for 1990-1994. How many more international tourists visited Palm Beach in 1994 than in 1991?

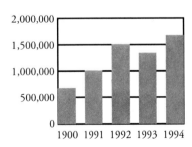

A. 100,000

B. 600,000

C. 1,600,000

D. 8,000,000

(Easy) (Skill 5.1)

48. Consider the graph of the distribution of the length of time it took individuals to complete an employment form.

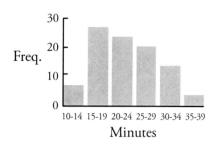

Approximately how many individuals took less than 15 minutes to complete the employment form?

A. 35

B. 28

C. 7

D. 4

(Easy) (Skill 5.1)

49. Which statement is true about George's budget?

A. George spends the greatest portion of his income on food

B. George spends twice as much on utilities as he does on his mortgage

C. George spends twice as much on utilities as he does on food

D. George spends the same amount on food and utilities as he does on mortgage

(Easy) (Skill 5.3)

50. Find the mean of the following numbers. Round to the nearest tenth.

92.7, 33.4, 17.8, 87.2, 143.1

A. 74.9

B. 75

C. 74.8

D. 70

(Average) (Skill 5.3)

51. What is the mode of the data in the following sample?

9, 10, 11, 9, 10, 11, 9, 13

A. 9

B. 9.5

C. 10

D. 11

(Rigorous) (Skill 5.3)

52. Mary did comparison shopping on her favorite brand of coffee. Over half of the stores priced the coffee at $1.70. Most of the remaining stores priced the coffee at $1.80, except for a few who charged $1.90. Which of the following statements about the distribution of prices is true?

A. The mean and the mode are the same

B. The mean is greater than the mode

C. The mean is less than the mode

D. The mean is less than the median

(Rigorous) (Skill 5.4)

53. Corporate salaries are listed for several employees. Which is the best measure of central tendency?

$24,000, $24,000, $26,000, $28,000, $30,000, $120,000

A. Mean

B. Median

C. Mode

D. There is no best measure

(Rigorous) (Skill 5.5)

54. The table below shows the distribution of majors for a group of college students.

MAJOR	PROPORTION OF STUDENTS
Mathematics	0.32
Photography	0.26
Journalism	0.19
Engineering	0.21
Criminal Law	0.02

If we know that a student, chosen at random, is not majoring in mathematics or engineering, what is the probability that the student is majoring in journalism?

A. 0.19

B. 0.36

C. 0.40

D. 0.81

(Rigorous) (Skill 5.5)

55. What is the probability of drawing two consecutive aces from a standard deck of cards?

A. $\frac{3}{51}$

B. $\frac{1}{221}$

C. $\frac{2}{104}$

D. $\frac{2}{52}$

(Rigorous) (Skill 5.5)

56. A drawer contains 5 black socks, 3 blue socks, and 2 red socks. Without looking at the socks you draw, what is the probability that you will draw two black socks in two draws?

A. $\frac{2}{9}$

B. $\frac{1}{4}$

C. $\frac{17}{18}$

D. $\frac{1}{18}$

Answer Key: Mathematics

1. A	11. B	21. A	31. C	41. B	51. A
2. C	12. A	22. C	32. B	42. C	52. B
3. C	13. C	23. B	33. D	43. B	53. B
4. D	14. C	24. C	34. D	44. A	54. C
5. D	15. B	25. C	35. D	45. B	55. B
6. A	16. C	26. B	36. C	46. C	56. A
7. C	17. B	27. D	37. B	47. B	
8. C	18. B	28. A	38. B	48. C	
9. B	19. A	29. D	39. B	49. C	
10. D	20. A	30. C	40. B	50. C	

Rigor Table

RIGOR TABLE		
Rigor level	**Questions**	**TOTALS**
Easy 20%	1, 2, 4, 15, 22, 30, 31, 47, 48, 49, 50	11 (19.64%)
Average Rigor 40%	3, 5, 6, 7, 8, 9, 10, 11, 12, 18, 19, 23, 24, 28, 29, 32, 33, 35, 36, 38, 40, 42, 43, 51	23 (41.1%)
Rigorous 40%	13, 14, 16, 17, 20, 21, 25, 26, 27, 34, 37, 39, 41, 44, 45, 46, 52, 53, 54, 55, 56	22 (39.3%)

Sample Test with Rationales: Mathematics

(Easy) (Skill 1.1)

1. 0.74 =

   A. $\frac{74}{100}$

   B. 7.4%

   C. $\frac{33}{50}$

   D. $\frac{74}{10}$

   Answer: A. $\frac{74}{100}$

   In 0.74, the 4 is in the hundredths place, so the answer is $\frac{74}{100}$.

(Easy) (Skill 1.1)

2. Identify the missing term in the following harmonic sequence: $\frac{1}{3}, \frac{1}{6}, \frac{1}{9}, \frac{1}{12}, \frac{1}{15}, ?$

   A. $\frac{1}{16}$

   B. $\frac{1}{17}$

   C. $\frac{1}{18}$

   D. 18

   Answer: C. $\frac{1}{18}$

   The difference between the denominators is 3, so the next term in the progression is $\frac{1}{18}$.

(Average) (Skill 1.1)

3. Choose the set in which the members are not equivalent.

   A. $\frac{1}{2}$, 0.5, 50%

   B. $\frac{10}{5}$, 2.0, 200%

   C. $\frac{3}{8}$, 0.385, 38.5%

   D. $\frac{7}{10}$, 0.7, 70%

   Answer: C. $\frac{3}{8}$, 0.385, 38.5%

   $\frac{3}{8}$ is equivalent to .375 and 37.5%.

(Easy) (Skill 1.2)

4. 303 is what percent of 600?

   A. 0.505%

   B. 5.05%

   C. 505%

   D. 50.5%

   Answer: D. 50.5%

   Use x to represent the percent.
   $600x = 303$.
   $\frac{600x}{600} = \frac{303}{600} \rightarrow x = 0.505 = 50.5\%$

(Average) (Skill 1.2)

5. $\left(\frac{-4}{9}\right) + \left(\frac{-7}{10}\right) =$

   A. $\frac{23}{90}$

   B. $\frac{-23}{90}$

   C. $\frac{103}{90}$

   D. $\frac{-103}{90}$

   Answer: D. $\frac{-103}{90}$

   Find the LCD of $\frac{-4}{9}$ and $\frac{-7}{10}$. The LCD is 90, so you get $\frac{-40}{90} + \frac{-63}{90} = \frac{-103}{90}$.

(Average) (Skill 1.2)

6. $(5.6) \times (-0.11) =$

   A. -0.616

   B. 0.616

   C. -6.110

   D. 6.110

   Answer: A. -0.616

   This problem involves simple multiplication. The answer will be negative because a positive number times a negative number is a negative number. $5.6 \times -0.11 = -0.616$.

(Average) (Skill 1.2)

7. An item that sells for $375 is put on sale for $120. What is the percent of discount?

   A. 25%

   B. 28%

   C. 68%

   D. 34%

Answer: C. 68%

Use $(1 - x)$ as the discount. $375x = 120$. $375(1 - x) = 120 \rightarrow 375 - 375x = 120 \rightarrow 375x = 255 \rightarrow x = 0.68 = 68\%$.

(Average) (Skill 1.2)

8. Two mathematics classes have a total of 410 students. The 8:00 am class has 40 more than the 10:00 am class. How many students are in the 10:00 am class?

   A. 123.3

   B. 370

   C. 185

   D. 330

Answer: C. 185

Let x = # of students in the 8 am class and $x - 40$ = # of students in the 10 am class. $x + (x - 40) = 410 \rightarrow 2x - 40 = 410 \rightarrow 2x = 450 \rightarrow x = 225$. So there are 225 students in the 8 am class, and $225 - 40 = 185$ in the 10 am class.

(Average) (Skill 1.2)

9. A restaurant employs 465 people. There are 280 waiters and 185 cooks. If 168 waiters and 85 cooks receive pay raises, what percent of the waiters receive a pay raise?

   A. 36.13%

   B. 60%

   C. 60.22%

   D. 40%

Answer: B. 60%

The total number of waiters is 280 and only 168 of them receive a pay raise. Divide the number who receive a raise by the total number of waiters to get the answer. $\frac{168}{280} = 0.6 = 60\%$.

(Average) (Skill 1.2)

10. $\frac{7}{9} + \frac{1}{3} \div \frac{2}{3} =$

    A. $\frac{5}{3}$

    B. $\frac{3}{2}$

    C. 2

    D. $\frac{23}{18}$

Answer: D. $\frac{23}{18}$

First, do the division.
$\frac{1}{3} \div \frac{2}{3} = \frac{1}{3} \times \frac{3}{2} = \frac{1}{2}$
Add.
$\frac{7}{9} + \frac{1}{2} = \frac{14}{18} + \frac{9}{18} = \frac{23}{18}$.

(Average) (Skill 1.2)

11. The price of gas is $3.27 per gallon. Your tank holds 15 gallons of fuel. You are using two tanks of gas a week. Approximately how much will you save each week if the price of gas goes down to $2.30 per gallon?

    A. $26.00

    B. $29.00

    C. $15.00

    D. $17.00

Answer: B. $29.00

15 gallons × 2 tanks = 30 gallons a week
= 30 gallons × $3.27 = $98.10
30 gallons × $2.30 = $69.00
$98.10 − $69.00 = $29.10 is approximately $29.00.

(Average) (Skill 1.2)

12. **Choose the statement that is true for all real numbers.**

    A. $a = 0$, $b \neq 0$, then $\frac{b}{a}$ = undefined

    B. $-(a + (-a)) = 2a$

    C. $2(ab) = -(2a)b$

    D. $-a(b + 1) = ab - a$

    Answer: A. $a = 0$, $b \neq 0$,
    then $\frac{b}{a}$ = undefined.

    Option A is the correct answer because any number divided by 0 is undefined.

(Rigorous) (Skill 1.2)

13. **In a sample of 40 full-time employees at a particular company, 35 are also working a part-time job requiring at least 10 hours per week. If this proportion holds true for the entire company of 25,000 employees, how many full-time employees at this company are also working a part-time job at least 10 hours per week?**

    A. 714

    B. 625

    C. 21,875

    D. 28,571

    Answer: C. 21,875

$\frac{35}{40}$ full time employees have a part time job also. Out of 25,000 full time employees, the number that also have a part time job is $\frac{35}{40} = \frac{x}{25000} \rightarrow 40x = 875000 \rightarrow x = 21875$, so 21,875 full time employees also have a part time job.

(Rigorous) (Skill 1.2)

14. $4\frac{2}{9} \times \frac{7}{10} =$

    A. $4\frac{9}{10}$

    B. $\frac{266}{90}$

    C. $2\frac{43}{45}$

    D. $2\frac{6}{20}$

    Answer: C. $2\frac{43}{45}$

    Convert any mixed number to an improper fraction: $\frac{38}{9} \times \frac{7}{10}$. Since there are no common factors of the numerators or denominators, multiply the numerators and the denominators by each other $= \frac{266}{90}$. Convert back to a mixed number and reduce $2\frac{86}{90} = 2\frac{43}{45}$.

(Easy) (Skill 1.3)

15. **What is the greatest common factor of 16, 28, and 36?**

    A. 2

    B. 4

    C. 8

    D. 16

    Answer: B. 4

    The smallest number in this set is 16. Its factors are 1, 2, 4, 8, and 16. 16 is the largest factor, but it does not divide into 28 or 36. 8 does not divide into 28 or 36 either. 4 is the smallest factor of 16 that factors into both 28 and 36.

(Rigorous) (Skill 1.3)

16. $(-2.1 \times 10^4)(4.2 \times 10^{-5}) =$

    A. 8.82

    B. -8.82

    C. -0.882

    D. 0.882

    Answer: C. -0.882

    First, multiply -2.1 by 4.2 to get -8.82. Then, multiply 10^4 by 10^{-5} to get 10^{-1}. $-8.82 \times 10^{-1} = -0.882$.

(Rigorous) (Skill 1.3)

17. $\frac{2^{10}}{2^5} =$

    A. 2^2

    B. 2^5

    C. 2^{50}

    D. $2^{\frac{1}{2}}$

    Answer: B. 2^5

    The quotient rule of exponents says $\frac{a^m}{a^n} = a^{(m-n)}$ so $\frac{2^{10}}{2^5} = 2^{(10-5)} = 2^5$.

(Average) (Skill 1.4)

18. Choose the expression that is *not* equivalent to $5x + 3y + 15z$:

    A. $5(x + 3z) + 3y$

    B. $3(x + y + 5z)$

    C. $3y + 5(x + 3z)$

    D. $5x + 3(y + 5z)$

Answer: B. $3(x + y + 5z)$

$5x + 3y + 15z = (5x + 15z) + 3y = 5(x + 3z) + 3y$ A is equivalent

$= 5x + (3y + 15z) = 5x + 3(y + 5z)$ D is equivalent

$= 37 + (5x + 15z) = 37 + 5(x + 3z)$ C is equivalent

We can solve all of these using the associative property and then factoring. However, in B $3(x + y + 5z)$ by distributive property $= 3x + 3y + 15z$, which does not equal $5x + 37 + 15z$.

(Average) (Skill 1.4)

19. A sofa sells for $520. If the retailer makes a 30% profit, what is the whole-sale price?

    A. $400

    B. $676

    C. $490

    D. $364

Answer: A. $400

Let x be the wholesale price; then $x + .30x = 520$. $1.30x = 520$. Divide both sides by 1.30 to get $400.

(Rigorous) (Skill 1.4)

20. $(3 \times 9)^4 =$

    A. $(3 \times 9)(3 \times 9)(27 \times 27)$

    B. $(3 \times 9) + (3 \times 9)$

    C. (12×36)

    D. $(3 \times 9) + (3 \times 9) + (3 \times 9) + (3 \times 9)$

Answer: A. $(3 \times 9)(3 \times 9)(27 \times 27)$

$(3 \times 9)^4 = (3 \times 9)(3 \times 9)(3 \times 9)$ (3×9), which, when solving two of the parentheses, is $(3 \times 9)(3 \times 9)$ (27×27).

(Rigorous) (Skill 1.4)

21. **Choose the equation that is equivalent to the following:** $\frac{3x}{5} - 5 = 5x$

A. $3x - 25 = 25x$

B. $x - \frac{25}{3} = 25x$

C. $6x - 50 = 75x$

D. $x + 25 = 25x$

Answer: A. $3x - 25 = 25x$

Option A is correct because it is the original equation multiplied by 5. The other choices alter the answer to the original equation.

(Easy) (Skill 2.1)

22. **What unit of measurement could we use to record the distance traveled walking around a track?**

A. Degrees

B. Square meters

C. Kilometers

D. Cubic feet

Answer: C. Kilometers

Degrees measure angles, square meters measure area, cubic feet measure volume, and kilometers measure length. Kilometers is the only appropriate answer.

(Average) (Skill 2.1)

23. **What is the area of a square with a side measuring 13 feet?**

A. 169 feet

B. 169 square feet

C. 52 feet

D. 52 square feet

Answer: B. 169 square feet

Area = length times width (lw)
Length = 13 feet
Width = 13 feet, because the four sides of a square are always equivalent.
Area = $13 \times 13 = 169$ square feet (area is measured in square feet).

(Average) (Skill 2.1)

24. **What is the circumference of a circle with a diameter of 4 meters?**

A. 6.28 m

B. 25.12 m

C. 12.56 m

D. None of the above

Answer: C. 12.56 m

Since the diameter of the circle is 4 meters, use $C = \pi d$. $C = (3.14)(4) = 12.6$ meters.

(Rigorous) (Skill 2.1)

25. **What is the area of this triangle?**

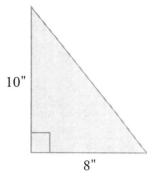

10"

8"

  A. 80 square inches

  B. 20 square inches

  C. 40 square inches

  D. 30 square inches

Answer: C. 40 square inches

The area of a triangle is $\frac{1}{2}bh$.
$\frac{1}{2} \times 8 \times 10 = 40$ square inches.

(Rigorous) (Skill 2.1)

26. **The trunk of a tree has a 2.1 meter radius. What is its circumference?**

  A. 2.1π square meters

  B. 4.2π meters

  C. 2.1π meters

  D. 4.2π square meters

Answer: B. 4.2π meters

Circumference is $2\pi r$, where r is the radius. The circumference is $2\pi 2.1 = 4.2\pi$ meters (not square meters because we are not measuring area).

(Rigorous) (Skill 2.1)

27. **The figure below shows a running track and the shape of an inscribed rectangle with semicircles at each end.**

Calculate the distance around the track.

  A. $6\pi y + 14x$

  B. $3\pi y + 7x$

  C. $6\pi y + 7x$

  D. $3\pi y + 14x$

Answer: D. $3\pi y + 14x$

The two semicircles of the track create one circle with a diameter $3y$. The circumference of a circle is $C = \pi d$ so $C = 3\pi y$. The length of both sides of the track is $7x$ each side, so the total circumference around the track is $3\pi y + 7x + 7x = 3\pi y + 14x$

(Average) (Skill 2.2)

28. **What unit of measurement could be used to describe the spread of a forest fire in a unit time?**

  A. 10 square yards per second

  B. 10 yards per minute

  C. 10 feet per hour

  D. 10 cubit feet per hour

Answer: A. 10 square yards per second

The only appropriate answer is one that describes an *area* of forest consumed per unit time. Only answer A is a unit of area measurement.

(Average) (Skill 2.2)

29. Given the formula $d = rt$, (where $d =$ distance, $r =$ rate, and $t =$ time), calculate the time required for a vehicle to travel 585 miles at a rate of 65 miles per hour.

    A. 8.5 hours

    B. 6.5 hours

    C. 9.5 hours

    D. 9 hours

    Answer: D. 9 hours

    We are given $d = 585$ miles and $r = 65$ miles per hour and $d = rt$. Solve for t. $585 = 65t \rightarrow t = 9$ hours.

(Easy) (Skill 2.4)

30. A teacher spends 45 minutes per day reading and replying to email messages. How many hours does the teacher devote to email correspondence during a five-day workweek?

    A. 4.25 hours

    B. 3.25 hours

    C. 3.75 hours

    D. 3.50 hours

    Answer: C. 3.75 hours

    45 minutes $\times$ 5 days = 225 minutes
    $\frac{225 \text{ minutes}}{60 \text{ minutes in an hour}} = 3.75$ hours.

(Easy) (Skill 2.5)

31. Round $1\frac{13}{16}$ of an inch to the nearest quarter of an inch.

    A. $1\frac{1}{4}$ inch

    B. $1\frac{5}{8}$ inch

    C. $1\frac{3}{4}$ inch

    D. 2 inches

Answer: C. $1\frac{3}{4}$ inch

$1\frac{13}{16}$ inches is approximately $1\frac{12}{16}$, which is also $1\frac{3}{4}$, which is the nearest $\frac{1}{4}$ of an inch.

(Average) (Skill 2.5)

32. A car gets 25.36 miles per gallon. The car has been driven 83,310 miles. What is a reasonable estimate of the total number of gallons of gas the car has used?

    A. 2,087 gallons

    B. 3,000 gallons

    C. 1,800 gallons

    D. 164 gallons

Answer: B. 3,000 gallons

Divide the number of miles by the miles per gallon to determine the approximate number of gallons of gas used. $\frac{83310 \text{ miles}}{25.36 \text{ miles per gallon}} = 3285$ gallons. This is approximately 3,000 gallons.

(Average) (Skill 2.5)

33. Estimate $5{,}743 - 318$ by front-end estimation.

    A. 5,430

    B. 5,420

    C. 5,425

    D. 5,400

Answer: D. 5,400

Using front-end estimation, $5{,}743 - 318 = 5{,}400$. Because 318 does not have a digit in the thousands place but 5,743 does, convert 318 to 300, not 310 or 320.

(Rigorous) (Skill 2.5)

34. The owner of a rectangular piece of land 40 yards in length and 30 yards in width wants to divide it into two parts. She plans to join two opposite corners with a fence as shown in the diagram below. The cost of the fence will be approximately $25 per linear foot. What is the estimated total cost for the fence?

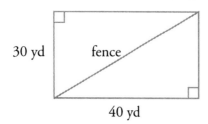

30 yd

fence

40 yd

A. $1,250

B. $62,500

C. $5,250

D. $3,750

Answer: D. $3,750

Find the length of the diagonal by using the Pythagorean theorem. Let x be the length of the diagonal.

$30^2 + 40^2 = x^2 \rightarrow 900 + 1600 = x^2$

$2500 = x^2 \rightarrow \sqrt{2500} = \sqrt{x^2}$

$x = 50$ yards

Convert to feet.

$\frac{50 \text{ yards}}{x \text{ feet}} = \frac{1 \text{ yard}}{3 \text{ feet}} \rightarrow 1500$ feet

The fence costs $25 per linear foot, so the cost is (1500 ft)($25) = $3,750.

(Average) (Skill 3.1)

35. What type of triangle is △ ABC?

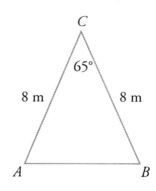

A. Right

B. Equilateral

C. Scalene

D. Isosceles

Answer: D. Isosceles

Two of the sides are the same length, so we know the triangle is either equilateral or isosceles. $\angle CAB$ and $\angle CBA$ are equal, because their sides are of equal length. Therefore, $180° = 65° - 2x = \frac{115°}{2} = 57.5°$. Because all three angles are not equal, the triangle is isosceles, not equilateral.

(Average) (Skill 3.1)

36. Consider the following statements:

I. All parallelograms are rectangles

II. Some rhombi are squares

A. Both statements are correct

B. Both statements are incorrect

C. Only statement II is correct

D. Only statement I is correct

Answer: C. Only statement II is correct

Statement I is false because only some parallelograms are rectangles.

(Rigorous) (Skill 3.1)

37. **Study figures A through D. Select the letter in which all triangles are similar.**

A.

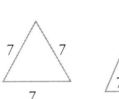

B.

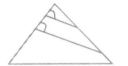

C.

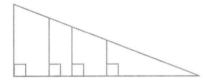

D.

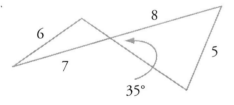

Answer: B.

Choice A is not correct because one triangle is equilateral and the other is isosceles. Choice C is not correct because the two smaller triangles are similar, but the larger triangle is not. Choice D is not correct because the lengths of the sides

and the angles are not proportional to each other. Therefore, the correct answer is B because all the triangles in this choice have the same angles.

(Average) (Skill 3.2)

38. **At the lake, the ratio is 16 ducks to 9 geese. Suppose there are 192 ducks. How many geese are there?**

A. 21

B. 108

C. 7

D. 1,728

Answer: B. 108

Set up the proportion: $\frac{16}{9} = \frac{192}{g}$.
Solve for g.
$16g = (192)(9)$
$16g = 1728$
$g = 108$

(Rigorous) (Skill 3.2)

39. **Which formula would you use to find the length of the hypotenuse in the figure shown below?**

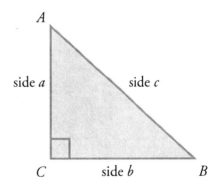

A. $(\frac{1}{2})bh$

B. $c^2 = a^2 + b^2$

C. $\frac{1}{2}h(b_1 + b_2)$

D. None of the above

Answer: B. $c^2 = a^2 + b^2$

Option A is the formula for finding the area of a triangle, while option C is the formula for the area of a trapezoid. Option B is the Pythagorean theorem, used to find the length of one side of a right triangle given the lengths of the other two sides.

(Average) (Skill 3.3)

40. **Find the slope of a line with points at (5, 3) and (8, 9).**

    A. $\frac{12}{13}$

    B. 2.0

    C. $\frac{27}{13}$

    D. −2.0

Answer: B. 2.0

Use the formula: slope $= \frac{y_2 - y_1}{x_2 - x_1}$.

$\frac{(9) - (3)}{(8) - (5)} = \frac{6}{3}$ This is rise over run. Solve for slope: $\frac{6}{3} = 2.0$.

(Rigorous) (Skill 3.3)

41. **What is the equation that expresses the relationship between x and y in the table below?**

x	-2	-1	0	1	2
y	4	1	-2	-5	-8

    A. $y = -x - 2$

    B. $y = -3x - 2$

    C. $y = 3x - 2$

    D. $y = \frac{1}{3}x - 1$

Answer: B. $y = -3x - 2$

Solve by plugging the values of x and y into the equations to see if they work. The answer is B because it is the only equation for which the values of x and y are correct.

(Average) (Skill 4.3)

42. **If $4x - (3 - x) = 7(x - 3) + 10$, then:**

    A. $x = 8$

    B. $x = -8$

    C. $x = 4$

    D. $x = -4$

Answer: C. $x = 4$

Solve for x.
$$4x - (3 - x) = 7(x - 3) + 10$$
$$4x - 3 + x = 7x - 21 + 10$$
$$5x - 3 = 7x - 11$$
$$5x = 7x - 11 + 3$$
$$5x - 7x = -8$$
$$-2x = -8$$
$$x = 4$$

(Average) (Skill 4.3)

43. **Solve for x: $3(5 + 3x) - 8 = 88$**

    A. 30

    B. 9

    C. 4.5

    D. 27

Answer: B. 9

$$3(5 + 3x) - 8 = 88$$
$$15 + 9x - 8 = 88$$
$$7 + 9x = 88$$
$$9x = 81$$
$$x = 9$$

(Rigorous) (Skill 4.3)

44. $3x - \frac{2}{3} = \frac{5x}{2} + 2$. Solve for x.

   A. $5\frac{1}{3}$

   B. $\frac{17}{3}$

   C. 2

   D. $\frac{16}{2}$

   Answer: A. $5\frac{1}{3}$

   $3x(6) - \frac{2}{3}(6) = \frac{5x}{2}(6) + 2(6)$
   6 is the LCD of 2 and 3
   $18x - 4 = 15x + 12$
   $18x = 15x + 16$
   $3x = 16$
   $x = \frac{16}{3} = 5\frac{1}{3}$

(Rigorous) (Skill 4.3)

45. **What is the x-intercept of the line represented by $4x + 2y = 12$?**

   A. $(0, 6)$

   B. $(3, 0)$

   C. $(0, 3)$

   D. $(0, 8)$

   Answer: B. $(3, 0)$

   Let $y = 0$ and solve for x:
   $4x + 2(0) = 12$
   $4x + 0 = 12$
   $4x = 12$
   $x = 3$
   $(3, 0)$ is the x-intercept

(Rigorous) (Skill 4.4)

46. **For each of the statements below, determine whether $x = \frac{1}{6}$ is a solution.**

   I. $6x \leq\ = 4x^2 + 2$

   II. $10x + 1 = 3(4x - 3)$

   III. $|x - 1| = x$

A. I, II, and III

B. I and III only

C. I only

D. III only

Answer: C. I only

Substitute $x = \frac{1}{6}$ into each equation and solve.

I. $6\left(\frac{1}{6}\right) \leq 4\left(\frac{1}{6}\right)^2 + 2 = 1 \leq 4\left(\frac{1}{36}\right) + 2 \rightarrow$
$1 \leq \frac{1}{9} + 2 \rightarrow 1 \leq 2\frac{1}{9}$ True.

II. $10\left(\frac{1}{6}\right) + 1 = 3\left(4\left(\frac{1}{6}\right) - 3\right) = 2\frac{2}{3}$
$= 3\left(\frac{2}{3} - 3\right) \rightarrow 2\frac{2}{3} = \frac{6}{3} - 9 \rightarrow 2\frac{2}{3} = -7$
          False.

III. $\left|\frac{1}{6} - 1\right| = \frac{1}{6} \rightarrow \left|\frac{1}{6} - \frac{6}{6}\right| = \frac{1}{6} \rightarrow \left|\frac{-5}{6}\right|$
$= \frac{1}{6} \rightarrow \frac{5}{6} = \frac{1}{6}$ False.

(Easy) (Skill 5.1)

47. **The following chart shows the yearly average number of international tourists visiting Palm Beach for 1990-1994. How many more international tourists visited Palm Beach in 1994 than in 1991?**

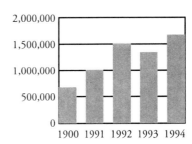

A. 100,000

B. 600,000

C. 1,600,000

D. 8,000,000

Answer: B. 600,000

The number of tourists in 1991 was 1,000,000 and the number in 1994 was 1,600,000. Subtract to get a difference of 600,000.

(Easy) (Skill 5.1)

48. **Consider the graph of the distribution of the length of time it took individuals to complete an employment form.**

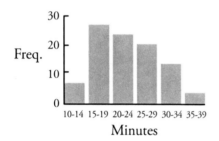

Approximately how many individuals took less than 15 minutes to complete the employment form?

A. 35

B. 28

C. 7

D. 4

Answer: C. 7

According to the chart, the number of people who took under 15 minutes is 7.

(Easy) (Skill 5.1)

49. **Which statement is true about George's budget?**

A. George spends the greatest portion of his income on food

B. George spends twice as much on utilities as he does on his mortgage

C. George spends twice as much on utilities as he does on food

D. George spends the same amount on food and utilities as he does on mortgage

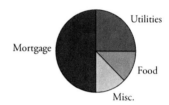

Answer: C. George spends twice as much on utilities as he does on food.

The wedge representing utilities is twice as large as the wedge representing food.

(Easy) (Skill 5.3)

50. **Find the mean of the following numbers. Round to the nearest tenth.**

92.7, 33.4, 17.8, 87.2, 143.1

A. 74.9

B. 75

C. 74.8

D. 70

Answer: C. 74.8

Add all the numbers: 92.7 + 33.4 + 17.8 + 87.2 + 143.1 = 374.2
Divide the sum by the number of items in the set: 374.2/5 = 74.84.
Round down to the nearest tenth to get 74.8.

(Average) (Skill 5.3)

51. What is the mode of the data in the following sample?

    9, 10, 11, 9, 10, 11, 9, 13

    A. 9

    B. 9.5

    C. 10

    D. 11

    Answer: A. 9

    The mode is the number that appears most frequently in a set. The number 9 appears three times, which is more frequently than the other numbers.

(Rigorous) (Skill 5.3)

52. Mary did comparison shopping on her favorite brand of coffee. Over half of the stores priced the coffee at $1.70. Most of the remaining stores priced the coffee at $1.80, except for a few who charged $1.90. Which of the following statements about the distribution of prices is true?

    A. The mean and the mode are the same

    B. The mean is greater than the mode

    C. The mean is less than the mode

    D. The mean is less than the median

    Answer: B. The mean is greater than the mode.

    Over half the stores priced the coffee at $1.70, so this is the mode. The mean is slightly over $1.70 because other stores priced the coffee at over $1.70.

(Rigorous) (Skill 5.4)

53. Corporate salaries are listed for several employees. Which is the best measure of central tendency?

    $24,000, $24,000, $26,000, $28,000, $30,000, $120,000

    A. Mean

    B. Median

    C. Mode

    D. There is no best measure

    Answer: B. Median

    The median provides the best measure of central tendency in this case because the mode is the lowest number and the mean is disproportionately skewed by the outlier $120,000.

(Rigorous) (Skill 5.5)

54. The table below shows the distribution of majors for a group of college students.

MAJOR	PROPORTION OF STUDENTS
Mathematics	0.32
Photography	0.26
Journalism	0.19
Engineering	0.21
Criminal Law	0.02

If we know that a student, chosen at random, is not majoring in mathematics or engineering, what is the probability that the student is majoring in journalism?

A. 0.19

B. 0.36

C. 0.40

D. 0.81

Answer: C. 0.40

The proportion of students majoring in math or engineering is 0.32 + 0.21 = 0.53. This means that the proportion of students not majoring in math or engineering is 1.00 − 0.53 = 0.47. The proportion of students majoring in journalism out of those not majoring in math or engineering is $\frac{0.19}{0.47}$ = 0.404.

(Rigorous) (Skill 5.5)

55. **What is the probability of drawing two consecutive aces from a standard deck of cards?**

A. $\frac{3}{51}$

B. $\frac{1}{221}$

C. $\frac{2}{104}$

D. $\frac{2}{52}$

Answer: B. $\frac{1}{221}$

There are 4 aces in the 52 card deck. $P(\text{first ace}) = \frac{4}{52}$. $P(\text{second ace}) = \frac{3}{51}$. $P(\text{first ace and second ace}) = P(\text{first ace}) \times P(\text{second ace}) = \frac{4}{52} \times \frac{3}{51} = \frac{1}{221}$.

(Rigorous) (Skill 5.5)

56. **A drawer contains 5 black socks, 3 blue socks, and 2 red socks. Without looking at the socks you draw, what is the probability that you will draw two black socks in two draws?**

A. $\frac{2}{9}$

B. $\frac{1}{4}$

C. $\frac{17}{18}$

D. $\frac{1}{18}$

Answer: A. $\frac{2}{9}$

In this example of conditional probability, the probability of drawing a black sock on the first draw is $\frac{5}{10}$. The problem implies that there is no replacement, so the probability of drawing a black sock on the second draw is $\frac{4}{9}$. Multiply the two probabilities and reduce to lowest terms.

SAMPLE TEST

English

DIRECTIONS: Choose the underlined word or phrase that is unnecessary within the context of the passage.

(Easy) (Skill 7.1)

1. The <u>expanding</u> number of television channels has <u>prompted</u> cable operators to raise their prices, <u>even though</u> many consumers do not want to pay a higher <u>increased</u> amount for their service.

    A. expanding

    B. prompted

    C. even though

    D. increased

(Average) (Skill 7.1)

2. <u>Considered by many to be</u> one of the worst <u>terrorist</u> incidents <u>on American soil</u> was the bombing of the Oklahoma City Federal Building, which will be remembered <u>for years to come</u>.

    A. Considered by many to be

    B. terrorist

    C. on American soil

    D. for years to come

(Average) (Skill 7.1)

3. The <u>flu</u> epidemic struck <u>most of</u> the <u>respected</u> faculty and students of The Woolbright School, forcing the Boynton Beach School Superintendent to close it down <u>for two weeks</u>.

    A. flu

    B. most of

    C. respected

    D. for two weeks

(Average) (Skill 7.1)

4. Many of the clubs in Boca Raton are noted for their _____ elegance.

    A. vulgar

    B. tasteful

    C. ordinary

(Average) (Skill 7.1)

5. When a student is expelled from school, the parents are usually _____ in advance.

    A. rewarded

    B. congratulated

    C. notified

(Average) (Skill 7.1)

6. Before appearing in court, the witness was _____ the papers requiring her to show up.

    A. condemned

    B. served

    C. criticized

(Average) (Skill 7.1)

7. Because George's _____ bothering him, he apologized forcrashing his father's car.

    A. feelings were

    B. conscience was

    C. guiltiness was

(Rigorous) (Skill 7.1)

8. The charity art auction _____ every year at Mizner Park includes a wide selection of artists showcasing their work.

    A. attended

    B. presented

    C. displayed

DIRECTIONS: For the underlined sentence(s), choose the option that expresses the meaning with the most fluency and the clearest logic within the context. If the underlined sentence should not be changed, Choose Option A, which shows no change.

(Average) (Skill 7.1)

9. John wanted to join his friends on the mountain-climbing trip. <u>Seeing that the weather had become dark and stormy, John knew he would stay safe indoors.</u>

    A. Seeing that the weather had become dark and stormy, John knew he would stay safe indoors.

    B. The weather had become dark and stormy, and John knew he would stay indoors, and he would be safe.

    C. Because the weather had become dark and stormy, John knew he would stay indoors, where he would be safe.

    D. Because the weather had become dark, as well as stormy, John knew he would stay safe indoors.

(Average) (Skill 7.1)

10. A few hours later, the storm subsided, so John left the cabin to join his friends. <u>Even though he was tired from the four-mile hike the day before; he climbed the mountain in a few hours.</u>

    A. Even though he was tired from the four-mile hike the day before, he climbed the mountain in a few hours.

    B. He was tired from the four-mile hike the day before; he climbed the mountain in a few hours.

    C. He climbed the mountain in a few hours, John was tired from the four-mile hike the day before.

    D. Seeing as he was tired from the day before, when he went on a four-mile hike, John climbed the mountain in a few hours.

(Rigorous) (Skill 7.1)

11. Selecting members of a President's cabinet can often be an aggravating process. <u>Either there are too many or too few qualified candidates for a certain position, and then they have to be confirmed by the Senate, where there is the possibility of rejection.</u>

    A. Either there are too many or too few qualified candidates for a certain position, and then they have to be confirmed by the Senate, where there is the possibility of rejection.

    B. Qualified candidates for certain positions face the possibility of rejection, when they have to be confirmed by the Senate.

    C. The Senate has to confirm qualified candidates, who face the possibility of rejection.

    D. Because the Senate has to confirm qualified candidates; they face the possibility of rejection.

(Rigorous) (Skill 7.1)

12. Treating patients for drug and/or alcohol abuse is sometimes a difficult process. <u>Even though there are a number of different methods for helping the patient overcome a dependency, there is no way of knowing which is best in the long-run.</u>

    A. Even though there are a number of different methods for helping the patient overcome a dependency, there is no way of knowing which is best in the long-run.

    B. Even though different methods can help a patient overcome a dependency, there is no way to know which is best in the long-run.

    C. Even though there is no way to know which way is best in the long run, patients can overcome their dependencies when they are helped.

    D. There is no way to know which method will help the patient overcome a dependency in the long-run, even though there are many different ones.

(Rigorous) (Skill 7.1)

13. Many factors account for the decline in quality of public education. <u>Overcrowding, budget cutbacks, and societal deterioration which have greatly affected student learning.</u>

    A. Overcrowding, budget cutbacks, and societal deterioration which have greatly affected student learning.

    B. Student learning has been greatly affected by overcrowding, budget cutbacks, and societal deterioration.

    C. Due to overcrowding, budget cutbacks, and societal deterioration, student learning has been greatly affected.

    D. Overcrowding, budget cutbacks, and societal deterioration have affected students learning greatly.

(Easy) (Skill 9.9)

14. Choose the sentence that logically and correctly expresses the comparison.

    A. The Empire State Building in New York is taller than buildings in the city.

    B. The Empire State Building in New York is taller than any other building in the city.

    C. The Empire State Building in New York is tallest than other buildings in the city.

DIRECTIONS: The passage below contains many errors. Read the passage. Then answer each test item by choosing the option that corrects an error in the underlined portion(s). No more than one underlined error will appear in each item. If no error exists, choose "No change is necessary."

Climbing to the top of Mount Everest is an adventure. One which everyone—whether physically fit or not—seems eager to try. The trail stretches for miles, the cold temperatures are usually frigid and brutal.

Climbers must endure severel barriers on the way, including other hikers, steep jagged rocks, and lots of snow. Plus, climbers often find the most grueling part of the trip is their climb back down, just when they are feeling greatly exhausted. Climbers who take precautions are likely to find the ascent less arduous than the unprepared. donning heavy flannel shirts, gloves, and hats, climbers prevented hypothermia, as well as simple frostbite. A pair of rugged boots is also one of the necesities. If climbers are to avoid becoming dehydrated, there is beverages available for them to transport as well.

Once climbers are completely ready to begin their lengthy journey, they can comfortable enjoy the wonderful scenery. Wide rock formations dazzle the observers eyes with shades of gray and white, while the peak forms a triangle that seems to touch the sky. Each of the climbers are reminded of the splendor and magnifisence of Gods great Earth.

(Rigorous) (Skill 8.3)

15. Climbing to the top of Mount Everest is an **adventure. One** which **everyone— whether** physically fit or not—**seems** eager to try.

  A. adventure, one

  B. everyone, whether

  C. seem

  D. No change is necessary

(Rigorous) (Skill 8.3)

16. The **trail** stretches for **miles,** the cold temperatures are **usually** frigid and brutal.

  A. trails

  B. miles;

  C. usual

  D. No change is necessary

(Average) (Skill 9.2)

17. By donning heavy flannel shirts, boots, and **hats, climbers prevented** hypothermia, as well as simple frostbite.

  A. hats climbers

  B. can prevent

  C. hypothermia;

  D. No change is necessary

(Average) (Skills 9.2, 9.4, and 9.11)

18. Plus, climbers often find the most grueling part of the trip is **their** climb back **down, just** when they **are** feeling greatly exhausted.

  A. his

  B. down; just

  C. were

  D. No change is necessary

(Easy) (Skill 9.3)

19. If climbers are to avoid **becoming** dehydrated, there **is** beverages available for **them** to transport as well.

  A. becomming

  B. are

  C. him

  D. No change is necessary

(Rigorous) (Skill 9.3)

20. Each of the climbers **are** reminded of the splendor and **magnificence** of **God's** great Earth.

  A. is

  B. magnifisence

  C. Gods

  D. No change is necessary

(Average) (Skill 9.8)

21. Once climbers are completely prepared for <u>their</u> lengthy <u>journey,</u> <u>they</u> can <u>comfortable</u> enjoy the wonderful scenery.

   A. they're

   B. journey; they

   C. comfortably

   D. No change is necessary

(Average) (Skills 9.9 and 9.11)

22. <u>Climbers who</u> take precautions are likely to find the ascent <u>less difficult</u> <u>than</u> the unprepared.

   A. Climbers, who

   B. least difficult

   C. then

   D. No change is necessary

(Rigorous) (Skill 9.10)

23. Climbers must endure <u>severel</u> barriers <u>on the way, including</u> other <u>hikers</u>, steep jagged rocks, and lots of snow.

   A. several

   B. on the way: including

   C. hikers'

   D. No change is necessary

(Rigorous) (Skill 9.11)

24. A pair of rugged boots <u>is</u> <u>also one</u> of the <u>necesities.</u>

   A. are

   B. also, one

   C. necessities

   D. No change is necessary

(Rigorous) (Skill 9.11)

25. Wide rock formations dazzle the <u>observers eyes</u> with shades of gray and <u>white,</u> <u>while</u> the peak <u>forms</u> a triangle that seems to touch the sky.

   A. observers' eyes

   B. white; while

   C. formed

   D. No change is necessary

DIRECTIONS: The passage below contains several errors. Read the passage. Then answer each test item by choosing the option that corrects an error in the underlined portion(s). No more than one underlined error will appear in each item. If no error exists, choose "No change is necessary."

Every job places different kinds of demands on their employees. For example, whereas such jobs as accounting and bookkeeping require mathematical ability; graphic design requires creative/artistic ability.

Doing good at one job does not usually guarantee success at another. However, one of the elements crucial to all jobs are especially notable: the chance to accomplish a goal.

The accomplishment of the employees vary according to the job. In many jobs the employees become accustom to the accomplishment provided by the work they do every day.

In medicine, for example, all doctors test them selves by treating badly injured or critically ill people. In the operating room, a team of Surgeons, is responsible for operating on many of these patients. In addition to the feeling of accomplishment that the workers achieve, some jobs also give a sense of identity to the employees'. Profesions like law, education, and sales offer huge financial or emotional rewards. Politicians are public servants: who work for the federal and state governments. President obama is basically employed by the American people to make laws and run the country.

Finally; the contributions that employees make to their companies and to the world cannot be taken for granted. Through their work, employees are performing a service for their employers and are contributing something to the world.

(Rigorous) (Skill 9.1)

26. The <u>accomplishment</u> of the <u>employees vary</u> according to the job.

A. accomplishment,

B. employee's

C. varies

D. No change is necessary

(Average) (Skill 9.2)

27. In many jobs the employees <u>become accustom</u> to the accomplishment <u>provided</u> by the work they do every day.

A. became

B. accustomed

C. provides

D. No change is necessary

(Rigorous) (Skill 9.3)

28. <u>However,</u> one of the elements crucial to all jobs <u>are</u> especially <u>notable:</u> the accomplishment of a goal.

A. However

B. is

C. notable;

D. No change is necessary

(Average) (Skill 9.4)

29. In medicine, for example, all doctors <u>test them self</u> by treating badly injured and critically ill people.

A. tests

B. themselves

C. critical

D. No change is necessary

(Rigorous) (Skill 9.4)

30. Every job <u>places</u> different kinds of demands on <u>their</u> <u>employees.</u>

A. place

B. its

C. employes

D. No change is necessary

(Rigorous) (Skill 9.8)

31. Doing <u>good</u> at one job does not <u>usually</u> guarantee <u>success</u> at another.

A. well

B. usualy

C. succeeding

D. No change is necessary

(Average) (Skill 9.10)

32. <u>Profesions</u> like law, <u>education,</u> and sales <u>offer</u> huge financial oremotional rewards.

    A. Professions

    B. education;

    C. offered

    D. No change is necessary

(Easy) (Skill 9.11)

33. Politicians <u>are</u> public <u>servants: who work</u> for the federal and state governments.

    A. were

    B. servants who

    C. worked

    D. No change is necessary

(Average) (Skill 9.11)

34. <u>For example,</u> <u>whereas</u> such jobs as accounting and bookkeeping require mathematical <u>ability;</u> graphic design requires creative/artistic ability.

    A. For example

    B. whereas,

    C. ability,

    D. No change is necessary

(Average) (Skills 9.10 and 9.11)

35. In addition to the feeling of accomplish-ment that the workers <u>achieve,</u> some jobs also <u>give</u> a sense of self-identity to the <u>employees'.</u>

    A. acheive

    B. gave

    C. employees

    D. No change is necessary

(Average) (Skill 9.11)

36. <u>Finally;</u> the contributions that employees make to <u>their</u> companies and to the world cannot be <u>taken</u> for granted.

    A. Finally,

    B. thier

    C. took

    D. No change is necessary

(Easy) (Skill 9.12)

37. In the <u>operating room,</u> a team of <u>Surgeons, is</u> responsible for operating on many of <u>these</u> patients.

    A. operating room:

    B. surgeons is

    C. those

    D. No change is necessary

(Easy) (Skill 9.12)

38. President <u>obama</u> is basically employed <u>by</u> the American people to <u>make</u> laws and run the country.

    A. Obama

    B. to

    C. made

    D. No change is necessary

DIRECTIONS: The passage below contains several errors. Read the passage. Then answer each test item by choosing the option that corrects an error in the underlined portion(s). No more than one underlined error will appear in each item. If no error exists, choose "No change is necessary."

The discovery of a body at Paris Point marina in Boca Raton shocked the residents of Palmetto Pines, a luxury condominium complex located next door to the marina.

The victim is a thirty-five year old woman who had been apparently bludgeoned to death and dumped in the ocean late last night. Many neighbors reported terrible screams, gunshots: as well as the sound of a car backfiring loudly to Boca Raton Police shortly after midnight. The woman had been spotted in the lobby of Palmetto Pines around ten thirty, along with an older man, estimated to be in his fifties, and a younger man, in his late twenties.

"Apparently, the victim had been driven to the complex by the older man, and was seen arguing with him when the younger man intervened," said Sheriff Fred Adams, "all three of them left the building together and walked to the marina, where gunshots rang out an hour later." Deputies found five bullets on the sidewalk and some blood, along with a steel pipe that is assumed to be the murder weapon. Two men were seen fleeing the scene in a red Mercedes short after, rushing toward the Interstate.

The Palm Beach County Coroner, Melvin Watts, said he concluded the victim's skull had been crushed by a blunt tool, which resulted in a brain hemorrhage. As of now, there is no clear motive for the murder.

(Rigorous) (Skill 9.2)

39. The victim <u>is</u> a thirty-five year old who had been apparently <u>bludgeoned</u> to death and dumped in the <u>ocean late</u> last night.

    A. was

    B. bludgoned

    C. ocean: late

    D. No change is necessary

(Rigorous) (Skill 9.2)

40. Deputies found five bullets on the sidewalk and some <u>blood</u>, along with a steel pipe that is <u>assumed</u> <u>to be</u> the murder weapon.

    A. blood;

    B. assuming

    C. to have been

    D. No change is necessary

(Easy) (Skill 9.8)

41. Two men <u>were</u> seen fleeing the scene in a red Mercedes <u>short</u> after, <u>rushing</u> toward the Interstate.

    A. are

    B. shortly

    C. rushed

    D. No change is necessary

(Rigorous) (Skill 9.10)

42. The <u>Palm Beach</u> County <u>Coroner,</u> Kelvin Watts, said he concluded the victim's skull had been crushed by a blunt tool, which resulted in a brain <u>hemorrage</u>.

   A. palm beach

   B. coroner:

   C. hemorrhage

   D. No change is necessary

(Easy) (Skills 9.2, 9.10, and 9.11)

43. As of <u>now,</u> there <u>is</u> no clear motive for the murder.

   A. now;

   B. their

   C. was

   D. No change is necessary

(Rigorous) (Skill 9.11)

44. Many <u>neighbors</u> reported terrible screams, <u>gunshots: as</u> well as the sound of a car backfiring <u>loudly</u> to Boca Raton Police shortly after midnight.

   A. nieghbors

   B. gunshots, as

   C. loud

   D. No change is necessary

(Rigorous) (Skill 9.11)

45. The woman <u>had</u> been spotted in the lobby of Palmetto Pines around ten <u>thirty,</u> along with an older <u>man, estimated</u> to be in his fifties, and a younger man in his late twenties.

   A. has

   B. thirty;

   C. man estimated

   D. No change is necessary

(Average) (Skills 9.11 and 9.12)

46. "Apparently, the victim had been driven to the complex by the older man, and was seen arguing with him when the younger man intervened," said <u>Sheriff Fred Adams, "all</u> three of them left the building together and walked to the marina, when gunshots rang out an hour later."

   A. sheriff Fred Adams, "all

   B. sheriff Fred Adams, "All

   C. Sheriff Fred Adams. "All

   D. No change is necessary

(Easy) (Skill 9.12)

47. The discovery of a body at Paris Point <u>marina</u> in Boca Raton shocked the <u>residents</u> of Palmetto Pines, a luxury <u>condominium</u> complex located next door to the Palmetto marina.

   A. Marina

   B. residence

   C. condomminium

   D. No change is necessary

Answer Key: English

1. D	11. C	21. C	31. A	41. B
2. A	12. B	22. D	32. A	42. C
3. C	13. B	23. A	33. B	43. D
4. B	14. B	24. C	34. C	44. B
5. C	15. A	25. A	35. C	45. C
6. B	16. B	26. C	36. A	46. C
7. B	17. B	27. B	37. B	47. A
8. B	18. D	28. B	38. A	
9. D	19. B	29. B	39. A	
10. A	20. A	30. B	40. C	

Rigor Table

RIGOR TABLE		
Rigor level	**Questions**	**TOTALS**
Easy 20%	1, 14, 19, 33, 37, 38, 41, 43, 47	9 (19.1%)
Average Rigor 40%	2, 3, 4, 5, 6, 7, 9, 10, 17, 18, 21, 22, 27, 29, 32, 34, 35, 36, 46	19 (40.4%)
Rigorous 40%	8, 11, 12, 13, 15, 16, 20, 23, 24, 25, 26, 28, 30, 31, 39, 40, 42, 44, 45	19 (40.4%)

Sample Test with Rationales: English

DIRECTIONS: Choose the underlined word or phrase that is unnecessary within the context of the passage.

(Easy) (Skill 7.1)

1. The <u>expanding</u> number of television channels has <u>prompted</u> cable operators to raise their prices, <u>even though</u> many consumers do not want to pay a higher <u>increased</u> amount for their service.

    A. expanding

    B. prompted

    C. even though

    D. increased

Answer: D. increased

The word *increased* is redundant when used after the word *higher* and should be removed. All the other words are necessary within the context of the sentence.

(Average) (Skill 7.1)

2. <u>Considered by many to be</u> one of the worst <u>terrorist</u> incidents <u>on American soil</u> was the bombing of the Oklahoma City Federal Building, which will be remembered <u>for years to come</u>.

    A. Considered by many to be

    B. terrorist

    C. on American soil

    D. for years to come

Answer: A. Considered by many to be

Considered by many to be is a wordy phrase and unnecessary in the context of the sentence. All other words are necessary within the context of the sentence.

(Average) (Skill 7.1)

3. The <u>flu</u> epidemic struck <u>most of</u> the <u>respected</u> faculty and students of The Woolbright School, forcing the Boynton Beach School Superintendent to close it down <u>for two weeks</u>.

    A. flu

    B. most of

    C. respected

    D. for two weeks

Answer: C. respected

The fact that the faculty might have been *respected* is not necessary to in the purpose of the sentence. The other words and phrases are all necessary to complete the meaning of the sentence.

(Average) (Skill 7.1)

4. Many of the clubs in Boca Raton are noted for their _____ elegance.

    A. vulgar

    B. tasteful

    C. ordinary

Answer: B. tasteful

Tasteful means beautiful or charming, which would correspond to an elegant club. The words *vulgar* and *ordinary* have negative connotations.

(Average) (Skill 7.1)

5. When a student is expelled from school, the parents are usually _____ in advance.

   A. rewarded

   B. congratulated

   C. notified

   Answer: C. notified

   Notified means informed or told, which fits into the logic of the sentence. The words *rewarded* and *congratulated* are positive actions, which don't make sense in the context of an expulsion.

(Average) (Skill 7.1)

6. Before appearing in court, the witness was _____ the papers requiring her to show up.

   A. condemned

   B. served

   C. criticized

   Answer: B. served

   Served means given, which makes sense in the context of the sentence. *Condemned* and *criticized* do not make sense within the context of the sentence.

(Average) (Skill 7.1)

7. Because George's _____ bothering him, he apologized forcrashing his father's car.

   A. feelings were

   B. conscience was

   C. guiltiness was

   Answer: B. conscience was

   Option B shows the correct word choice because a *conscience* would motivate someone to confess. Option A is incorrect because *feelings* is not as accurate as conscience. Option C is incorrect because *guiltiness* is less descriptive of George's motive for confession than conscience.

(Rigorous) (Skill 7.1)

8. The charity art auction _____ every year at Mizner Park includes a wide selection of artists showcasing their work.

   A. attended

   B. presented

   C. displayed

   Answer: B. presented

   The word presented makes more sense in the context of the sentence than *attended* or *displayed*.

DIRECTIONS: For the underlined sentence(s), choose the option that expresses the meaning with the most fluency and the clearest logic within the context. If the underlined sentence should not be changed, Choose Option A, which shows no change.

(Average) (Skill 7.1)

9. John wanted to join his friends on the mountain-climbing trip. <u>Seeing that the weather had become dark and stormy, John knew he would stay safe indoors.</u>

   A. Seeing that the weather had become dark and stormy, John knew he would stay safe indoors.

   B. The weather had become dark and stormy, and John knew he would stay indoors, and he would be safe.

   C. Because the weather had become dark and stormy, John knew he would stay indoors, where he would be safe.

   D. Because the weather had become dark, as well as stormy, John knew he would stay safe indoors.

   Answer: D. Because the weather had become dark, as well as stormy, John knew he would stay safe indoors.

   This sentence best subordinates the idea of dark and stormy weather to John's knowledge. Option A is incorrect because seeing that is an awkward construction. Option B does not subordinate any idea to any other. Option C is incorrect because the idea that John would be safe shouldn't be subordinate to staying indoors.

(Average) (Skill 7.1)

10. A few hours later, the storm subsided, so John left the cabin to join his friends. <u>Even though he was tired from the four-mile hike the day before; he climbed the mountain in a few hours.</u>

    A. Even though he was tired from the four-mile hike the day before, he climbed the mountain in a few hours.

    B. He was tired from the four-mile hike the day before; he climbed the mountain in a few hours.

    C. He climbed the mountain in a few hours, John was tired from the four-mile hike the day before.

    D. Seeing as he was tired from the day before, when he went on a four-mile hike, John climbed the mountain in a few hours.

    Answer: A. Even though he was tired from the four-mile hike the day before, he climbed the mountain in a few hours.

    The idea that John was tired from the four-mile hike the day before is subordinate to the idea of John climbing the mountain. Options B and C do not subordinate the idea of John being tired from the four-mile hike to John climbing the mountain. In Option D, the modifying phrase *Seeing as... before* makes no logical sense in the context of the sentence.

(Rigorous) (Skill 7.1)

11. Selecting members of a President's cabinet can often be an aggravating process. <u>Either there are too many or too few qualified candidates for a certain position, and then they have to be confirmed by the Senate, where there is the possibility of rejection.</u>

    A. Either there are too many or too few qualified candidates for a certain position, and then they have to be confirmed by the Senate, where there is the possibility of rejection.

    B. Qualified candidates for certain positions face the possibility of rejection, when they have to be confirmed by the Senate.

    C. The Senate has to confirm qualified candidates, who face the possibility of rejection.

    D. Because the Senate has to confirm qualified candidates; they face the possibility of rejection.

    Answer: C. The Senate has to confirm qualified candidates, who face the possibility of rejection.

    Option C is the most straightforward and concise sentence. Option A is too unwieldy with the wordy *Either... or* phrase at the beginning. Option B doesn't make it clear that candidates face rejection by the Senate. Option D illogically implies that candidates face rejection because they have to be confirmed by the Senate.

(Rigorous) (Skill 7.1)

12. Treating patients for drug and/or alcohol abuse is sometimes a difficult process. <u>Even though there are a number of different methods for helping the patient overcome a dependency, there is no way of knowing which is best in the long-run.</u>

    A. Even though there are a number of different methods for helping the patient overcome a dependency, there is no way of knowing which is best in the long-run.

    B. Even though different methods can help a patient overcome a dependency, there is no way to know which is best in the long-run.

    C. Even though there is no way to know which way is best in the long run, patients can overcome their dependencies when they are helped.

    D. There is no way to know which method will help the patient overcome a dependency in the long-run, even though there are many different ones.

    Answer: B. Even though different methods can help a patient overcome a dependency, there is no way to know which is best in the long-run.

    Option B is concise and logical. Option A tends to ramble with the use of *there are* and the verbs *helping* and *knowing*. Option C is awkwardly worded and repetitive in the first part of the sentence, and vague in the second part because it never indicates how the patients can be helped. Option D contains the unnecessary phrase *even though there are many different ones.*

(Rigorous) (Skill 7.1)

13. Many factors account for the decline in quality of public education. <u>Overcrowding, budget cutbacks, and societal deterioration which have greatly affected student learning.</u>

    A. Overcrowding, budget cutbacks, and societal deterioration which have greatly affected student learning.

    B. Student learning has been greatly affected by overcrowding, budget cutbacks, and societal deterioration.

    C. Due to overcrowding, budget cutbacks, and societal deterioration, student learning has been greatly affected.

    D. Overcrowding, budget cutbacks, and societal deterioration have affected students learning greatly.

    Answer: B. Student learning has been greatly affected by overcrowding, budget cutbacks, and societal deterioration.

    Option B is concise and best explains the causes of the decline in student learning. The unnecessary use of *which* in Option A makes the sentence feel incomplete. Option C makes a weak connection between the reasons for the decline in public education and the fact that student learning has been affected. Option D incorrectly places the adverb *greatly* after the noun *learning*, instead of before *affected*.

(Easy) (Skill 9.9)

14. Choose the sentence that logically and correctly expresses the comparison.

    A. The Empire State Building in New York is taller than buildings in the city.

    B. The Empire State Building in New York is taller than any other building in the city.

    C. The Empire State Building in New York is tallest than other buildings in the city.

    Answer: B. The Empire State Building in New York is taller than any other building in the city.

    Because the Empire State Building is a building in New York City, the phrase *any other* must be included. Option A is incorrect because the Empire State Building is implicitly compared to itself since it is one of the buildings. Option C is incorrect because *tallest* is the incorrect form of the adjective.

    DIRECTIONS: The passage below contains many errors. Read the passage. Then answer each test item by choosing the option that corrects an error in the underlined portion(s). No more than one underlined error will appear in each item. If no error exists, choose "No change is necessary."

    Climbing to the top of Mount Everest is an adventure. One which everyone—whether physically fit or not—seems eager to try. The trail stretches for miles, the cold temperatures are usually frigid and brutal.

    Climbers must endure severel barriers on the way, including other hikers, steep jagged rocks, and lots of snow. Plus, climbers often find the most grueling part of the trip is their climb back down, just when they are feeling greatly exhausted. Climbers who take precautions are likely to find the ascent less arduous than the unprepared. donning heavy flannel shirts, gloves, and hats, climbers prevented hypothermia, as well as simple frostbite. A pair of rugged boots is also one of the necesities. If climbers are to avoid becoming dehydrated, there is beverages available for them to transport as well.

Once climbers are completely ready to begin their lengthy journey, they can comfortable enjoy the wonderful scenery. Wide rock formations dazzle the observers eyes with shades of gray and white, while the peak forms a triangle that seems to touch the sky. Each of the climbers are reminded of the splendor and magnifisence of Gods great Earth.

(Rigorous) (Skill 8.3)

15. **Climbing to the top of Mount Everest is an <u>adventure. One</u> which <u>everyone— whether</u> physically fit or not—<u>seems</u> eager to try.**

    A. adventure, one

    B. everyone, whether

    C. seem

    D. No change is necessary

    Answer: A. adventure, one

    A comma is needed between *adventure* and one to avoid making the second part of the sentence a fragment. In Option B a comma after *everyone* would not be appropriate when a dash is used on the other side of *not*. In Option C the singular verb *seems* is needed to agree with the singular subject *everyone*.

(Rigorous) (Skill 8.3)

16. **The <u>trail</u> stretches for <u>miles</u>, the cold temperatures are <u>usually</u> frigid and brutal.**

    A. trails

    B. miles;

    C. usual

    D. No change is necessary

    Answer: B. miles;

    A semicolon, not a comma, is needed to separate the first independent clause from the second independent clause. Option A is incorrect because the plural subject *trails* needs the singular verb *stretch*. Option C is incorrect because the adverb form *usually*, not the adjective *usual*, is needed to modify the adjective *frigid*.

(Average) (Skill 9.2)

17. **By donning heavy flannel shirts, boots, and <u>hats, climbers prevented</u> hypothermia, as well as simple frostbite.**

    A. hats climbers

    B. can prevent

    C. hypothermia;

    D. No change is necessary

    Answer: B. can prevent

    The verb *prevented* is in the past tense and must be changed to the present *can prevent* to be consistent. Option A is incorrect because a comma is needed after a long introductory phrase. Option C is incorrect because the semicolon creates a fragment of the phrase *as well as simple frostbite*.

(Average) (Skills 9.2, 9.4, and 9.11)

18. Plus, climbers often find the most grueling part of the trip is <u>their</u> climb back <u>down, just</u> when they <u>are</u> feeling greatly exhausted.

    A. his

    B. down; just

    C. were

    D. No change is necessary

Answer: D. No change is necessary

The present tense must be used consistently throughout, therefore Option C is incorrect. Option A is incorrect because the singular pronoun *his* does not agree with the plural antecedent *climbers*. Option B is incorrect because a comma, not a semicolon, is needed to separate the dependent clause from the main clause.

(Easy) (Skill 9.3)

19. If climbers are to avoid <u>becoming</u> dehydrated, there <u>is</u> beverages available for <u>them</u> to transport as well.

    A. becomming

    B. are

    C. him

    D. No change is necessary

Answer: B. are

The plural verb *are* must be used with the plural subject *beverages*. Option A is incorrect because *becoming* is spelled with only one *m*. Option C is incorrect because the plural pronoun *them* is needed to agree with the plural referent *climbers*.

(Rigorous) (Skill 9.3)

20. Each of the climbers <u>are</u> reminded of the splendor and <u>magnificence</u> of <u>God's</u> great Earth.

    A. is

    B. magnifisence

    C. Gods

    D. No change is necessary

Answer: A. is

The singular verb *is* agrees with the singular subject each. Option B is incorrect because *magnificence* is misspelled. Option C is incorrect because an apostrophe is needed to show possession.

(Average) (Skill 9.8)

21. Once climbers are completely prepared for <u>their</u> lengthy <u>journey,</u> <u>they</u> can <u>comfortable</u> enjoy the wonderful scenery.

    A. they're

    B. journey; they

    C. comfortably

    D. No change is necessary

Answer: C. comfortably

The adverb form *comfortably*, not the adjective *comfortable*, is needed to modify the verb phrase can enjoy. Option A is incorrect because the possessive plural pronoun is spelled *their*. Option B is incorrect because a semicolon would make the first half of the item seem like an independent clause when the subordinating conjunction *once* makes that clause dependent.

(Average) (Skills 9.9 and 9.11)

22. **Climbers who** take precautions are likely to find the ascent **less difficult than** the unprepared.

    A. Climbers, who

    B. least difficult

    C. then

    D. No change is necessary

Answer: D. No change is necessary

No change is needed. Option A is incorrect because a comma would make the phrase *who take precautions* seem less restrictive or less essential to the sentence. Option B is incorrect because *less* is appropriate when two items—the prepared and the unprepared—are compared. Option C is incorrect because the comparative adverb *than*, not *then*, is needed.

(Rigorous) (Skill 9.10)

23. **Climbers must endure severel barriers on the way, including other hikers, steep jagged rocks, and lots of snow.**

    A. several

    B. on the way: including

    C. hikers'

    D. No change is necessary

Answer: A. several

The word several is misspelled in the text. Option B is incorrect because a comma, not a colon, is needed to set off the modifying phrase. Option C is incorrect because no apostrophe is needed after *hikers* since it is not a possessive form.

(Rigorous) (Skill 9.11)

24. **A pair of rugged boots is also one of the necesities.**

    A. are

    B. also, one

    C. necessities

    D. No change is necessary

Answer: C. necessities

The word *necessities* is misspelled in the text. Option A is incorrect because the singular verb *is* must agree with the singular noun *pair* (a collective singular). Option B is incorrect because if *also* is set off with commas (which is a potential correction), it must be set off on both sides.

(Rigorous) (Skill 9.11)

25. **Wide rock formations dazzle the observers eyes with shades of gray and white, while the peak forms a triangle that seems to touch the sky.**

    A. observers' eyes

    B. white; while

    C. formed

    D. No change is necessary

Answer: A. observers' eyes

An apostrophe is needed to show the plural possessive form *observers' eyes*. Option B is incorrect because the semicolon would make the second half of the item seem like an independent clause when the subordinating conjunction *while* makes that clause dependent. Option C is incorrect because *formed* is in the wrong tense.

DIRECTIONS: The passage below contains several errors. Read the passage. Then answer each test item by choosing the option that corrects an error in the underlined portion(s). No more than one underlined error will appear in each item. If no error exists, choose "No change is necessary."

Every job places different kinds of demands on their employees. For example, whereas such jobs as accounting and bookkeeping require mathematical ability; graphic design requires creative/artistic ability.

Doing good at one job does not usually guarantee success at another. However, one of the elements crucial to all jobs are especially notable: the chance to accomplish a goal.

The accomplishment of the employees vary according to the job. In many jobs the employees become accustom to the accomplishment provided by the work they do every day.

In medicine, for example, all doctors test themselves by treating badly injured or critically ill people. In the operating room, a team of Surgeons, is responsible for operating on many of these patients. In addition to the feeling of accomplishment that the workers achieve, some jobs also give a sense of identity to the employees'. Profesions like law, education, and sales offer huge financial or emotional rewards. Politicians are public servants: who work for the federal and state governments. President obama is basically employed by the American people to make laws and run the country.

Finally; the contributions that employees make to their companies and to the world cannot be taken for granted. Through their work, employees are performing a service for their employers and are contributing something to the world.

(Rigorous) (Skill 9.1)

26. The <u>accomplishment</u> of the <u>employees</u> <u>vary</u> according to the job.

   A. accomplishment,

   B. employee's

   C. varies

   D. No change is necessary

Answer: C. varies

The singular verb *varies* is needed to agree with the singular subject *accomplishment*. Option A is incorrect because a comma after *accomplishment* would suggest that the modifying phrase *of the employees* is not essential to the sentence. Option B is incorrect because *employees* is not possessive.

(Average) (Skill 9.2)

27. In many jobs the employees <u>become</u> <u>accustom</u> to the accomplishment <u>provided</u> by the work they do every day.

   A. became

   B. accustomed

   C. provides

   D. No change is necessary

Answer: B. accustomed

The past participle accustomed is needed with the verb *become*. Option A is incorrect because the verb tense does not need to change to the past *became*. Option C is incorrect because *provides* is the wrong tense.

(Rigorous) (Skill 9.3)

28. <u>However,</u> one of the elements crucial to all jobs <u>are</u> especially <u>notable:</u> the accomplishment of a goal.

    A. However

    B. is

    C. notable;

    D. No change is necessary

    Answer: B. is

    The singular verb *is* agrees with the singular subject *one*. Option A is incorrect because a comma is needed to set off the transitional word *however*. Option C is incorrect because a colon, not a semicolon, is needed to set off an item.

(Average) (Skill 9.4)

29. In medicine, for example, all doctors <u>test them self</u> by treating badly injured and critically ill people.

    A. tests

    B. themselves

    C. critical

    D. No change is necessary

    Answer: B. themselves

    The reflexive pronoun *themselves* is needed (them self is nonstandard and never correct). Option A is incorrect because the plural verb test is needed to agree with the plural subject doctors. Option C is incorrect because the adverb *critically* is needed to modify the adjective *ill*.

(Rigorous) (Skill 9.4)

30. Every job <u>places</u> different kinds of demands on <u>their</u> <u>employees</u>.

    A. place

    B. its

    C. employes

    D. No change is necessary

    Answer: B. its

    The singular possessive pronoun *its* must agree with its antecedent *job*, which is singular also. Option A is incorrect because place is a plural form and the subject, job, is singular. Option C is incorrect because the correct spelling of *employees* is given in the sentence.

(Rigorous) (Skill 9.8)

31. Doing <u>good</u> at one job does not <u>usually</u> guarantee <u>success</u> at another.

    A. well

    B. usualy

    C. succeeding

    D. No change is necessary

    Answer: A. well

    The adverb *well* modifies the verb *doing*. Option B is incorrect because *usually* is spelled correctly in the sentence. Option C is incorrect because *succeeding* is in the wrong tense.

(Average) (Skill 9.10)

32. <u>Profesions</u> like law, <u>education,</u> and sales <u>offer</u> huge financial oremotional rewards.

    A. Professions

    B. education;

    C. offered

    D. No change is necessary

Answer: A. Professions

Option A is correct because *professions* is misspelled in the sentence. Option B is incorrect because a comma, not a semicolon, is needed after *education*. In Option C *offered* is in the wrong tense.

(Easy) (Skill 9.11)

33. Politicians <u>are</u> public <u>servants: who</u> <u>work</u> for the federal and state governments.

    A. were

    B. servants who

    C. worked

    D. No change is necessary

Answer: B. servants who

A colon is not needed to set off the introduction of the sentence. In Option A, *were* is the incorrect tense of the verb. In Option C *worked* is in the wrong tense of the verb.

(Average) (Skill 9.11)

34. <u>For example</u>, <u>whereas</u> such jobs as accounting and bookkeeping require mathematical <u>ability;</u> graphic design requires creative/artistic ability.

    A. For example

    B. whereas,

    C. ability,

    D. No change is necessary

Answer: C. ability

An introductory dependent clause is set off with a comma, not a semicolon. Option A is incorrect because the transitional phrase *for example* should be set off with a comma. Option B is incorrect because the adverb *whereas* functions like *while* and does not need a comma after it.

(Average) (Skills 9.10 and 9.11)

35. **In addition to the feeling of accomplishment that the workers <u>achieve</u>, some jobs also <u>give</u> a sense of self-identity to the <u>employees'</u>.**

    A. acheive

    B. gave

    C. employees

    D. No change is necessary

Answer: C. employees

Option C is correct because *employees* is not possessive. Option A is incorrect because *achieve* is spelled correctly in the sentence. Option B is incorrect because *gave* is the wrong tense.

(Average) (Skill 9.11)

36. <u>Finally;</u> the contributions that employees make to <u>their</u> companies and to the world cannot be <u>taken</u> for granted.

   A. Finally,

   B. thier

   C. took

   D. No change is necessary

Answer: A. Finally,

Finally is a reposition that usually heads a dependent sentence, so a comma is needed to separate *Finally* from the rest of the sentence. Option B is incorrect because *their* is misspelled. Option C is incorrect because *took* is the wrong form of the verb.

(Easy) (Skill 9.12)

37. In the <u>operating room,</u> a team of <u>Surgeons, is</u> responsible for operating on many of <u>these</u> patients.

   A. operating room:

   B. surgeons is

   C. those

   D. No change is necessary

Answer: B. surgeons is

Surgeons is not a proper name so it does not need to be capitalized. Also, a comma is not needed to break up a *team of surgeons* from the rest of the sentence. Option A is incorrect because a comma, not a colon, is needed to set off an item. Option C is incorrect because *those* is an incorrect pronoun.

(Easy) (Skill 9.12)

38. President <u>obama</u> is basically employed <u>by</u> the American people to <u>make</u> laws and run the country.

   A. Obama

   B. to

   C. made

   D. No change is necessary

Answer: A. Obama

Obama is a proper name and should be capitalized. Option B *to*, does not fit with the verb employed. Option C uses the wrong form of the verb.

DIRECTIONS: The passage below contains several errors. Read the passage. Then answer each test item by choosing the option that corrects an error in the underlined portion(s). No more than one underlined error will appear in each item. If no error exists, choose "No change is necessary."

The discovery of a body at Paris Point marina in Boca Raton shocked the residents of Palmetto Pines, a luxury condominium complex located next door to the marina.

The victim is a thirty-five year old woman who had been apparently bludgeoned to death and dumped in the ocean late last night. Many neighbors reported terrible screams, gunshots: as well as the sound of a car backfiring loudly to Boca Raton Police shortly after midnight. The woman had been spotted in the lobby of Palmetto Pines around ten thirty, along with an older man, estimated to be in his fifties, and a younger man, in his late twenties.

"Apparently, the victim had been driven to the complex by the older man, and was seen arguing with him when the younger man intervened," said Sheriff Fred Adams, "all three of them left the building together and walked to the marina, where gunshots rang out an hour later." Deputies found five bullets on the sidewalk and some blood, along with a steel pipe that is assumed to be the murder weapon. Two men were seen fleeing the scene in a red Mercedes short after, rushing toward the Interstate.

The Palm Beach County Coroner, Melvin Watts, said he concluded the victim's skull had been crushed by a blunt tool, which resulted in a brain hemorrhage. As of now, there is no clear motive for the murder.

(Rigorous) (Skill 9.2)

39. **The victim is a thirty-five year old who had been apparently bludgeoned to death and dumped in the ocean late last night.**

    A. was

    B. bludgoned

    C. ocean: late

    D. No change is necessary

    Answer: A. was

    The past tense *was* is needed to maintain consistency. Option B creates a misspelling. Option C incorrectly uses a colon where it is not needed.

(Rigorous) (Skill 9.2)

40. **Deputies found five bullets on the sidewalk and some blood, along with a steel pipe that is assumed to be the murder weapon.**

    A. blood;

    B. assuming

    C. to have been

    D. No change is necessary

    Answer: C. to have been

    The past tense *to have been* is needed to maintain consistency. Option A incorrectly uses a semicolon instead of a comma. Option B uses the wrong form of the verb *assumed*.

(Easy) (Skill 9.8)

41. **Two men were seen fleeing the scene in a red Mercedes short after, rushing toward the Interstate.**

    A. are

    B. shortly

    C. rushed

    D. No change is necessary

    Answer: B. shortly

    The adverb *shortly* is needed to modify the adverb *after*, not the adjective *short*. Option A incorrectly uses the present tense *are* instead of the past tense *were*. Option C *rushed*, is the wrong form of the verb.

(Rigorous) (Skill 9.10)

42. The <u>Palm Beach</u> County <u>Coroner,</u> Kelvin Watts, said he concluded the victim's skull had been crushed by a blunt tool, which resulted in a brain <u>hemorrage</u>.

   A. palm beach

   B. coroner:

   C. hemorrhage

   D. No change is necessary

   Answer: C. hemorrhage

   Option C uses the correct spelling of *hemorrhage*. Option A is incorrect because *Palm Beach* is a proper name and needs to be capitalized. Option B incorrectly uses a colon when a comma is needed to separate the items.

(Easy) (Skills 9.2, 9.10, and 9.11)

43. As of <u>now,</u> <u>there</u> <u>is</u> no clear motive for the murder.

   A. now;

   B. their

   C. was

   D. No change is necessary

   Answer: D. No change is necessary

   Option A is incorrect because a comma, not a semicolon, is needed to separate the independent clause from the dependent clause. Option B creates a misspelling. Option C uses the incorrect tense, *was*, which doesn't fit with the present tense phrase *as of now*.

(Rigorous) (Skill 9.11)

44. Many <u>neighbors</u> reported terrible screams, <u>gunshots: as</u> well as the sound of a car backfiring <u>loudly</u> to Boca Raton Police shortly after midnight.

   A. nieghbors

   B. gunshots, as

   C. loud

   D. No change is necessary

   Answer: B. gunshots, as

   Option B correctly uses a comma, not a colon, to separate the items. Option A creates a misspelling. Option C incorrectly changes the adverb into an adjective.

(Rigorous) (Skill 9.11)

45. The woman <u>had</u> been spotted in the lobby of Palmetto Pines around ten <u>thirty,</u> along with an older <u>man, estimated</u> to be in his fifties, and a younger man in his late twenties.

   A. has

   B. thirty;

   C. man estimated

   D. No change is necessary

   Answer: C. man estimated

   A comma is not needed to separate the item because *an older man estimated to be in his fifties* is one complete fragment. Option A incorrectly uses the present tense *has* instead of the past tense *had*. Option B incorrectly uses a semicolon when a comma is needed.

(Average) (Skills 9.11 and 9.12)

46. "Apparently, the victim had been driven to the complex by the older man, and was seen arguing with him when the younger man intervened," said <u>Sheriff Fred Adams, "all</u> three of them left the building together and walked to the marina, when gunshots rang out an hour later."

    A. sheriff Fred Adams, "all

    B. sheriff Fred Adams, "All

    C. Sheriff Fred Adams. "All

    D. No change is necessary

    Answer: C. Sheriff Fred Adams. "All

    The quote's source comes in the middle of two independent clauses, so a period should follow *Adams*. Option A is incorrect because titles, when they come before a name, must be capitalized. The punctuation in Option A is also faulty. Option B is incorrect because the word *Adams* ends a sentence; a comma is not strong enough to support two sentences.

(Easy) (Skill 9.12)

47. The discovery of a body at Paris Point <u>marina</u> in Boca Raton shocked the <u>residents</u> of Palmetto Pines, a luxury <u>condominium</u> complex located next door to the Palmetto marina.

    A. Marina

    B. residence

    C. condomminium

    D. No change is necessary

    Answer: A. Marina

    Marina is part of a specific name that needs to be capitalized. Options B and C create misspellings.

SAMPLE TEST
Reading

Read the following passage and answer the questions that follow.

This writer has often been asked to tutor hospitalized children with cystic fibrosis. While undergoing all the precautionary measures to see these children (for example, scrubbing thoroughly and donning a face mask and sterile gown), she has wondered why parents subject these children to the pressures of schooling and trying to catch up on what they have missed because of hospitalization, which is a normal part of cystic fibrosis patients' lives. These children undergo so many tortuous treatments a day that it seems cruel to expect them to learn as normal children do, especially when their life expectancies are so short.

(Average) (Skill 10.1)

1. **What is the main idea of this passage?**

   A. There is a lot of preparation involved in visiting a patient with cystic fibrosis

   B. Children with cystic fibrosis are incapable of living normal lives

   C. Certain concessions should be made for children with cystic fibrosis

   D. Children with cystic fibrosis die young

(Easy) (Skill 10.2)

2. **How is the author so familiar with the procedures used when visiting a child with cystic fibrosis?**

   A. She has read about it

   B. She works in a hospital

   C. She is the parent of one

   D. She often tutors them

(Average) (Skill 10.3)

3. **What is meant by the word "precautionary" in the second sentence?**

   A. Careful

   B. Protective

   C. Medical

   D. Sterilizing

(Average) (Skill 11.1)

4. **What is the author's purpose?**

   A. To inform

   B. To entertain

   C. To describe

   D. To narrate

(Rigorous) (Skill 11.2)

5. **What type of organizational pattern does the author use?**

   A. Classification

   B. Example, clarification, and definition

   C. Comparison and contrast

   D. Cause and effect

(Rigorous) (Skill 11.3)

6. **The author states that it is "cruel" to expect children with cystic fibrosis to learn as "normal" children do. Is this a fact or an opinion?**

   A. Fact

   B. Opinion

(Rigorous) (Skill 11.4)

7. **Is there evidence of bias in this paragraph?**

   A. Yes

   B. No

(Rigorous) (Skill 11.5)

8. **What is the author's tone?**

   A. Sympathetic

   B. Cruel

   C. Disbelieving

   D. Cheerful

(Rigorous) (Skill 11.6)

9. **What organizational structure is used in the last sentence of this passage?**

   A. Addition

   B. Summary

   C. Example

   D. Comparison and contrast

(Rigorous) (Skill 11.7)

10. **Is the author's argument about schooling children with cystic fibrosis valid or invalid?**

    A. Valid

    B. Invalid

Read the following passage, and answer the questions that follow.

Disciplinary practices have been found to affect diverse areas of child development such as moral values, obedience to authority, and performance at school. Even though the dictionary has a specific definition for the word "discipline," the concept is still open to interpretation by people of different cultures.

There are four types of disciplinary styles: assertion of power, withdrawal of love, reasoning, and permissiveness. Assertion of power involves the use of force to discourage unwanted behavior. Withdrawal of love involves making the love of a parent or authority figure a condition of a child's good behavior. Reasoning involves persuading a child to behave one way rather than another. Permissiveness involves allowing children to do as they please and face the consequences of their actions.

(Average) (Skill 10.1)

11. **What is the main idea of this passage?**

    A. Different people have different ideas of what discipline is

    B. Permissiveness is the most widely used disciplinary style

    C. Most people agree on their definition of discipline

    D. There are four disciplinary styles

(Easy) (Skill 10.2)

12. **Name the four types of disciplinary styles.**

    A. Reasoning, power assertion, morality, and permissiveness

    B. Morality, reasoning, permissiveness, and withdrawal of love

    C. Withdrawal of love, permissiveness, assertion of power, and reasoning

    D. Permissiveness, morality, reasoning, and power assertion

(Easy) (Skill 10.2)

13. **What does the technique of reasoning involve?**

    A. Persuading children to behave in a certain way

    B. Allowing children to do as they please

    C. Using force to discourage unwanted behavior

    D. Making love a condition of good behavior

(Easy) (Skill 10.3)

14. **What is the meaning of the word "diverse" in the first sentence?**

    A. Many

    B. Related to children

    C. Disciplinary

    D. Moral

(Easy) (Skill 11.1)

15. **What is the author's purpose in writing this passage?**

    A. To describe

    B. To narrate

    C. To entertain

    D. To inform

(Rigorous) (Skill 11.2)

16. **What is the overall organizational pattern of this passage?**

    A. Statement support

    B. Cause and effect

    C. Classification

    D. Summary

(Rigorous) (Skill 11.3)

17. **What organizational structure is used in the first sentence of the second paragraph?**

    A. Addition

    B. Location/spatial order

    C. Clarification

    D. Example

(Average) (Skill 11.3)

18. **The author states that "assertion of power involves the use of force to discourage unwanted behavior." Is this a fact or an opinion?**

    A. Fact

    B. Opinion

(Average) (Skill 11.4)

19. **Is this passage biased?**

    A. Yes

    B. No

(Average) (Skill 11.5)

20. **What is the author's tone?**

    A. Disbelieving

    B. Angry

    C. Informative

    D. Optimistic

(Rigorous) (Skill 11.8)

21. **From reading this passage we can conclude that:**

    A. The author is a teacher

    B. The author has many children

    C. The author has written a book about discipline

    D. The author has done research on discipline

Read the following passage, and answer the questions that follow.

One of the most difficult problems plaguing American education is the assessment of teachers. No one denies that teachers should be answerable for what they do, but what exactly does that mean? The Oxford American Dictionary defines accountability as the obligation to give a reckoning or explanation for one's actions.

Do students have to learn for teaching to have taken place? Historically, teaching has not been defined in this restrictive manner; teachers were thought to be responsible for the quantity and quality of material covered and for the way in which it was presented. However, some definitions of teaching now imply that students must learn in order for teaching to have taken place.

As a teacher who tries <u>my</u> best to keep current on all the latest teaching strategies, I believe that those teachers who do not bother even to pick up an educational journal every once in a while should be kept under close watch. There are many teachers out there who have been teaching for decades and refuse to change their ways even if research has proven that their methods are outdated and ineffective. There is no place in the profession of teaching for these types of individuals. It is time that the

American educational system clean house, for the sake of our children.

(Average) (Skill 10.1)

22. **What is the main idea of the passage?**

    A. Teachers should not be answerable for what they do

    B. Teachers who do not do their job should be fired

    C. The author is a good teacher

    D. Assessment of teachers is a serious problem in society today

(Easy) (Skill 10.2)

23. **The author states that teacher assessment is a problem for:**

    A. Elementary schools

    B. Secondary schools

    C. American education

    D. Families

(Easy) (Skill 10.2)

24. **Where does the author get her definition of "accountability?"**

    A. *Webster's Dictionary*

    B. *Encyclopedia Brittanica*

    C. *The Oxford American Dictionary*

    D. *World Book Encyclopedia*

(Easy) (Skill 10.3)

25. **What is meant by the word "plaguing" in the first sentence?**

    A. Causing problems

    B. Causing illness

    C. Causing anger

    D. Causing failure

(Average) (Skill 10.3)

26. **What is the meaning of the word "reck-oning" in the third sentence?**

    A. Thought

    B. Answer

    C. Obligation

    D. Explanation

(Average) (Skill 11.1)

27. **What is the author's purpose in writing this?**

    A. To entertain

    B. To narrate

    C. To describe

    D. To persuade

(Average) (Skill 11.2)

28. **What is the author's overall organizational pattern?**

    A. Classification

    B. Cause and effect

    C. Definition

    D. Comparison and contrast

(Rigorous) (Skill 11.2)

29. **What is the organizational pattern of the second paragraph?**

    A. Cause and effect

    B. Classification

    C. Addition

    D. Example, clarification, and definition

(Average) (Skill 11.3)

30. **"Teachers who do not keep current on educational trends should be fired." Is this a fact or an opinion?**

    A. Fact

    B. Opinion

(Rigorous) (Skill 11.4)

31. **Is there evidence of bias in this passage?**

    A. Yes

    B. No

(Average) (Skill 11.5)

32. **The author's tone is one of:**

    A. Disbelief

    B. Excitement

    C. Support

    D. Concern

(Rigorous) (Skill 11.7)

33. **Is this a valid argument?**

    A. Yes

    B. No

(Rigorous) (Skill 11.8)

34. **From the passage, one can infer that:**

    A. The author considers herself a good teacher

    B. Poor teachers will be fired

    C. Students have to learn for teaching to take place

    D. The author will be fired

Read the following paragraph, and answer the questions that follow.

Mr. Smith gave instructions for the painting to be hung on the wall. And then it leaped forth before his eyes: the little cottages on the river, the white clouds floating over the valley, and the green of the towering mountain ranges that were seen in the distance. The painting was so vivid that it seemed almost real. Mr. Smith was now absolutely certain that the painting had been worth the money.

(Average) (Skill 10.1)

35. **What is the main idea of this passage?**

  A. The painting that Mr. Smith purchased was expensive

  B. Mr. Smith purchased a painting

  C. Mr. Smith was pleased with the quality of the painting he had purchased

  D. The painting depicted cottages and valleys

(Average) (Skill 10.3)

36. **What does the author mean by the expression "it leaped forth before his eyes"?**

  A. The painting fell off the wall

  B. The painting appeared so real it was almost three-dimensional

  C. The painting struck Mr. Smith in the face

  D. Mr. Smith was hallucinating

(Average) (Skill 10.3)

37. **What is the meaning of the word "vivid" in the third sentence?**

  A. Lifelike

  B. Dark

  C. Expensive

  D. Big

(Rigorous) (Skill 11.1)

38. **The author's purpose is to:**

  A. Inform

  B. Entertain

  C. Persuade

  D. Narrate

(Rigorous) (Skill 11.4)

39. **Is this passage biased?**

  A. Yes

  B. No

(Rigorous) (Skill 11.8)

40. **From the last sentence, one can infer that:**

  A. The painting was expensive

  B. The painting was cheap

  C. Mr. Smith was considering purchasing the painting

  D. Mr. Smith thought the painting was too expensive and decided not to purchase it

Answer Key: Reading

1. C	11. A	21. D	31. A
2. D	12. C	22. D	32. D
3. B	13. A	23. C	33. B
4. C	14. A	24. C	34. A
5. B	15. D	25. A	35. C
6. B	16. C	26. D	36. B
7. A	17. D	27. D	37. A
8. A	18. A	28. C	38. D
9. B	19. B	29. D	39. B
10. B	20. C	30. B	40. A

Rigor Table

RIGOR TABLE		
Rigor level	**Questions**	**TOTALS**
Easy 20%	2, 12, 13, 14, 15, 23, 24, 25,	8 (20.0%)
Average Rigor 40%	1, 3, 4, 11, 18, 19, 20, 22, 26, 27, 28, 30, 32, 35, 36, 37	16 (40.0%)
Rigorous 40%	5, 6, 7, 8, 9, 10, 16, 17, 21, 29, 31, 33, 34, 38, 39, 40	16 (40.0%)

Sample Test with Rationales: Reading

Read the following passage and answer the questions that follow.

This writer has often been asked to tutor hospitalized children with cystic fibrosis. While undergoing all the precautionary measures to see these children (for example, scrubbing thoroughly and donning a face mask and sterile gown), she has wondered why parents subject these children to the pressures of schooling and trying to catch up on what they have missed because of hospitalization, which is a normal part of cystic fibrosis patients' lives. These children undergo so many tortuous treatments a day that it seems cruel to expect them to learn as normal children do, especially when their life expectancies are so short.

(Average) (Skill 10.1)

1. **What is the main idea of this passage?**

   A. There is a lot of preparation involved in visiting a patient with cystic fibrosis

   B. Children with cystic fibrosis are incapable of living normal lives

   C. Certain concessions should be made for children with cystic fibrosis

   D. Children with cystic fibrosis die young

   Answer: C. Certain concessions should be made for children with cystic fibrosis

   The author states that she wonders "why parents subject these children to the pressures of schooling," and that "it seems cruel to expect them to learn as normal children do." In making these statements, she seems to express the belief that these children should not have to

do everything that "normal" children do. They have enough to deal with—their illness itself.

(Easy) (Skill 10.2)

2. **How is the author so familiar with the procedures used when visiting a child with cystic fibrosis?**

   A. She has read about it

   B. She works in a hospital

   C. She is the parent of one

   D. She often tutors them

   Answer: D. She often tutors them

   The writer states this fact in the opening sentence as a supporting detail.

(Average) (Skill 10.3)

3. **What is meant by the word "precautionary" in the second sentence?**

   A. Careful

   B. Protective

   C. Medical

   D. Sterilizing

   Answer: B. Protective

   Details such as "sterilized gown" and "scrubbing thoroughly" help readers understand the meaning of the word "precautionary" in this context.

(Average) (Skill 11.1)

4. **What is the author's purpose?**

   A. To inform

   B. To entertain

   C. To describe

   D. To narrate

   Answer: C. To describe

   This author is simply describing her experience in working with children with cystic fibrosis.

(Rigorous) (Skill 11.2)

5. **What type of organizational pattern does the author use?**

   A. Classification

   B. Example, clarification, and definition

   C. Comparison and contrast

   D. Cause and effect

   Answer: B. Example, clarification, and definition

   The author mentions tutoring children with cystic fibrosis in her opening sentence and goes on to explain and elaborate on her main idea. She focuses extensively on how little time the children have due to hospitalization and a shortened life span.

(Rigorous) (Skill 11.3)

6. **The author states that it is "cruel" to expect children with cystic fibrosis to learn as "normal" children do. Is this a fact or an opinion?**

   A. Fact

   B. Opinion

   Answer: B. Opinion

   The fact that she states that it "seems" cruel indicates that there is no evidence to support this belief.

(Rigorous) (Skill 11.4)

7. **Is there evidence of bias in this paragraph?**

   A. Yes

   B. No

   Answer: A. Yes

   The writer clearly feels sorry for these children, and her writing reflects these personal feelings.

(Rigorous) (Skill 11.5)

8. **What is the author's tone?**

   A. Sympathetic

   B. Cruel

   C. Disbelieving

   D. Cheerful

   Answer: A. Sympathetic

   The author states that "it seems cruel to expect them to learn as normal children do," thereby indicating that she feels sorry for them.

(Rigorous) (Skill 11.6)

9. **What organizational structure is used in the last sentence of this passage?**

   A. Addition

   B. Summary

   C. Example

   D. Comparison and contrast

   Answer: B. Summary

   In mentioning that their life expectancies are short, she is reiterating her point that it is cruel to expect them to learn as normal children do.

(Rigorous) (Skill 11.7)

10. **Is the author's argument about schooling children with cystic fibrosis valid or invalid?**

    A. Valid

    B. Invalid

    Answer: B. Invalid

    Even though the writer's argument may make good sense to many readers, it is biased and is not supported by any concrete facts or evidence.

Read the following passage, and answer the questions that follow.

Disciplinary practices have been found to affect diverse areas of child development such as moral values, obedience to authority, and performance at school. Even though the dictionary has a specific definition for the word "discipline," the concept is still open to interpretation by people of different cultures.

There are four types of disciplinary styles: assertion of power, withdrawal of love, reasoning, and permissiveness. Assertion of power involves the use of force to discourage unwanted behavior. Withdrawal of love involves making the love of a parent or authority figure a condition of a child's good behavior. Reasoning involves persuading a child to behave one way rather than another. Permissiveness involves allowing children to do as they please and face the consequences of their actions.

(Average) (Skill 10.1)

11. **What is the main idea of this passage?**

    A. Different people have different ideas of what discipline is

    B. Permissiveness is the most widely used disciplinary style

    C. Most people agree on their definition of discipline

    D. There are four disciplinary styles

    Answer: A. Different people have different ideas of what discipline is

    Choice C is not true; in fact, the passage states the opposite. Choice B could be true, but the passages does not give any evidence to support this. Choice D is one of the many facts listed in the passage, not the main idea.

(Easy) (Skill 10.2)

12. **Name the four types of disciplinary styles.**

    A. Reasoning, power assertion, morality, and permissiveness

    B. Morality, reasoning, permissiveness, and withdrawal of love

    C. Withdrawal of love, permissiveness, assertion of power, and reasoning

    D. Permissiveness, morality, reasoning, and power assertion

    Answer: C. Withdrawal of love, permissiveness, assertion of power, and reasoning

    This supporting detail is directly stated in the second paragraph.

(Easy) (Skill 10.2)

13. **What does the technique of reasoning involve?**

    A. Persuading children to behave in a certain way

    B. Allowing children to do as they please

    C. Using force to discourage unwanted behavior

    D. Making love a condition of good behavior

    Answer: A. Persuading children to behave in a certain way

    This supporting fact is directly stated in the second paragraph.

(Easy) (Skill 10.3)

14. **What is the meaning of the word "diverse" in the first sentence?**

    A. Many

    B. Related to children

    C. Disciplinary

    D. Moral

    Answer: A. Many

    Any of the other choices would be redundant in this sentence, and none are correct definitions of the word "diverse."

(Easy) (Skill 11.1)

15. **What is the author's purpose in writing this passage?**

    A. To describe

    B. To narrate

    C. To entertain

    D. To inform

    Answer: D. To inform

    The author is providing the reader with information about disciplinary practices.

(Rigorous) (Skill 11.2)

16. **What is the overall organizational pattern of this passage?**

    A. Statement support

    B. Cause and effect

    C. Classification

    D. Summary

Answer: C. Classification

The author has taken a subject, in this case the subject of discipline, and developed it point by point by stating the general category and then explaining its related styles.

(Rigorous) (Skill 11.3)

17. **What organizational structure is used in the first sentence of the second paragraph?**

    A. Addition

    B. Location/spatial order

    C. Clarification

    D. Example

    Answer: D. Example

    The author states the types of disciplinary styles and then gives an example of each.

(Average) (Skill 11.3)

18. **The author states that "assertion of power involves the use of force to discourage unwanted behavior." Is this a fact or an opinion?**

    A. Fact

    B. Opinion

    Answer: A. Fact

    The author is stating an established definition of assertion of power.

(Average) (Skill 11.4)

19. **Is this passage biased?**

    A. Yes

    B. No

    Answer: B. No

    A reader could research discipline and find this information.

(Average) (Skill 11.5)

20. **What is the author's tone?**

    A. Disbelieving

    B. Angry

    C. Informative

    D. Optimistic

    Answer: C. Informative

    The author appears to simply be stating facts.

(Rigorous) (Skill 11.8)

21. **From reading this passage we can conclude that:**

    A. The author is a teacher

    B. The author has many children

    C. The author has written a book about discipline

    D. The author has done research on discipline

    Answer: D. The author has done research on discipline

    Given all the facts mentioned in the passage, this is the only inference one can make. The other answers, while possibly true statements about the author, are not supported by any evidence in the content or style of the passage.

Read the following passage, and answer the questions that follow.

One of the most difficult problems plaguing American education is the assessment of teachers. No one denies that teachers should be answerable for what they do, but what exactly does that mean? The Oxford American Dictionary defines accountability as the obligation to give a reckoning or explanation for one's actions.

Do students have to learn for teaching to have taken place? Historically, teaching has not been defined in this restrictive manner; teachers were thought to be responsible for the quantity and quality of material covered and for the way in which it was presented. However, some definitions of teaching now imply that students must learn in order for teaching to have taken place.

As a teacher who tries my best to keep current on all the latest teaching strategies, I believe that those teachers who do not bother even to pick up an educational journal every once in a while should be kept under close watch. There are many teachers out there who have been teaching for decades and refuse to change their ways even if research has proven that their methods are outdated and ineffective. There is no place in the profession of teaching for these types of individuals. It is time that the American educational system clean house, for the sake of our children.

(Average) (Skill 10.1)

22. **What is the main idea of the passage?**

   A. Teachers should not be answerable for what they do

   B. Teachers who do not do their job should be fired

   C. The author is a good teacher

   D. Assessment of teachers is a serious problem in society today

   Answer: D. Assessment of teachers is a serious problem in society today

   Most of the passage is dedicated to elaborating on why teacher assessment is such a problem.

(Easy) (Skill 10.2)

23. **The author states that teacher assessment is a problem for:**

   A. Elementary schools

   B. Secondary schools

   C. American education

   D. Families

   Answer: C. American education

   This fact is directly stated in the first paragraph.

(Easy) (Skill 10.2)

24. **Where does the author get her definition of "accountability?"**

   A. *Webster's Dictionary*

   B. *Encyclopedia Brittanica*

   C. *The Oxford American Dictionary*

   D. *World Book Encyclopedia*

Answer: C. *The Oxford American Dictionary*

The supporting details in the first paragraph make this definition clear.

(Easy) (Skill 10.3)

25. **What is meant by the word "plaguing" in the first sentence?**

    A. Causing problems

    B. Causing illness

    C. Causing anger

    D. Causing failure

    Answer: A. Causing problems

    Other words in the first sentence, such as "difficult" and "problems," help define "plaguing" in this context.

(Average) (Skill 10.3)

26. **What is the meaning of the word "reckoning" in the third sentence?**

    A. Thought

    B. Answer

    C. Obligation

    D. Explanation

    Answer: D. Explanation

    The meaning of this word is directly stated in the same sentence.

(Average) (Skill 11.1)

27. **What is the author's purpose in writing this?**

    A. To entertain

    B. To narrate

    C. To describe

    D. To persuade

Answer: D. To persuade

The majority of the statements in this passage are opinions seemingly intended to convince the reader that teachers who are lazy or who do not keep current should be fired.

(Average) (Skill 11.2)

28. **What is the author's overall organizational pattern?**

    A. Classification

    B. Cause and effect

    C. Definition

    D. Comparison and contrast

    Answer: C. Definition

    The author identifies teacher assessment as a problem and spends the rest of the passage defining why it is considered a problem.

(Rigorous) (Skill 11.2)

29. **What is the organizational pattern of the second paragraph?**

    A. Cause and effect

    B. Classification

    C. Addition

    D. Example, clarification, and definition

    Answer: D. Example, clarification, and definition

    The author states a question in the first paragraph. The second paragraph explains and expands upon this question.

(Average) (Skill 11.3)

30. "Teachers who do not keep current on educational trends should be fired." Is this a fact or an opinion?

   A. Fact

   B. Opinion

   Answer: B. Opinion

   There may be those who feel they can be good teachers by using old methods.

(Rigorous) (Skill 11.4)

31. Is there evidence of bias in this passage?

   A. Yes

   B. No

   Answer: A. Yes

   The entire third paragraph is the author's opinion on the matter, with no supporting facts or examples.

(Average) (Skill 11.5)

32. The author's tone is one of:

   A. Disbelief

   B. Excitement

   C. Support

   D. Concern

   Answer: D. Concern

   The author appears concerned with the future of education.

(Rigorous) (Skill 11.7)

33. Is this a valid argument?

   A. Yes

   B. No

   Answer: B. No

   In the third paragraph, the author appears to be resentful of lazy teachers.

(Rigorous) (Skill 11.8)

34. From the passage, one can infer that:

   A. The author considers herself a good teacher

   B. Poor teachers will be fired

   C. Students have to learn for teaching to take place

   D. The author will be fired

   Answer: A. The author considers herself a good teacher

   The first sentence of the third paragraph alludes to this.

Read the following paragraph, and answer the questions that follow.

Mr. Smith gave instructions for the painting to be hung on the wall. And then it leaped forth before his eyes: the little cottages on the river, the white clouds floating over the valley, and the green of the towering mountain ranges that were seen in the distance. The painting was so vivid that it seemed almost real. Mr. Smith was now absolutely certain that the painting had been worth the money.

(Average) (Skill 10.1)

35. **What is the main idea of this passage?**

    A. The painting that Mr. Smith purchased was expensive

    B. Mr. Smith purchased a painting

    C. Mr. Smith was pleased with the quality of the painting he had purchased

    D. The painting depicted cottages and valleys

    Answer: C. Mr. Smith was pleased with the quality of the painting he had purchased

    Every sentence in the paragraph alludes to this fact.

(Average) (Skill 10.3)

36. **What does the author mean by the expression "it leaped forth before his eyes"?**

    A. The painting fell off the wall

    B. The painting appeared so real it was almost three-dimensional

    C. The painting struck Mr. Smith in the face

    D. Mr. Smith was hallucinating

    Answer: B. The painting appeared so real it was almost three-dimensional

    This is almost directly stated in the third sentence.

(Average) (Skill 10.3)

37. **What is the meaning of the word "vivid" in the third sentence?**

    A. Lifelike

    B. Dark

    C. Expensive

    D. Big

    Answer: A. Lifelike

    This is reinforced by the second half of the same sentence.

(Rigorous) (Skill 11.1)

38. **The author's purpose is to:**

    A. Inform

    B. Entertain

    C. Persuade

    D. Narrate

    Answer: D. Narrate

    The author is simply narrating or telling the story of Mr. Smith and his painting.

(Rigorous) (Skill 11.4)

39. **Is this passage biased?**

    A. Yes

    B. No

    Answer: B. No

    The author appears to be simply relating what happened when Mr. Smith had his new painting hung on the wall.

(Rigorous) (Skill 11.8)

40. **From the last sentence, one can infer that:**

    A. The painting was expensive

    B. The painting was cheap

    C. Mr. Smith was considering purchasing the painting

    D. Mr. Smith thought the painting was too expensive and decided not to purchase it

    Answer: A. The painting was expensive

    The correct answer is A. Choice B is incorrect because, had the painting been cheap, chances are that Mr. Smith would not have considered his purchase. Choices C and D are ruled out by the fact that the painting had already been purchased, as is clear in the phrase "...the painting had been worth the money."

Constructed Response Writing Preview

After the sample test questions conclude, you will be asked to write an essay of your own. The testing people will present you with what is known as a test-prompt, question, situation, or passage, upon which you will be asked to write an opinion.

Assert yourself in a thesis statement. Take a stance in which you believe; do not worry if you are right or wrong. This test does not evaluate you or judge you on your opinion. It judges you on how well and confidently you can express your opinion. So you need to believe in yourself, and express yourself with conviction.

Second, you need to convey *why* you feel the way you do. A really good essay goes beyond merely asserting a belief: it offers a variety of reasons in support of this belief.

These reasons flow as naturally from the pen as if you were explaining to a friend why, for instance, you had decided to become a teacher in the first place—or any key decision in your life that matters. Why did you choose teaching? Why the certain specialty within teaching that you are now seeking? What are your greatest hopes from the career in that specialty (the subject and age group)? You can see that the reasons lead to more specific levels of inquiry.

In keeping with the above, include concrete details that readers can visualize to help support your reasons; these are known as examples.

Again, to liken essay writing to conversation, you ought to be a friendly neighbor. Try to find some good in the viewpoint opposing yours; it may come naturally to the person sitting across from you. You ought to include the merits of the opposite viewpoint in the body of your essay.

Overall, however, you will want to conclude by restating your personal conviction, giving it a new and resounding emphasis.

Sample question prompt

Topic: classroom safety

In the past few years, we have seen a rise in the sudden eruption of violence in secondary schools, leading to permanent trauma and loss of life. Given the copy-cat nature of this situation, should students in public secondary schools be submitted to random searches?

While an imperfect instrument, search would benefit the students, the schools, and the community. Searches can benefit the school's students as a whole. They can contribute to the safety of the student group in the most literal sense of this word. Students should not feel they are entering a high-risk situation when they attend school, but rather feel free to immerse themselves in learning without fear or nervousness. In order for this to happen, the students must feel that someone has instituted safeguards for them. If the whole student body is routinely, or randomly, searched as they enter the building through a backpack or belongings search, real and felt security will come into play. It will then affect both the real safely level of the student community, and their comfort level—and level of trust.

Others to benefit from these searches are the teachers and administrators themselves. It is preposterous to think of these nurturing adults as in the front line of fire. Nor should the leaders of the school in any way be "set against" the students in this battle to establish a safe environment: for the truth is that the safety is something all crave, and it is therefore imperative that such searches as are beneficial be carried out by security people—such as police officers—from outside the school, rather than by the administration or the teachers themselves, whose bond with students is implicitly one of mutual trust. All students must be deemed alike in school policy eyes, for the true community to function.

This last point highlights a possible drawback of searches. If student searches go too far, they break down the sense of community by creating divisiveness; then their very mission of community healing has failed. If they are too vigorously pursued in a sort of witch-hunt style, causing a mob vigilantism to arise within the student body, this could happen. Worse, certain students could get singled out or targeted unfairly, or certain groups within the school become the unjustifiable victims of a restless search. This kind of treatment might engender the very ostracism that community-building struggles to discourage; or might simply be unreasonably deplorable.

Hence, searches must be applied equally to all, by an outside force, presumably a police force. They must be explained to the students as a system for enforcing the peace deserved by all.

Analysis of essay

When you approach the topic of the *Sample Question Prompt,* your job is to adopt a position toward it. Your position is your point of view on the matter presented to you in the *Question Stem.* You cannot simply repeat the fact contained within the stem; you must assert an opinion that is reasonable and comes naturally to you on the matter under consideration. Be sure to stick with the topic raised by the *Question Stem,* which the testing people have provided to stimulate a response they can compare in all of their test-takers, who will all respond to the same *prompt.*

In the example above, it is the opinion of our author that searches are a good idea. But he does not stop at that. A more accurate statement of the author's position would be: "Searches are a good idea because they promote and restore school community."

One way we can test this restatement of the author's position is by looking at how he suggests the searches be conducted and at the problems he concedes might arise with searches. All of these points have to do with potential conflict and division in the community, teacher against student or student against student. The author wants searches to strengthen, not weaken, school community.

When you choose a position, and make your point known by strongly asserting it, go beyond just saying what you think: say why you think your viewpoint would turn things around for the better.

It is especially convincing for the reader to see the bright light at the end of the tunnel. If you can suggest the illumination you envision in detail, readers will want to go your way!

Most of all, write with confidence and conviction, and let one thought lead to another. Remember to include your assertion and two to three reasons that support your idea. Also remember to integrate a concession to the other side. Wrap up strongly by reasserting the merit of your idea.

Constructed Response Structure Summary

1. Assert your thesis

2. Support your argument with reasons why (2-3)

3. Make a concession to the "other side"

4. Wrap up strongly with a thesis reassertion

Teaching in another state? XAMonline carries 14 other state-specific series including the GACE, NYSTCE and MTEL. Also check out our 30+ Praxis titles!

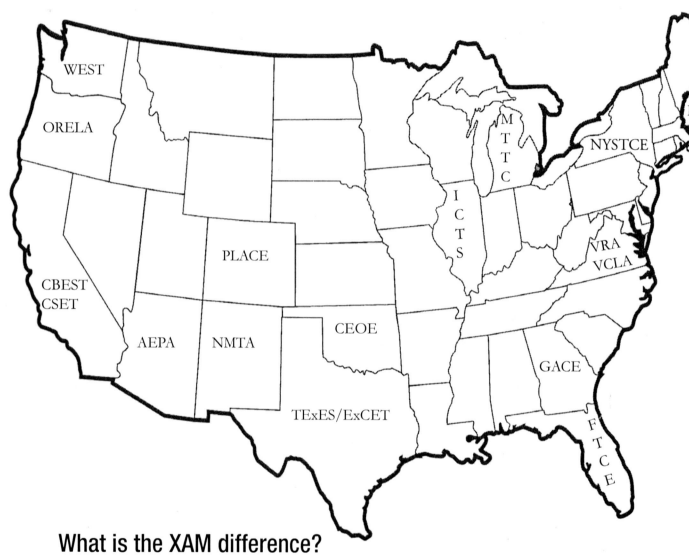

WEST

ORELA

CBEST
CSET

AEPA

NMTA

PLACE

CEOE

TExES/ExCET

M
T
T
C

I
C
T
S

NYSTCE

M

VRA
VCLA

GACE

F
T
C
E

What is the XAM difference?

- State-aligned, current and comprehensive content
- Reviews all required competencies and skills
- Practice test questions aligned to actual test in both number and rigor level
- Questions include full answer rationale and skill reference for easy, efficient study
- Additional resources available online: diagnostic tests, flashcards, timed and scored practice tests and study/test tips